Turning Points
of the Civil War

TURNING POINTS
OF THE
CIVIL WAR

JAMES A. RAWLEY

UNIVERSITY OF NEBRASKA PRESS · LINCOLN

First Bison Book printing March, 1968
Bicentennial Reissue May, 1974

Most recent printing shown by first digit below:

3   4   5   6   7   8   9   10

Bison Book edition reproduced from the first edition by
arrangement with the author.

For
John and James, Jr.

Acknowledgment

The present-day historian inevitably incurs a heavy debt of obligation to other historians and friends of scholarship. My bibliography is one acknowledgment of that debt. In addition I express my thanks to President Anne G. Pannell of Sweet Briar College for granting a year's leave and to Miss Tyler Gemmell and her staff of the Mary Helen Cochran Library at Sweet Briar College for many kindnesses rendered. Special thanks are owing Mr. John Cook Wyllie and his staff of the Alderman Library at the University of Virginia for a year's hospitality. The University of Nebraska has extended favors too numerous to be recorded here. My wife, Ann, alone knows the depth of my obligation to her in the writing of this book. And my sons, to whom this book is dedicated, have throughout the research and writing demonstrated a patience with their abstracted parent above and beyond the call of filial duty.

Contents

Introduction

The Civil War was a turning point in American history. On its outcome hinged the perpetuation of the nation, the maintenance of majority rule, and the success of the American experiment in liberty and equality. The war originated—in no simple sense—in slavery, and by the war slavery was extinguished in the nation, thereby not merely preserving but extending the American commitment to liberty and equality. These results are well known, but the outcome might have been different had the war, at one place or another, taken a different course.

At first sight, believers in historical determinism might think the North was bound to win. Its manpower and economic strength far exceeded that of the South. The nineteenth century seemed pitted against the eighteenth: industry against agriculture, nationalism against state particularism, freedom against slavery. How futile, in this view, was a cause so weak in material and so flawed in moral resources!

But there was another side to the matter. Subjugation might be impossible, for the South occupied an area almost as large as western Europe; and it was the North's strategic assignment to invade and conquer the Confederacy. "The task of suppressing so great a rebellion was herculean. All the world except the Americans of the northern states—and some even of these—believed it to be impossible," exclaimed the historian John Fiske. One side, then, must use its superiority in the costly business of taking the war to the enemy, while the other side need only defend itself.

Nor was idealism or morality all with one party in the strife. Southerners were fighting for self-determination, independence, self-government, the preservation of a distinctive way of life. Nobility and sentiment filled the minds and hearts of Southerners as they fought for Dixie—the land of chivalry and cotton. In his message of April 29, 1861, to his Congress, Jefferson Davis expressed the sincerity of the Southern purpose: "We feel that our cause is just and holy. . . . In independence we seek no conquest, no aggrandizement, no cession of any kind from the States with which we have lately confederated. All we ask is to be let alone . . . ." The belief in the justice of their cause is an important explanation of the prolonged and stubborn resistance by Southerners.

In the North, the war opened the wellsprings of American nationality. Lincoln appealed to this source of strength—in vain so far as the seceded states were concerned—in the closing paragraph of his first inaugural address:

> The mystic chords of memory, stretching from every battlefield, and patriot grave, to every living heart and hearthstone, all over this broad land, will yet swell the chorus of the Union, when again touched, as surely they will be, by the better angels of our nature.

Following the call to arms, Democrats, Whigs, Know-Nothings, Liberty Party men, and Free-Soilers joined Republicans in a rush to the colors. The Charleston *Mercury* exclaimed in dismay, "The North is a unit for the Union." Lincoln's political rival, Stephen A. Douglas, who had held the victor's hat at the inaugural ceremony, declaimed (just before his untimely death in the summer of 1861): "I express it as my conviction before God that it is the duty of every American citizen to rally round the flag of his country." The belief in the justice of their cause is an important explanation of the prolonged and stubborn insistence by Northerners on the main-tenance of the Union and the principles it lived by.

The predominance of the North in population and in financial and industrial strength was conspicuous. Twenty-three states, with a population of 22 million (augmented during the conflict by immigra-tion, with 400,000 foreign-born in the Union army), stood arrayed against eleven states, with a population of 9 million, of whom $3\frac{1}{2}$ million were Negro slaves (with few immigrants in the section).

The North boasted a complex economy, in contrast to the relatively simple, agricultural economy of the South. Having reached a takeoff point in the 1840s, the industrial revolution surged forward in the North. By 1860, industrial centers, although on a small scale, dotted the map of New England, the Middle States, and the Ohio Valley. The census-takers in 1860 had enumerated more factories in New England alone than in all the South, and had counted

111,000 laborers in the latter—and 392,000 in New England. Commercial farming and diversified agriculture, moreover, characterized a region that was learning the use of technology and science to grow food for cities and foreign markets. The banking institutions of the nation were concentrated in the Northeast, together with the merchandising, shipping, and insurance concerns.

The transportation revolution in the generation before the war favored the North. With public planning and assistance, and sometimes outright ownership—as in the case of the Erie Canal—the North was laced together with man-made waterways and a railroad grid that consolidated the resources, united the section, and enhanced a sense of homogeneity among the people. Three-fourths of the railroad mileage in the United States belonged to the North; and the main lines linked the eastern ports of Boston, New York, Philadelphia, and Baltimore with the interior. In the pre-war decade, rails had reached out to the Old Northwest, diverting trade from the Ohio and Mississippi rivers to eastern markets. Besides the political advantage augured by the railroad nexus, the logistical advantage in the event of war was vast.

The Union began the war with an established government. It was recognized and accredited abroad, and it was accustomed to the discharge of its daily responsibilities at home. Its machinery of laws, revenues, and courts was functioning. It possessed the regular army and navy almost intact, though the loss of key army officers was serious. It was a developed, living organism, although it had lost, as if by amputation, a large segment of its body.

South of the Potomac, stretching from the Atlantic Ocean to the Gulf of Mexico, stood a region individualistic and rural, at whose center was plantation agriculture. The production of staples—cotton, tobacco, rice, etc.—with the use of slave labor dominated the agricultural and political life of the section. An underdeveloped area, it lacked fluid capital and technology. About a third of the capital invested in industry in the South was Northern. Abundant resources of iron, coal, and timber lay unexploited for want of money, skill, and equipment.

A modest railroad system, poorly constructed and made up of local lines, and with gaps in key places, failed to integrate a sprawling, sparsely populated land. There were, for example, no connections between Danville, Virginia and Greensboro, North Carolina, or between Meridian, Mississippi and Selma, Alabama. Both of these connections were made before the war ended, but, on the matter of producing supplies, we may listen to the lament of the superintendent of railroad transport in February, 1865: "...not a single bar of railroad iron has been rolled in the Confederacy since [the beginning of] the war."

The South, in short, suffered all the disadvantages that industrial change might have overcome. She appeared woefully unprepared to wage a modern war.

Nor was geography wholly on the side of the South. Though she had an extended coastline of 3,500 miles, counting the Florida peninsula, she boasted few good harbors. The long coastline favored small blockade runners; the small number of harbors favored a naval blockade. The Confederacy's shortage of rail transportation was partially offset by her riverways, but these, in turn, offered natural routes for Northern invaders, down the Mississippi, and up the Tennessee, the Cumberland, the Shenandoah, and the James.

In men, money, iron, food, railroads, and ships, the North enjoyed the advantages. Yet it took four years and 600,000 lives before Northern might prevailed. In seceding, the Southern states accepted a calculated risk. Many Southerners cherished the delusion that the North would not fight. The belief in the right of peaceable secession, a political credo in the South, deepened this miscalculation. In the unlikely event that the North fought, secessionists overrated the extent of their influence. They counted upon the border slave states to adhere to the Confederate cause. Overlooking the new rail tentacles that pulled the region to the Northeast, they believed the Upper Mississippi Valley was dependent upon the river as its lifeline, and would therefore support the South. Overlooking the surplus of cotton in English warehouses, new sources, and other offsets to foreign intervention, they believed, moreover, that Britain and France were dependent upon Southern raw cotton, and would therefore support the South. Secessionists, in striking out for self-government, assumed they could govern themselves. The conflict of individualism and state rights with mobilization of a national war effort upset yet another calculation of Southern political capacity.

Part of the Southern strategic advantage in fighting a defensive war was that the defender could afford to lose battles, even whole campaigns, without losing the war. The defender's aim was to wear out the enemy; a victory by attrition was as good as a victory by assault. Southerners held an optimistic belief that their way of life made for superior soldiers. Outdoor life, the habit of command, familiarity with firearms, liking for military life—all these factors, it was felt, would make the Southerner a better fighting man than the Yankee clerk or mechanic.

What was not perceived in this optimistic outlook was the necessity for men who were expert at the multiform tasks of modern war, who could fight, produce, organize, administer, and adapt. No one today can doubt the valor of the Union soldier, and no one can underestimate the work of Thomas Scott, the president of the Pennsylvania Railroad, who served as assistant secretary of war; of John Ericsson, who designed and built the *Monitor*; of Montgomery Meigs, who worked wonders as quartermaster general; and of Jay Cooke, who sold $2½ billion worth of U.S. government bonds.

The phrase *turning point* is in common use among historians. It suggests important junctures in the course of history when force meets counterforce with such intensity as to make possible a change in the expected direction of development. So it was during the American Civil War. The North, with its preponderance of strength, might have been expected inevitably to win; but not even the fact that the Union invoked the aid of the strongest forces of the nineteenth century—nationalism, industrialism, and universal liberty— doomed the Confederate ship of state, barnacled through it was with state rights, agrarianism, and Negro slavery. Nor did the unexampled statesmanship of Abraham Lincoln—marked by reasoned nationalism, a deep faith in democracy, a conviction that slavery was wrong, and political pragmatism—assure victory to Union arms. At a number of times the war might have taken a different course, and the Union—in the final outcome—might have "snatched defeat from the jaws of victory."

This book examines seven turning points of the American Civil War; each is a major episode of the war, for I have avoided caprice, vagary, and whim in favor of pivotal situations. At a given turning point, however, small and erratic forces were often at work. For example, in Kentucky's neutrality, a major turning point, divers historians have discerned a variety of factors that kept the state in the Union: the "Lincoln guns" (Albert D. Kirwan), the superior wisdom of Union trade policy (E. M. Coulter), the legislature's vote to be neutral (N. S. Shaler), the influence of John J. Crittenden (James G. Blaine), the fact that the Kentucky legislature was not in session when Lincoln called for troops and when Virginia seceded (A. M. Stickles), and Lincoln's policy of forbearance toward Kentucky (H. S. Commager).

Broadly speaking, there are two ways of looking at historical development. One of these may be defined as determinism: a belief in fundamental, shaping forces, which may be described as Fate, as the ancients saw the movement of history; or God, in St. Augustine's view; or law, as Newton, Marx, and Darwin regarded the "automatic" unfolding of man's destiny. Throughout most of man's past, the conception of historical change has been supported by one or another of these powerful buttresses: theology or science.

The other major outlook is to consider history as operating through human will, or libertarianism, or contingency; individuals (great or small), free will, and chance turn the course of history. Napoleon, the boy with his thumb in the dike, the resolution of Robert Bruce, and the "Protestant wind" that blew the Spanish Armada off course are familiar illustrations. The polarity is an old one: from the Pelagian challenge to the Augustinian view, through the Arminian confrontation of the Calvinists, to the twentieth-century interpretation of the past.

The major bent of American historical writing was long toward determinism. George Bancroft surveyed the history of the United States from the discovery of America to the close of the Revolutionary War, and found God "visible in history." The Johns Hopkins historian, Herbert Baxter Adams, subscribing to a "germ theory" of history and under the influence of science, discerned the evolutionary growth of Teutonic "germs" (or racial qualities) on the American scene. Henry Adams, falling under the spell of new theories of physics, formulated a "scientific law": the dynamic theory of history.

The Wisconsin-born historian, Frederick Jackson Turner, reacted strongly against the germ theory of his Johns Hopkins mentor. The frontier and the section, he propounded, not the Teutonic inheritance, molded the contours of American history. Though impressed by Turner's keen insight into the shaping influence of frontier environment and geographical sections, the Middle Westerner Charles A. Beard, in his early writings, emphasized economic forces as determinants of history. As Beard continued to write, however, he came to see historical change caused less by economic determinism and more by a plurality of forces. American civilization had risen under the propulsion of numerous energies. A score of years after Beard had made his influential economic interpretation of the framing of the American Constitution, he was describing objectivity in history as a "noble dream." The historian, he held, selected the record from available facts in the light of his own interpretation.

Charles Beard's transit from determinism to relativism represents a longer journey than most of today's historians care to make. Somewhere in mid-passage they have found a way of looking at history as developing neither by destiny nor by chance. They see not one but many fundamental forces at work, which in varying measure limit the operation of chance or contingency. History moves, however, not in a course predetermined by will or law, not in a predictable cycle, not inevitably upwards or downwards, but, as it were, along a line with many possible turnings.

The most dramatic turnings are often personified by individuals, as can be suggested by three questions: Would the course of history have been different if Lincoln had lived? If Wilson had not been stricken with paralysis? If Franklin D. Roosevelt had not overcome his paralysis sufficiently to become president? In an impersonal realm, historians have speculated that there would have been no War of 1812 if a trans-Atlantic cable had existed, and that there would have been an Anglo-Union war in 1861 if the cable had existed. In presidential elections, historians have speculated how the result would have been different if old Stephen Van Rensselaer had not changed his House vote to Adams in 1824, if Clay had not written his "Raleigh letter" in 1844, if Blaine had not failed to rebuke the

Rev. Samuel Burchard for uttering the phrase "Rum, Romanism, and Rebellion" in 1884.

The turning points in this book are not, contrary to what one might expect, "decisive" battles—or, indeed, military events alone. Military history, to be sure, has an indispensable function in the volume, but stress is laid upon politics, personalities, diplomacy, and statesmanship. Military questions are not seen in the narrow view of a technical study of campaigns but rather in the wider sweep of the interrelationships of policy and politics. Strategy is an expression of the political conditions that underlay the struggle. War, as Clausewitz remarked, is a phase of politics. The turning points are therefore set in a broad context of the war. The reader of this volume should not expect detailed descriptions of battles.

Though it is tempting to study the episodes by which war might have been averted, this book rigorously confines itself to the actual war years. The main theme is the examination of seven events, between 1861 and 1865, from which flowed large consequences—when the outcome of the war might have been different. This is not to say *if* at one of these crises history had taken a different turn, the North would necessarily have lost the war; but it *did* take the North four full years to subdue the South, and the South *did* at times seem close to realizing its independence. Each of these seven crises changed the shape of the war, and a different turn of events would have made a far different future. With the recognition that no one can be sure *how* the outcome might have been different if events had turned the other way, I have throughout tried to be moderate in making my appraisals.

A series of minor threads runs throughout the work: slavery, democracy, British policy, military organization and progress, and the roles of Lincoln, McClellan, Grant, Davis, and Lee. These provide a warp, for which the woof is a set of lessons and principles: political pragmatism, military preparedness, realism in foreign relations, balanced military-civil relationships, politics of race, and democracy in wartime.

To examine this fabric, let us first turn to the curious behavior of Kentucky and the Borderland in 1861.

Kentucky and the Borderland

> I think to lose Kentucky is nearly the
> same as to lose the whole game.
> Abraham Lincoln

"I hope to have God on my side, but I must have Kentucky," Abraham Lincoln is reported to have remarked. The President's hope for Kentucky's allegiance to the Union cause was not merely the patriotism of a native son. Kentucky was, in fact, the keystone in the arch of border slave states, and its adherence to the North was fundamental to winning the war for the Union. "The country at large never has had an adequate conception of the sacrifices made and the work done by the Union men of the Border Slave States," wrote Supreme Court Justice John M. Harlan, a Union veteran and a native Kentuckian. "It is not too much to say that if the people of those States had been as favorable to secession as were the people of the Cotton States, it would, most probably, have been impossible to prevent the dissolution of the Union."[1]

Before March 4, 1861, the day Lincoln swore to "preserve, protect and defend the Constitution of the United States," seven slave states had already seceded and styled themselves a new nation: the Confederate States of America. The withdrawal of these states of the Lower South left eight slave states swaying in the balance between the old Union and the new Confederacy. Lincoln's call for troops to suppress insurrection, following the fall of Fort Sumter, drove four additional states—Virginia, Arkansas, Tennessee, and North Carolina—to find common cause with the Confederacy. It remained now for the slaveholding Borderland, stretching from the Atlantic Ocean to the lower reaches of the Missouri River, and covering the seat of national government as well as the vital arteries of commerce —the Ohio and Mississippi rivers—to determine its destiny.

Nearly 2,600,000 white people, almost half again the white population of the eleven seceded states, lived in the four closely interknit border states—Delaware, Maryland, Kentucky, and Missouri. Another half million loyal whites dwelt in western Virginia

[1] Thomas Speed, *The Union Cause in Kentucky, 1860–1865* (New York: G. P. Putnam's Sons, 1907), pp. v–vi.

11

and eastern Tennessee, and if these were subtracted from the Southern population, the Confederate total would be cut to about five million. The Union recruited well over a quarter million men from the four border slave states.[2]

Delaware, with a population of 90,000 whites and only 1,798 slaves, figured the least among the four. Athwart Maryland and Kentucky lay the western counties of Virginia, locked between the Appalachians and the Ohio River, and long resentful of political domination by the eastern counties. Owning fewer than 13,000 slaves, and differing from the cis-Appalachian region in national origins, religious predilection, and ways of making a living, western Virginians, numbering a third of a million, were to seize the opportunity offered by the sundering of the nation to become a separate state.

Beyond Kentucky stood Missouri, on the western flank of both sections—the home of 1,182,012 people in 1860. Missouri had already contributed not a little to the strife that had now erupted in civil war. It has been remarked that the conflict developed within her limits. Her application for admission to the Union had provoked the great sectional crisis of 1819–21, when the slave states had first drawn together in common fear of Northern proscription of slavery in new states and territories. The resulting Missouri Compromise had held the republic together for a long generation, until its repeal in 1854. From then on, there was no peace, and Missourians—the famous "border ruffians," who helped make Kansas a bloody rehearsal ground for civil war, and the Negro Dred Scott—had figured in fomenting the fury that broke in April of 1861.

Why did Kentucky possess such crucial significance—why not Missouri? Maryland? Delaware? Delaware was never in doubt; and Maryland alone of these three had a Unionist governor, Thomas Hicks, who hesitantly exerted the weight of his executive office in favor of the North. His state posed a clear and present danger to the military prosecution of the war, as well as to the Federal oasis in Washington. So patent was this danger that the Federal government

[2] Frederick Phisterer, *Statistical Record of the Armies of the United States* (New York: Charles Scribner's Sons, 1883), p. 10; J. G. Randall and David Donald, *The Civil War and Reconstruction* (2d ed.; Boston: D. C. Heath & Co., 1961), pp. 227–242.

applied force to quelling insurrection in the state. Federal intervention, which lasted through the fall elections, made Maryland secure.

As for Missouri, it was the only state in the Union to cast its 1860 electoral vote for Stephen A. Douglas, candidate of the Northern Democrats. Delaware had gone for Breckinridge, candidate of the Deep South, as had Maryland. Kentucky, like Virginia and Tennessee, had declared for Bell, the Constitutional Union nominee. Of the four states, Lincoln had polled his largest vote in Missouri: Missouri, 17,028; and Delaware, 3,815; Maryland, 2,294; Kentucky, 1,364. Lincoln was not only the weakest of the four presidential candidates in the four states, he was weakest of all in Kentucky.[3]

In 1864, Missourians would give their popular vote to Lincoln by a two-to-one margin, and Marylanders would vote for Lincoln by a substantial majority; but Kentuckians would plump for McClellan in excess of a two-to-one margin. In the presidential contest of 1860, Missouri had presented a strong contender for the Republican nomination, Edward Bates, who became Lincoln's attorney general. A second cabinet member, Montgomery Blair, though resident in Maryland, belonged to an influential Missouri dynasty and served as another link between the state and the union.

Social patterns are also revealing. In 1860 Kentucky held twice as many slaves as Missouri—225,483 as against 114,931. In the course of the war the Missouri legislature abolished slavery in the state, in contrast to the Kentucky legislature. Moreover, Missouri's population included 88,000 German-Americans, compared to only 27,000 in Kentucky;[4] and the German-American element in Missouri, more than three times as numerous as the slaveowners, was a political force for Union. Exposed on three sides to "free soil," Missouri slaveholders risked loss of fugitive slaves, without hope of recovery, should their state secede.

Loyalty in the border slave states may be partly measured by their responses to Lincoln's April 15 call for 75,000 militia. Maryland and Kentucky refused to furnish any men. Delaware met her quota,

[3] Edward C. Smith, *The Borderland in the Civil War* (New York: The Macmillan Co., 1927), *passim*; Edward McPherson, *Handbook of Politics for 1868* (Washington: Philip & Solomons, 1868), p. 372.

[4] Randall and Donald, *Civil War*, p. 68; Smith, *Borderland*, p. 14, n. 7.

except for five men. Missouri, assigned a quota of 3,123 men, furnished 10,591—three times the quota—despite the governor's denunciation of the requisition.[5]

The gravest threat Missouri posed to the Union was strategic. In Confederate hands, the state could interdict commerce on the middle span of the Mississippi and could become a base for thrusts into southern Illinois, Kentucky, and Tennessee. A Confederate Missouri would have complicated Union mastery of the Mississippi; and yet, located beyond the great river, situated on the western flank, at the hither edge of population, and exposed to invasion from Iowa, Illinois, and Kansas, it presented less menace to successful conduct of the war than Kentucky—east of the Mississippi and south of the Ohio, fronting on Tennessee. A Confederate Kentucky would have thrown the Southern frontier to the Ohio, fronting on the southern portions of Ohio, Indiana, and Illinois—where 2,600,000 persons had a sentimental attachment to the South. Kentucky, separated from free states by rivers, stood less vulnerable to attack than Missouri, which had no river boundaries on the north or west to impede Union onslaughts.[6]

Kentucky rivaled Missouri in total population—there was a difference of 27,000 inhabitants. It had the largest slave element, absolutely and proportionately, of the four loyal slave states. It was the central and longest connecting link in the chain that stretched from the Atlantic Ocean to the Missouri River. Its northern river boundary could afford a natural military frontier for the Southern armies. It gave evidence in the election of 1860 of a decidedly neutralist tendency. It offered a problem of peculiar delicacy to Union statesmanship. It could not be taken easily, like Delaware; coerced, like Maryland; or garrisoned, like Missouri. Unique, it had to be nursed out of neutrality. Of the significance of Kentucky we have the contemporary appraisal of Lincoln: "I think to lose Kentucky is nearly the same as to lose the whole game."

[5] Phisterer, *Statistical Record*, p. 3.

[6] Edward Channing, *A History of the United States* (6 vols.; New York: The Macmillan Co., 1927), VI, 374–394; Carl R. Fish, "The Decision of the Ohio Valley," *Annual Report of the American Historical Association for 1910* (Washington: The Smithsonian Institution, 1912), pp. 153–164.

Kentucky ranked ninth in the nation in numbers of slaves, higher than three states that adhered to the Confederacy. Yet its pattern of ownership showed wide dispersion, for of the 38,645 slaveowners only seventy owned over fifty slaves, and the state ranked third in the nation in number of slaveowners. Few slaves were kept in the mountainous eastern section; most of them lived in the Blue Grass or upper central section, and in the western counties where tobacco was cultivated.

White Kentuckians, whether slaveowners or not, were haunted by the question raised by abolitionist exhortations; they wondered what impact emancipation would have upon their way of life. Indeed, they had grown more reactionary toward slavery in the 1850s. A mob ran the Kentucky abolitionist, John G. Fee, and his following out of Madison County, and mass meetings supported this mob act. The legislature repealed the ban on importing slaves, passed new restrictive measures against incendiary literature, prohibited free Negroes from entering the state, and forbade manumission unless the freedman left the state. Many Kentuckians, however, believed there was greater security for slavery within the Union than outside it. Disunion would make impossible recapture of fugitive slaves, and would destroy slavery itself. If Kentucky should join the Confederacy, warned the influential Joseph Holt, slavery would "perish away...as a ball of snow would melt in a summer's sun."[7]

With regard to trade relations, the southward currents of the Ohio and Mississippi had long pulled Kentucky's exports toward New Orleans, but with the coming of the canals and especially the railroads, the configuration of commerce changed. By 1861, railroads from the North had reached the yet unbridged Ohio River at a dozen points opposite Kentucky; in contrast, only two railheads provided connection with the South. River and rail vied for Kentucky's trade, and the Mississippi remained the state's lifeline. But many Kentuckians feared that a Confederate government, practicing free trade, would impose an onerous direct tax; and they were

[7] E. Merton Coulter, *The Civil War and Readjustment in Kentucky* (Chapel Hill: University of North Carolina Press, 1926), pp. 6–12, quotation on p. 12.

aware that north of the Ohio River lived five and a half million people who, in the event of hostilities, could overwhelm the less than one million citizens of the Bluegrass State. For imports except coffee, moreover, Kentuckians were dependent upon the North. Emphasizing that the state might be caught between conflicting commercial interests, the Louisville *Democrat* demanded in 1860: "Are the Northwestern States willing to give the outlet at the mouth of the Mississippi to the Southern States?"[8]

"Right here, in the very center of the Mississippi Valley, lying like a crouching lion, stretched east and west, is Kentucky, the thoroughfare of the continent," an enthusiastic citizen once exulted. From the days of Daniel Boone, Virginians had passed through Cumberland Gap and down the rivers in such great numbers that Kentucky was often called "the child of Virginia." As late as 1860, the largest number of citizens born outside the state had come from Virginia; in ethnic origin, the state was distinctly Southern. In turn, Kentucky had sent her pioneers beyond the Ohio, beyond the Wabash, beyond the Mississippi. The state of Missouri, with 100,000 citizens of Kentucky birth in 1860, was the child of Kentucky; Indiana in that same year numbered 68,000 citizens born in Kentucky; and Illinois held 60,000. In all, a third of a million Kentuckians had found homes in other states, and very few of them in the South. Thus the bonds of kinship stretched in two directions.[9] Although Kentuckians had ancestors in Virginia, they had descendants in the North and West.

For all of these reasons, Kentuckians were Southern in their hearts, but they thought as national citizens. They were conservatives, who disapproved unilateral exercise of the right of secession— as well as use of force against seceded states. Variety of topography exerted some influence upon political views, with free-soil thinking strong in the non-slaveholding and urban areas; but Justice J. M. Harlan long ago scotched the myth that the Unionists (such as Lincoln) came only from the "thinner" soils while Kentucky Confederates were gentlemen of property from the Blue Grass.

[8] Quoted in Wilson P. Shortridge, "Kentucky Neutrality in 1861," *Mississippi Valley Historical Review*, IX (March, 1923), 284, n. 6.

[9] Coulter, *Civil War*, pp. 13–15.

Historical theories of geographic determinism, political allegiance, or religious affiliation, moreover, fall short of explaining the divisions within families, as Breckinridges, Crittendens, Todds, and other leading folk split in their loyalties. Robert J. Breckinridge served as temporary chairman of the Union (Republican) convention in 1864; he had sons in the Confederate and the Union armies, and his nephew had been the presidential nominee of the Southern extremists in 1860. Senator J. J. Crittenden, architect of the attempted compromise of 1860–61, had two sons, each a major general, on opposing sides in the armies. Mrs. Abraham Lincoln lost three brothers who had borne Confederate arms, and her husband had kin in the same service. N. S. Shaler, Kentucky-born Harvard paleontologist and historian, looking back to the year 1861, reminisced: "I do not know of a single large family in the state where all the men were arrayed on one side…"[10]

Ties of blood as well as commerce, then, tugged at Kentucky from both sides. Was the pull of equal strength, or would one side draw her into its camp? This was the great question confronting Kentuckians in April of 1861 as the sections rushed to war—the Union headed by one native son and the Confederacy by another. Abraham Lincoln, born in Hardin County in 1809, and Jefferson Davis, born in Christian County a year earlier, might each be expected to do his level best to gather the state to his own government, but which leader would exercise greater statesmanship in trying?

Kentucky had dispersed the family of one of these sons to the southern zone of the Old Northwest; and Abraham Lincoln, at the age of fifty-two, brought considerable reputation as a public figure but small experience as a public official to the high office he occupied in 1861. To be sure, he had served four terms in the Illinois legislature, and one term in the Congress (1847–49), but he had never gained administrative experience as a state governor. Further, he had been defeated for the U.S. Senate; and, though one of the nominees for the vice-presidency in 1856, he had not been the convention's choice.

He had begun to emerge from relative obscurity in 1854 with his stout opposition to the reopening of the Louisiana Purchase area to

[10] Speed, *Union Cause*, p. vii; N. S. Shaler, "Border State Men of the Civil War," *Atlantic Monthly*, lxix (February, 1892), 255.

slavery, a provision of the Kansas–Nebraska Act, which sparked the formation of the Republican party. Lincoln rose to national prominence as a moderate opponent of slavery through a notable series of speeches delivered between 1856 and 1860. Standing somewhere between abolitionists and conservative Unionists, he took what seemed his most extreme position in 1858, when in accepting nomination to the U.S. Senate he had ringingly declared: "A house divided against itself cannot stand." Though the candidate's phrase probably was meant to be prophecy rather than policy, it aggravated Southern distrust of him in the crisis of 1860–61.

Although elected a captain of volunteers in the tiny Black Hawk War, he had never seen combat service; a congressional critic of the Polk administration's motives in the Mexican War, he had no background in military affairs—unlike Jefferson Davis. A provincial Westerner, he had visited in New England and New York, and, as a young man, he had made a flatboat journey down the Mississippi to New Orleans, but he had seen little of the United States, and had never set foot outside the country. In the spring of 1861, he appeared singularly ill-equipped to hold the executive power of the nation, be commander-in-chief of the armed forces, or direct the course of American foreign policy.[11]

Soon after Jefferson Davis was born, his parents moved from Kentucky to Mississippi. In contrast with the Union president, he had received a classical education, at Transylvania University, and military training, at West Point. For eight years an officer of the United States army, he had seen service in the Black Hawk and the Mexican wars. Between terms as U.S. senator, Davis had been a very able secretary of war (1853–57). He championed, throughout the 1850s, the South's right to expand slavery in the territories (as well as in Cuba) and the South's need to develop economically to offset the growth of the North. The Davis resolutions of 1860, invoking Constitutional claims that slavery was immune from Federal interference and was entitled to Federal protection in the territories until they reached statehood, expressed the creedal faith of the land of cotton.

[11] Benjamin Thomas, *Abraham Lincoln* (New York: Alfred A. Knopf, Inc., 1952), *passim*.

Standing between the fire-eaters and the Southern Unionists, he was a compromise choice for the Confederate presidency in 1861. Perhaps no other Southerner was as well equipped by training and experience as Jefferson Davis to administer the affairs—civil and military—of the Confederate States of America. Like Lincoln, and most Americans, however, he was not knowledgeable in foreign relations. Catapulted into the presidency by secession, he looked the part of planter and aristocrat, his fine and sensitive features contrasting with the gaunt, swarthy countenance of his opposite number in Washington.

Faced with instituting a new nation among an individualistic people dedicated to state rights and slavery, in the spring of 1861, he would find that centralizing a war state and winning foreign sympathy were problems of peculiar obduracy. His pride in his military prowess did not in fact fit him to be a civilian commander-in-chief. His narrowness, morbid sensitivity, vulnerability to charges of favoritism in appointments and of interference in field operations, and his inability to mold public opinion could not readily be foreseen when he was inaugurated—the Confederacy's only president.[12]

Lincoln's secretaries tell us "from the beginning Lincoln felt that Kentucky would be a turning weight in the war." And Davis's biographer, Hudson Strode, declares: "Jefferson Davis hoped with all his heart for the border states of Kentucky and Missouri, because he felt that if Kentucky would secede along with Missouri, the nearer balance in strength would prevent the North from its purposed subjugation."[13]

Kentucky statesmen, for their part, had long striven to avert the schism that now had opened. Henry Clay, a native of Virginia, had thoroughly identified himself with the ideal of American nationalism; and his skillful moderating influence in the crises over the admission of Missouri, over South Carolina's nullification, and over the

[12] William E. Dodd, *Jefferson Davis* (Philadelphia: G. W. Jacobs & Co., 1907), *passim*; Hudson Strode, *Jefferson Davis, American Patriot, 1809–1861* (New York: Harcourt, Brace & World, 1955), *passim*.

[13] Quoted in Speed, *Union Cause*, p. 55; Hudson Strode, "Jefferson Davis, His Ideals of Honor Were Born in Kentucky," *Courier-Journal*, "The Civil War in Kentucky," November 20, 1960, p. 24.

complex of grievances smoothed out in 1850 had earned him the sobriquet, "the Great Compromiser." His mantle had fallen upon Senator John J. Crittenden, who in the crisis of 1860–61 had endeavored to unite the nation by dividing the territories.

Presiding over the Senate during this vain effort was Kentucky's youthful and handsome John C. Breckinridge, elected vice-president of the United States at the age of thirty-five, and the recent but unsuccessful nominee of the Southern Rights men for the presidency. A power in his state, he had failed to carry it in the election of 1860. The grandson of Thomas Jefferson's lieutenant, John Breckinridge, who had maneuvered the particularist Kentucky resolutions of 1798 through the state legislature, the younger Breckinridge now urged the Senate to adopt the Crittenden compromise. Well in advance of the expiration of the venerable Crittenden's term, the Kentucky legislature had elected Breckinridge to succeed Crittenden in the Senate scheduled to meet in 1861. Breckinridge believed in the right of secession, but he did not favor its exercise in the interval before Lincoln's call for troops. The call to arms, he thought, dissolved the Union, for he argued there was no Constitutional warrant to coerce a state.[14]

In political affiliation, Kentucky had through the days of Clay's supremacy given her ballots to the Whig party—often termed, if imprecisely, "the Party of Nationalism and Business." But the Whig party "went smash" in 1852, with only four states—Kentucky among them—supporting General Winfield Scott for the presidency. Clay went to his grave that year; and bewildered Whigs, unwilling to join the Democrats, at first flirted with the Know-Nothings (who elected a governor in 1855), and then—with a lamentable lack of imagination—called themselves "the Opposition," and lost the governorship in 1859 to the Democrat Beriah Magoffin.

In the election of 1860, four presidential candidates competed for Kentucky's votes: native sons Lincoln and Breckinridge (farthest apart of the four in political principles), Tennessee's John Bell (the nominee of moderation), and Stephen A. Douglas (champion of

[14] Albert D. Kirwan, *John J. Crittenden, The Struggle for the Union* (Lexington: University of Kentucky Press, 1962); Lucille Stillwell, *John C. Breckinridge* (Caldwell, Ida.: Caxton Press, 1936).

popular sovereignty). The election had been designed to resolve, at the grass roots, the national debate over the extension of slavery. With a cavalier disregard for native-son sentiment, Kentucky gave 45 per cent of its vote to Bell, 36 per cent to Breckinridge, 18 per cent to Douglas, and less than 1 per cent to Lincoln. Kentucky thereby placed moderation above admiration for a popular local leader.[15]

Beriah Magoffin, the Democratic governor of Kentucky in this crisis, united in his makeup the inheritance of an Irish father from county Down and a mother of Kentucky pioneer stock. A graduate at the age of twenty of Kentucky's Centre College, he had finished the law course at Transylvania University three years later, in 1838, and had practiced law and played with politics until he had been chosen governor over the "Opposition" candidate by a plurality of over 8,000 votes (in 1859). Strongly pro-Southern in his sympathies, from early in the secession winter he had worked for a compromise that would protect slavery. Before South Carolina seceded, he had sent a circular letter to the governors of the slave states advocating a Constitutional amendment that would divide the territories and assure recovery of fugitive slaves. He supported the Crittenden proposals—similar in essence to his—but a few days later the Kentucky senator offered a compromise plan in Congress.

Magoffin would have preferred cooperative action by the slave states. (He once told commissioners from Alabama that a slave state convention could agree in forty-eight hours on reasonable amendments to the Constitution that would win approval of enough Northerners to save the nation.) But the development of the secessionist movement, through independent state action, impelled him to place himself at the head of the Breckinridge element in the state, to call the legislature into special session, and to lead a drive to hold a state convention aimed at taking Kentucky out of the Union.[16]

[15] James R. Robertson, "Sectionalism in Kentucky from 1855 to 1865," *Mississippi Valley Historical Review*, IV (June, 1917), 57; Shortridge, "Kentucky Neutrality in 1861," *MVHR*, IX, 284.

[16] "Beriah Magoffin," Allen Johnson and Dumas Malone (eds.), *Dictionary of American Biography* (22 vols. and supplements; New York: Charles Scribner's Sons, 1928—), XII, 199–200.

"That Kentucky was confronted with the most serious problem that had ever arisen within the span of her entire existence was evident to all," historian E. M. Coulter has observed. Union men in the state—including Robert J. Breckinridge, Garret Davis, who had been a leader of the Bell party, and editor George D. Prentice of the Louisville *Journal* (as well as others)—began to organize in order to frustrate the convention movement and keep Kentucky in the Union.[17]

In his message to the legislature he had summoned to meet January 17, Magoffin disclosed a secessionist spirit. "We, the people, of the United States are no longer one people, united and friendly." He asked for approval of the Crittenden resolutions, to which it appeared (he said) the North stood opposed. Then he declared that the November election showed the North's purpose to administer the Federal government detrimentally to the South. He proclaimed that Kentucky would not submit to inequalities in the Union, and he pointed to the action of Kentucky's neighbors, Virginia and Tennessee, in calling state conventions. He asked the legislature to consider providing for a convention to determine at an early day "the future Federal and interstate relations of Kentucky." Of the seceded states he said: "Their cause is our right and they have our sympathies"; and of Federal coercion: "Kentucky will not be an indifferent observer of the force policy." Furthermore, he asked the legislature to arm and equip the state guard.[18]

Still clinging to the notion that the slave states acting together might yet find a Union-saving formula, Magoffin recommended that a convention of border slave states meet in early February. Magoffin had probably been obliged to abandon his plan for an all-Southern convention by the precipitate secession of the Lower South, for, by the time of his message, four states (South Carolina, Mississippi, Florida, and Alabama) had avowed themselves independent, and a fifth, Georgia, had made plain her purpose to follow speedily. The scheme of a border slave state convention, though perhaps futile in hindsight, recognized the weight of the Borderland and sought to use its leverage to restore the Union.

[17] Coulter, *Civil War*, p. 26.
[18] Speed, *Union Cause*, p. 27.

The nationalists in Kentucky busied themselves on behalf of their cause. Though the legislature was the same body that had elected Breckinridge to the U.S. Senate, the Breckinridge men failed to muster enough votes to call a state convention or to arm the state guard. Both houses passed resolutions that protested against Federal coercion and urged Southern states to halt the revolution. On February 11 the legislature adjourned, and the first phase of the struggle in Kentucky to call a secessionist convention had ended.

During that tense winter and spring of 1861, Kentucky lawmakers met three times. The failure of national attempts to find a formula of compromise drove Unionist and Southern Rights men to intensify their efforts within the state. Bell and Douglas forces, taking the name Union Democracy, labored to keep the state a member of the nation through compromise, forestallment of a convention, and inaction. Southern Rights forces organized clubs, circulated petitions, and called a state convention to meet in Frankfort the same day the legislature was to convene—March 20.

In the state senate, Union men preponderated by a slight majority, but in the house the division was about even; in each chamber the balance of power was held by a small group of legislators who opposed both secession and the active support of the Federal government. Unionist strategy aimed to avoid driving these men to the Southern Rights side. The second session lasted but a fortnight. The Union forces succeeded in preventing a vote upon a state secessionist convention. The session's most important work was to essay the role of mediator by calling a border slave state convention, with the hope of steering the nation from a collision course. The session, which ended April 4, made no provision for a convention.[19]

It was fortunate for the national cause that the Kentucky legislature, with its Confederate susceptibilities, was not sitting when shooting began at Fort Sumter. On April 15—two days after the Federal commander, Major Robert Anderson of Kentucky, surrendered his garrison—Lincoln hurled his thunderbolt. By

[19] Coulter, *Civil War*, pp. 36–37; *The American Annual Cyclopaedia and Register of Important Events of the Year 1861* (New York: D. Appleton & Co., 1866), pp. 396–397; Shortridge, "Kentucky Neutrality," *MVHR*, IX, *passim*; Speed, *Union Cause*, p. 39.

executive proclamation (Congress was not sitting), the President announced his policy of coercion. He called forth the militia of the several states to suppress "combinations" in the seven seceded states that were "too powerful to be suppressed by the ordinary course of judicial proceedings." Without consulting Congress, he had in effect declared the existence of a state of war.

It was this coercive measure, as we have said, that pushed four additional states into the new Southern nation. Outrage and indignation were widespread throughout the Borderland. Without hesitation, Governor Magoffin sent a defiant reply to Washington: "I say, *emphatically*, Kentucky will furnish no troops for the wicked purpose of subduing her sister states." He spoke the sentiment of most Kentuckians—if his tone was perhaps exceptionable. Unionist editor Prentice declared: "We are struck with mingled amazement. ...The Administration is not of our choosing. We did not bring it into power. It is composed of our deadly political foes."[20]

Kentucky's neighbors were also in convulsion. Her mother state, Virginia, in convention assembled, branded the President's proclamation a signal for the invasion of the South. The Old Dominion seceded April 17. Would the silver cord pull her daughter into the Confederacy? A portent of Kentucky's future appeared when the schismatic character of the diverse interests at stake impelled a group of citizens in western Virginia, on April 23, to set in train their own separatist movement, which ultimately led to the disruption of Virginia.

Governor John Letcher, uneasy about the possible use by the Union of the Baltimore and Ohio Railroad, which ran through the northwestern counties of Virginia, sent troops to obstruct passage, "even to the destruction of the road and bridges."[21] The consequent cutting of the line prompted the incursion of Federal troops from Ohio, who defeated the Virginia forces at Philippi on June 3.

The importance of Federal force in effecting the dismemberment of Virginia can scarcely be overstressed; though sectional conflict explains the new state movement, as historians have long stated, the

[20] Coulter, *Civil War*, p. 38.
[21] Festus P. Summers, *The Baltimore and Ohio in the Civil War* (New York: G. P. Putnam's Sons, 1939), p. 242, n. 27.

notion of Union solidarity in the fifty counties has been exposed as a myth. Half the counties, comprising almost two-thirds of the state's land area, opposed dismemberment and favored the Confederacy. The wartime West Virginia government never controlled more than half of the counties in the new state. Governor Henry A. Wise described West Virginia as the bastard child of a political rape.

Union strength in West Virginia lay in twenty-four counties along the banks of the Ohio, where about 60 per cent of the new state's population resided, and where Union sentiment overwhelmingly preponderated. These northwestern counties reckoned many citizens of Northern origin. Their trade moved in the Ohio River Valley, passing to Baltimore and Philadelphia; they owned almost no slaves, and looked to industrial development, especially iron and salt, instead of to agriculture as most Virginians did. It was this loyalist majority in the northwest that created the new state, arbitrarily incorporating the secessionist counties to the east and south—perhaps in order to place the Baltimore and Ohio Railroad entirely outside the Old Dominion. Western Virginians, their position strengthened by the presence of Federal troops, went securely ahead with formation of a new state, at Wheeling, on June 11.[22]

The decision of Missouri—to secede or not to secede—was second in consequence to the Union's retention of the Borderland only to the outcome in Kentucky. Bordering on the Father of Waters, flanking Illinois, and neighbor of Arkansas and pivotal Kentucky, Missouri had newly inaugurated a secessionist governor, Claiborne F. Jackson. Her legislature, like Kentucky's, was more pro-Southern than her people.

Early in January, in an address to a joint session of the legislature, Jackson identified Missouri's interests with those of the slaveholding South, and he asked the legislators to call a state convention. However, with an eye more to discussion of the national crisis than to secession, the lawmakers issued the call; and Unionists stipulated that an ordinance of secession must be submitted to popular ratification. When Missourians voted for delegates to the convention, they

[22] Richard O. Curry, "A Reappraisal of Statehood Politics in West Virginia," *Journal of Southern History*, XXVIII (November, 1962), 403–421.

cast 110,000 ballots for Conditional and Unconditional Unionist candidates, as opposed to 30,000 for secessionist candidates. More than half of the delegates were of Virginia and Kentucky ancestry.

The convention met in St. Louis from March 9 to March 22. Its report, submitted by Hamilton R. Gamble, favored the Crittenden compromise and declared that Missouri had no adequate cause for withdrawal from the Union. Compromise and Union represented the sentiment of Missourians at this time.

Meanwhile the St. Louis *Missouri Republican*, the principal conservative organ, had been developing the economic argument for rejection of secession. Disunion, it pointed out, would encourage slaves to flee; Confederate free-trade policy would ruin the hemp industry, where most slaves were employed; and needed Eastern capital would not be forthcoming to foster the mineral industry of the state.

St. Louis contained a subtreasury and a Federal arsenal—with $400,000 and 60,000 muskets in the respective repositories. Early in February, eighty U.S. regular troops, commanded by Captain Nathaniel Lyon, arrived to reinforce the small guard sent to the subtreasury a month earlier. A New Englander of rigid anti-slavery and Unionist principles—with a tendency toward martyrdom—Lyon zealously tried to save Missouri for the Union. After Governor Jackson denounced Lincoln's call for 75,000 militia as "illegal, unconstitutional, and revolutionary, in its object, inhuman and diabolical," Lyon secured authority from the secretary of war to recruit 10,000 men "for the protection of the peaceable inhabitants of Missouri."

On May 10, 1861, Lyon inaugurated war in Missouri; and during the ensuing four years the state would be a turbulent partner in the Union. State militia, numbering 700, had established a camp on hills overlooking the arsenal. Fearful of the loss of arms, Lyon had earlier shipped large quantities of them across the river into Illinois. Although his forces greatly outnumbered the militia, and the arms had been removed, Lyon forced the surrender of Camp Jackson and arrested the militiamen. The needless incident provoked mob action that resulted in the death of twenty-eight persons.

These events spread terror among the St. Louis disunionists; they also impelled the legislature to approve the governor's military measures, and they drove many Conditional Union men—including former governor Sterling Price—into secessionist ranks. This turbulence in Missouri sprang in part from a vacillating policy pursued by the Lincoln administration. Lyon worked hand in glove with Frank Blair, leader of the Unconditional Union men in Missouri and brother of Postmaster General Montgomery Blair. Lincoln placed too much reliance on the Blairs for guidance in his Missouri policy. At Blair's advice, the President on April 21 relieved Brigadier General William S. Harney of command of the Department of the West and gave Lyon temporary command of the forces around St. Louis. After the Camp Jackson fracas, Harney resumed command, reducing Lyon again to a subordinate position. Mistrustful of Harney, the Blairs persuaded the reluctant Lincoln to approve an order removing Harney, should his removal seem "indispensable" to Frank Blair.

Harney entered into an agreement with Sterling Price that effected a truce between the state and national governments. The Harney-Price agreement (May 21) was a statesmanlike act to maintain order and peace; and it was followed by Price's dispersal of troops from the state capital. But Unionists were dismayed, and Blair, on May 30—believing state authorities were violating the agreement— handed Harney his dismissal orders.

Lyon now came into temporary command of the Department of the West. On the night of June 11, at the end of a stormy four-hour meeting at the Planters' House in St. Louis, Lyon advised Governor Jackson: "In one hour one of my officers will call for you and conduct you out of my lines." Jackson fled to the capital, Jefferson City, where he issued a proclamation calling for 50,000 volunteers. He then repaired to Boonville, which he thought more easily defensible than Jefferson City.

At the head of 2,000 men, Lyon occupied the capital on June 15. Two days later he drove the state forces into southwest Missouri. The legal government of Missouri had been overturned by Union military strength. Lyon's attack on Camp Jackson had been a political blunder. The Harney-Price accord had been a viable arrangement that might have spared Missouri further bloodshed and guerrilla warfare. Federal interference turned Missouri into a "dark and bloody battleground" for Missourians.

Fighting continued throughout the summer, while Kentucky made its decision; and late in July Major General John C. Frémont, U.S.A., arrived in St. Louis to command the western department. Within a short time, despite a crisis of his own creation, he had established military control that cinched Missouri to the North.[23]

In Maryland, the focal point of danger was secessionist Baltimore. When the Sixth Massachusetts attempted to pass through the city, on April 19, a mob fell upon it; and in the fray four soldiers and at least nine civilians died. The secessionists tore up the railroad track, bridges and telegraph wires that connected Baltimore and Washington, and isolated the Federal capital for six frightening days. Soon a new Massachusetts force, commanded by iron-fisted Major General Benjamin F. Butler, arrived by ship and took military possession of Baltimore and Annapolis. Maryland gave no further important resistance to Federal troop movements.

Governor Thomas Hicks, for his part, flatly refused to summon a special session of the legislature in late December. Under the impact of the April riots, he called a session (for the 26th) to meet in Frederick rather than perfervid Baltimore. The legislature protested the governor's proposal of neutrality, denounced military occupation of the state, and resolved in favor of Southern independence; beyond this it would not go. On May 15 Governor Hicks called out four regiments to meet the month-old call. It was too late for ninety-day men, but Maryland from then on furnished volunteers for the Union, and came close to meeting her quotas.[24]

Would Kentucky now summon the sovereign convention that would align her with Virginia, Tennessee (which had seceded May 7), and the cause of Southern Rights? Rioting in Maryland, skirmishes in western Virginia—where the rail connection with Chesapeake Bay was threatened—and unrest in Missouri marked the days as the convention movement in Kentucky entered its climactic phase. Governor Magoffin called the legislature to meet May 6 to provide for a sovereignty convention.

[23] William E. Parrish, *Turbulent Partnership, Missouri and the Union, 1861–1865* (Columbia: University of Missouri Press, 1963), chs. 1–2.

[24] Allan Nevins, *The War for the Union* (2 vols.; New York: Charles Scribner's Sons, 1959–60), I, 80–87, 137–139.

Keenly disappointed by Congress's failure to adopt the compromise measures he had sponsored, John Jordan Crittenden now wielded his pacificatory influence upon state sentiment. A towering figure in this time of travail, vigorous and white-haired at seventy-three, he was credited by the perceptive contemporary politician, James G. Blaine, as being more responsible than any other man for saving Kentucky from rebellion. "But for his strong hold upon the sympathy and pride of Kentucky, the malign influence of Breckinridge might have forced the State into the Confederacy," Blaine wrote. For a half century Crittenden had been conspicuous in politics: in the state legislature, where he had served as speaker; in both houses of Congress; and as attorney general of the United States. He had capped his last term in the Senate with the abortive Crittenden compromise, intended to bag the stormy winds blowing over the issues of Negro fugitives and slavery in the territories.[25]

Erect and spare, Crittenden made a notable speech at Lexington on April 17, an expression of the Kentucky mind. Kentucky, he said, had not brought on this war; she had labored to avert it. She should now refuse help to either belligerent party and occupy a position between the foes as friendly mediator—a suggestion quickly taken up by Union men as a means of preventing secession. Crittenden toured the state, championing the doctrine of neutrality as a means toward compromise and peace.

On April 18 John C. Breckinridge made an ardent address to a gathering in Lexington. The former vice-president declared that the "only means by which a general civil war can be prevented is to confront Mr. Lincoln with fifteen united compact States to warn him that his unholy war is to be waged against 13,000,000 of freemen and fifteen sovereign States."[26] The struggle to sway Kentucky went on. The election of delegates to the border slave state convention took place May 4. It was a victory for moderation, since the Unionist delegates polled 106,863 votes against a mere 4,262—and Crittenden

[25] Kirwan, *Crittenden*, esp. pp. 431–432; James G. Blaine, *Twenty Years of Congress.* . . (2 vols.; Norwich, Conn.: Henry Hill Publishing Co., 1884–86), I, 330–331.

[26] Robert M. McElroy, *Kentucky in the Nation's History* (New York: Moffat, Yard & Co., 1909), p. 514.

was among those elected. But the convention itself, which met at Frankfort from May 27 to June 3, with Crittenden presiding, was a lame affair, drawing representatives only from Missouri and Kentucky, and recommending the discredited Crittenden resolutions.[27]

Union supporters were active in many ways, issuing addresses to the people, holding mass meetings, and turning to Lincoln for external aid. The President was by conviction a staunch nationalist and by virtue of his office the Commander-in-chief of the armed forces. He had been defied by a state governor, when Magoffin had refused to furnish Kentucky's quota of troops. What could he now do—throw Federal armies into the state, or draw the veil on Kentucky's assertion of her sovereignty? On April 26 the Kentucky Unionist Garret Davis had an interview with the President, and liked what he heard. Lincoln spoke with an enlightened pragmatism that was to characterize his skillful handling of Kentucky's peculiar behavior throughout the fateful summer months. Davis learned from the President that he had no military movements in mind requiring sending troops through Kentucky, and if Kentucky made no military move against the Federal government he would not molest her.[28]

A formidable state guard had been organized under the zealous leadership of Simon Bolivar Buckner, a graduate of West Point and a Southern sympathizer, who imbued the guard with his views. Governor Magoffin tried to persuade the legislature to strengthen this force, only to have action impeded by Unionists, who distrusted his purposes. On the last day of the third session (May 24), the legislature passed measures to arm the state, but at the same time it wrested control from Magoffin and vested it in an unconstitutional military board. It also established a rival home guard for defense of the counties, to share equally in appropriations with the state guard. Now the Southern Rights and Unionist factions each had its military organization, neither of which could legally be employed against North or South, but the danger of internal strife had grown.[29]

[27] Shortridge, "Kentucky Neutrality," *MVHR*, IX, 291–293; Kirwan, *Crittenden*, pp. 437–438; Stillwell, *Breckinridge*, p. 98.

[28] Coulter, *Civil War*, p. 54.

[29] *Ibid.*, pp. 86–91.

The Confederacy, perhaps misled by Kentucky's defiance of Lincoln, on April 22 called on Magoffin "to furnish one regiment, without delay" to Harper's Ferry. Magoffin promptly refused, but he secretly began to connive with Confederate recruiters in his state. A former naval officer, William Nelson, conferred with Lincoln and described the danger of losing Kentucky to the Confederacy. The President partially abandoned his "hands off" policy, and secretly began to furnish the "Lincoln guns"—renowned in the state's history—to a select committee of Kentucky Unionists. The committee, which included Nelson, Crittenden, Garret Davis, and others, allocated about 10,000 muskets in critical areas in early May. "These arms gave assurance and confidence to Kentucky Unionists and may have been a decisive factor in saving the state from secession," Kentucky historian Albert D. Kirwan has judged.[30]

Before the end of May, following the failure of the border slave state convention, came the climax of the struggle to hold a secessionist convention. On May 16 the lower house of the state legislature adopted the course of action prescribed by Crittenden, and virtually his language, when it resolved that Kentucky "should take no part in the civil war now being waged, except as mediator and friends to the belligerent parties, and that Kentucky should, during the contest, occupy the position of strict neutrality." The resolution was so broadly worded it could be endorsed by extremists from both sides, and it passed 69–26. Then the Unionists brought forward a resolution, far more definite in provisions, that would have restricted the activities of the secessionists. Complicated parliamentary fencing ensued, and the secessionists managed to defeat the second resolution by a single vote, 47–48. "They lost heart from that vote," N. S. Shaler records. "Some of them at once left their places for the Confederate army, convinced that nothing but the invasion of Kentucky by an army from the Southern States would give them mastery."[31]

The legislature sustained the governor's refusal to furnish troops upon the call of the executive authority of the United States. Four

[30] Kirwan, *Crittenden*, p. 436.
[31] Speed, *Union Cause*, p. 32; N. S. Shaler, *Kentucky. A Pioneer Commonwealth* (4th ed.; Boston: Houghton Mifflin & Co., 1888), p. 246.

days later Magoffin issued his own lengthy proclamation of armed neutrality and prohibited the movement of any outside forces, whether Federal or Confederate, upon the soil of Kentucky. An hour before the session adjourned, the senate (on May 24) adopted the policy of armed neutrality.[32]

"Utter fallacy ... useless inertia and quasi-treason," editorialized the *New York Times* on Kentucky's neutrality.[33] Others impeached Kentuckians of cowardice. Properly understood, neutrality was the expression of Kentucky's uniqueness; it was not the outgrowth of timidity. The 100,000 men—white and Negro—who wore the blue uniform and the estimated 40,000 who wore the gray are the refutation of that libel. Neutrality was a wise response to the state's dilemma and a logical result of her history. It echoed Clay's impassioned appeal to the Senate for compromise in 1850. It evidenced the people's reluctance to accept the madness and tragedy of a brothers' war. It clung to the hope that Kentucky might yet be the *mediator*, the significant word of the legislature's resolution, in the fratricidal strife. It meant an interim victory for the anti-secessionist forces, and was perhaps the only course that could keep the state from seceding. Neutrality also served the short-range political ends of both extremes during a period of agonizing incertitude. It spared the state the guerrilla combat that bloodied the ground of Missouri. Finally, neutrality provided a cooling-off period for the sorely divided commonwealth until sentiment could crystallize.

In May of 1861 it was equally harrowing for Kentuckians to contemplate withdrawing from the Federal union or raising a hand against their sister states. Ultimately untenable in a protracted war, neutrality was the happiest expedient that could be devised in that hour's quandary. And as this move of the Democratic legislature and the Democratic governor faced Kentucky away from secession, it may also have kept the Union from ultimate disintegration.[34] An exuberant local poet cried:

[32] Randall and Donald, *Civil War*, p. 229; also see Coulter, *Civil War*, p. 56.

[33] *New York Times*, May 12, 1861.

[34] Shaler, "Border State Men," *Atlantic Monthly*, LXIX; Randall and Donald, *Civil War*, p. 22.

Orbed in order, crowned with olives, there invoking peace,
  she stands;
Wreck and roar of revolution,
Anarchy and dissolution.
In the music and the glory, of the good old Constitution,
Sphered forever, there she stands!
It is there Kentucky stands![35]

In proclaiming her neutrality, Kentucky had claimed state sovereignty for herself as fully as South Carolina had in nullifying the tariff in 1832—and almost as fully as the Southern states had in seceding from the Union. Neutrality is a position that may be taken by an *independent* nation toward a *foreign* war, as the United States had done in the wars of the French Revolution and Napoleon. But Kentucky was a member of the Federal union; and its legislators and executive officers had taken an oath to support the Constitution, the supreme law of the land. Kentucky had flouted the Constitutional Commander-in-chief by refusing to furnish soldiers and by prohibiting Federal troops from "trespassing" on her "sovereign" soil.

Thus Kentucky's neutrality, unheard of in the Constitution, was a direct challenge to President Lincoln, who had promised in his inaugural address: "I shall take care, as the Constitution itself expressly enjoins upon me, that the laws of the Union be faithfully executed in all the states." Before Kentucky officially adopted her position, Lincoln, as we have seen, had quietly given assurances he would not send troops through the state and had secretly armed friends of the Union. Would he now accord recognition to this defiant doctrine, or would he—consistent with his nationalist principles—insist that Kentucky meet her responsibilities as a state in the Federal union?

The President continued to practice his pragmatic circumvention of the issue. A little more than a week after the governor's proclamation, the Federal government set up the Military Department of Kentucky, embracing only that part of the state within one hundred miles of the Ohio River (a generally loyal portion), and gave command to the Kentucky hero, Major Robert Anderson of Sumter fame. Sage General-in-chief Winfield Scott in Washington explained: "It is deemed here unwise to send to Kentucky a commander or

[35] Quoted in Coulter, *Civil War*, p. 42.

troops not natives and residents of the state." After western Virginia had been made secure, another Kentuckian, William Nelson of the "Lincoln guns" affair, was ordered to start recruiting in Kentucky, confining his activities to the Unionist southeastern region.[36]

Lincoln came to feel, however, that he could not only *not* recognize the policy of armed neutrality, he must officially repudiate it, though very likely he meant nothing more at the moment than to expose its fallacy. In his message to the special session of Congress that sat July 4, 1861, he spoke forthrightly on the policy of armed neutrality favored by some persons in the border states.

> An arming of those States to prevent the Union forces passing one way, or the disunion the other, over their soil ... would be disunion completed.... for, under the guise of neutrality, it would tie the hands of the Union men, and freely pass supplies from among them to the insurrectionists.... It recognizes no fidelity to the Constitution, no obligation to maintain the Union.[37]

Strong language from the Commander-in-chief! And John J. Crittenden, now a member of the House of Representatives, went along to the White House with Simon B. Buckner, the emissary Magoffin had sent to ask the President whether he intended to order troops into Kentucky. Lincoln assured them he had no present purpose to do so, and said he hoped he would have none, but he would say nothing that might later embarrass him in performance of his duty. The President wrote this out on a paper that he prudently refused to sign, but Crittenden inscribed his own initials to prove its authenticity. Lincoln had again demonstrated his pragmatism in indicating he would not force a showdown on the conflicting principles of state neutrality and national supremacy. At the same time, he had not bound himself as to future action, nor had he said anything officially.[38]

The special session of Congress, it will be remembered, had been summoned by President Lincoln in his proclamation of April 15,

[36] *Ibid.*, pp. 99–100.

[37] Roy P. Basler *et al.* (eds.), *The Collected Works of Abraham Lincoln* (9 vols.; New Brunswick, N.J., Rutgers University Press, 1953–55), IV, 428, and nn. 42–44.

[38] Coulter, *Civil War*, pp. 99–100.

but he had called the session for July 4, rather than immediately. One of the reasons for deferral, it has been suggested, was the election struggle in Kentucky. The state held a special election June 20—a month after the decision to be neutral—to name its representatives. The voters demonstrated their latent unionism by choosing nine Unionists, including former U.S. senator Crittenden, and one Southern Rights representative.

In the halls of Congress, Crittenden would confront his successor in the Senate, John C. Breckinridge, as a main antagonist.[39] Crittenden gave one last great service to the nation and a final witness of the principle for which he and Kentucky historically stood. Having failed to compromise the sectional conflict, he now essayed to moderate its fury. He succeeded in getting congressional endorsement of his celebrated resolution on war aims. The Crittenden Resolution disavowed the spirit of subjugation or oppression and any intention to interfere with slavery, and declared the war was being waged for two objects: "to defend and maintain the supremacy of the Constitution and to preserve the Union with all the dignity, equality, and rights of the several States unimpaired." As soon as these aims were accomplished, "the war ought to cease."[40] In short, no emancipation and no reconstruction.

The resolution was approved by the House with only two dissenting votes, by the Senate with only five. Breckinridge, one of the dissenters, told the Senate he could not vote for the resolution because he could not agree with its statement of facts. He believed the war was already being fought in a spirit of subjugation and emancipation; and he said a recent speech by Senator John Sherman of Ohio indicated it might become a war of extermination. Throughout the session Breckinridge opposed the President's war policy, refusing to vote men or money. A dramatic highlight of the session occurred when Senator Edward D. Baker of Oregon, wearing the full uniform of an army colonel, with fine presence and commanding voice, eloquently denounced the senator from Kentucky. A few months later Baker fell, fatally wounded, at Ball's Bluff. By that time

[39] Shortridge, "Kentucky Neutrality," *MVHR*, IX, 297.

[40] Edward McPherson, *Political History of the United States during the Rebellion* (Washington: Philip & Solomons, 1865), p. 122.

Breckinridge was wearing the uniform of a Confederate general, and the Senate when it convened in regular session voted his expulsion.[41]

The summer of 1861 was a troubled and tense time in Kentucky. A secret pro-Confederate order, the Knights of the Golden Circle, engaged in stealthy activities. State guards and home guards drilled and girded for fighting, and Confederate and Union recruiters solicited soldiers for the gray and the blue. The Union defeat at Bull Run, on July 21, electrified sentiment and heartened the secessionist element. A Kentuckian who was in the state capital recalled: "It was a day long to be remembered. The young men almost went wild; and I heard, as the Confederate flag waved through the streets ... 'we'll follow that flag, and cheer it even in hell!'"[42] Bull Run also dispelled hopes that Kentucky might mediate between the sections.

While spirited young men moved north and south to join the colors that summer, anxious citizens signed petitions that Kentucky stay neutral. Business conditions were in disarray, and prices and values were unstable as both Congresses sought to supervise trade between the sections. The Union, though enunciating a policy in opposition to trade with the rebel states, in practice allowed trade with the South. The Confederate Congress, less wise than the Federal government, permitted export of her chief crops only through her own seaports or across the Mexican border, thus cutting off Kentucky. "The Federal government worked toward ultimate ends, and it won the bigger reward," E. M. Coulter has judged. "The South, too impatient to be tolerant and too impetuous to be tactful, lost the greatest prize of the West—Kentucky."[43]

Unlike many of the seceding states, where the public pulse on secession was not carefully taken, Kentucky had the good fortune to conduct three special elections in 1861: for the border slave state convention, for Congress, and for the state legislature. Each eventuated in a Union victory—not meaning, to be sure, the Union at any price but the Union in preference to secession, unless there was provocation. In the special election of August 5 to choose a new

[41] *Annual Cyclopaedia ... 1861*, pp. 242–244; James K. Hosmer, *The Appeal to Arms* (New York: Harper & Brothers, 1907), p. 67.

[42] Coulter, *Civil War*, pp. 105–106.

[43] *Ibid.*, p. 80.

legislature, the Unionists won 76 of 100 seats in the house and 27 of 38 seats in the senate. This election, like its immediate predecessor, reflected a desire for peace; it was not an endorsement of Lincoln's war policy.[44]

The victory, nonetheless, emboldened the Lincoln administration, for the next day General William Nelson moved his headquarters to within thirty miles of Lexington, where he established Camp Dick Robinson and concentrated Federal troops, composed solely of Kentuckians. Governor Magoffin sent two commissioners to Washington to ask Lincoln to remove the Federal troops; this the President refused to do. In his reply to Magoffin, Lincoln spoke of his regret he could not find any "intimation that you entertain any desire for the preservation of the Federal Union."[45]

The Confederacy meanwhile began to accept all troops offered from Kentucky. On August 30 the Confederate Congress passed a measure providing for setting up recruiting stations in Kentucky. On the same day it secretly appropriated one million dollars "to aid the people of Kentucky in repelling any invasion or occupation of their soil by the armed forces of the United States." Jefferson Davis later observed: "The people of Kentucky were at that time regarded as allies of the Confederacy, sympathizing with its cause .... The appropriation was in its nature a subsidy to an ally."[46]

On the very day of this Confederate measure, a rash Union general almost demolished the delicate balance within the state, almost drove Kentucky into the arms of its "ally." General John C. Frémont, commanding guerrilla-ridden Missouri, issued a sweeping proclamation that established a Draconian martial law throughout the state and emancipated the slaves of all persons resisting the United States. Lincoln was aghast at the unauthorized proclamation. He promptly intervened, modifying the severity of martial law and countermanding the edict of proclamation.

In a letter to a protesting friend and member of Congress, Lincoln

[44] Shortridge, "Kentucky Neutrality," *MVHR*, IX, 297, and n. 73.
[45] Coulter, *Civil War*, p. 104; Basler (ed.), *Collected Works*, IV, 494.
[46] Dunbar Rowland (ed.), *Jefferson Davis, Constitutionalist* (10 vols.; Jackson, Miss.: Mississippi Department of Archives and History, 1923), VI, 157.

justified his intervention on the ground of reversing an act of military dictatorship, but he went on to point out the implications for Kentucky.

> The Kentucky legislature would not budge till that proclamation was modified; and Gen. Anderson telegraphed me that on the news of Gen. Frémont having actually issued deeds of manumission, a whole company of our Volunteers threw down their arms and disbanded. I was so assured, as to think it probable, that the very arms we had furnished Kentucky would be turned against us....
>
> I think to lose Kentucky is nearly the same as to lose the whole game. Kentucky gone, we can not hold Missouri, nor, as I think, Maryland. These all against us, and the job on our hands is too large for us. We would as well consent to separation at once, including the surrender of this capitol.[47]

He had in fact sent his instructions to Frémont before hearing from Kentucky, but it was well for the Union that he acted; and the legislature thanked him for his intervention.

The end of Kentucky's neutrality therefore came not because of General Frémont but because of the struggle for western Kentucky. The southwestern corner of the state—the Purchase—was an area of first importance to winning the Mississippi Valley. Four great rivers come together here: the Cumberland, the Tennessee, the Ohio, and the Mississippi. The first two rivers were the gateway to the Southeast—the means to a strategic thrust down the Mississippi Valley (to eventual conquest of the Father of Waters) and to the penetration of Tennessee and Georgia (to eventual attainment of the Atlantic). For some time a Union army, under General U. S. Grant, had occupied Cairo, Illinois, at the junction of the Ohio and Mississippi rivers; and for some time Federal and Confederate forces had staged raids into neutral Kentucky. The situation had already grown acute when Fremont published his proclamation.

On September 2, Federal troops occupied Belmont, Missouri, below Cairo and opposite Columbus, Kentucky. Nervous about the Federals' next move, and mistakenly believing Kentuckians would rise in support of Southern forces, Major General Leonidas Polk occupied Columbus. President Davis explained the crucial decision to the Confederate Congress on November 18, 1861.

[47] Basler (ed.), *Collected Works*, IV, 532.

Finding that the Confederate States were about to be invaded through Kentucky, and that her people, after being deceived into a mistaken security, were unarmed and in danger of being subjugated by the Federal forces, our armies were marched into that State to repel the enemy and prevent their occupation of certain strategic points which would have given them great advantages in the contest.[48]

The Confederate government had by proclamation announced a desire to respect the state's neutrality, and had never intended to conquer or coerce, Davis maintained; and it would have withdrawn had the federal troops done so.

General Grant now ordered troops to cross the Ohio and to occupy Paducah, Kentucky, at the mouth of the Tennessee—a town so Southern in sentiment it was nicknamed "Little Charleston." To the South's dismay, the Kentuckians did not rally to the Stars and Bars. The newly elected pro-Unionist legislature, fortunately for the North, was in session, and on September 7 it ordered the United States flag raised over the capitol at Frankfort. On the eleventh, it instructed Governor Magoffin to have the Confederate troops withdraw. Magoffin vetoed the resolution, but the legislature passed it over his veto. A week later the legislators implemented their instruction; they put Robert Anderson in charge of the Kentucky volunteers to expel the Confederates, told the governor to call out the militia, and asked aid of the Federal government. When Magoffin vetoed this action, the lawmakers again overrode him, and they refused to ask the Union forces to leave the state.

The next day, September 19, at the instance of the presiding officers of both houses of the legislature, an expedition under Colonel Thomas Bramlette (who would be elected governor in 1863) marched toward Lexington with the twofold purpose of forestalling a great peace meeting scheduled for the twenty-first and arresting the junior U.S. senator from Kentucky, John C. Breckinridge. A delay permitted Breckinridge to make his escape; and, after publishing an *apologia*, he donned the Confederate uniform.[49]

[48] Coulter, *Civil War*, p. 106; Rowland (ed.), *Davis*, V, 168.
[49] Shortridge, "Kentucky Neutrality," *MVHR*, IX, 300; Frank H. Heck, "John C. Breckinridge in the Crisis of 1860–1861," *Journal of Southern History*, XXI (August, 1955), 316–346.

Leaving no doubt that neutrality was no longer the policy of Kentucky, the legislature issued an address that called upon Kentuckians to "put forth the whole energies of the Commonwealth till the rebellion shall be overthrown, and the just supremacy of the National Government shall be restored." The address pinned the war guilt upon the disunionists, laid down the Crittenden Resolution as the "rule of action" from which the national government could not depart, and affirmed "that slavery is a State institution."[50]

The *New York Times* rejoiced at the turn of events in Kentucky.

It is now clear to us that the invasion of Kentucky by the rebels was, on their part, a crowning blunder, as it rendered her a staunch supporter of the National Government, led to the raising of her quota of troops and gave us among friends just the base we wanted for operations against Tennessee and further South.[51]

The legislature, obviously, could not speak for all the people, with their multiform opinions. In addition to Breckinridge, Kentucky sent other eminent citizens to leadership of the grayclad armies— among them Albert Sidney Johnston, John B. Hood, and Simon B. Buckner, each of whom saw significant action in the Mississippi Valley. Kentucky soldiers in the Confederate service, on hearing of the work of the regular legislature, called a convention to meet at Russellville on the southern border. It drew up a declaration of independence, set up a provisional government with Colonel George W. Johnson as governor (he was killed at Shiloh less than five months later), made Bowling Green the capital, and took steps to bring Kentucky into the Confederacy. The Confederate Congress admitted Kentucky into the Confederacy on December 10; and the state was allotted twelve seats in the Confederate House of Representatives. "Confederate Kentucky," however, never amounted to more than a rump of the people.[52]

Grant soon exploited his position by an amphibious movement up the Tennessee River to Fort Henry, which passed into his hands

[50] *Annual Cyclopaedia . . . 1861*, p. 402.

[51] *New York Times*, November 24, 1861.

[52] Henry S. Commager (ed.), *Documents of American History* (2 vols., 7th ed.; New York: Appleton-Century-Crofts, 1963), I, 401–402; Lewis Collins and Richard H. Collins, *History of Kentucky . . .* (2 vols.; Covington, Ky.: Collins & Co., 1882), I, 345.

February 6, 1862. Eleven miles away stood Fort Donelson, over-looking the Cumberland River. Its commander, Simon B. Buckner, was offered no terms but unconditional surrender, and on February 16 he capitulated to his former West Point comrade. Ironically, Buckner had been tendered a commission as brigadier general of volunteers by Lincoln the preceding August.

Grant was now ready to move south. Kentucky seemed secure for the Union, until—as we shall see—Braxton Bragg, C.S.A., invaded the state in the autumn. Meanwhile, John Breckinridge had been indicted in a Federal court for treason, and his place in the U.S. Senate had been taken by Unionist Garret Davis. As for Beriah Magoffin, his position became increasingly difficult, and in August of 1862 he was allowed to resign the governorship, with the privilege of naming a temporary successor. When the regular gubernatorial election took place in 1863, voters gave the Unionist candidate, Thomas Bramlette, a majority of over 50,000 votes.[53]

Let us now survey the outcome of the secessionist struggle in the other border slave states. From late April on, little Delaware supplied troops to the North—in all, 12,000 men. Its main obstruction to the war effort would come, as we shall see, by its unwillingness to embrace Lincoln's policy of compensated emancipation.[54]

Maryland remained under military surveillance until it had held its fall elections, with the secretary of war overseeing its political life. To assure the victory of the Unionist candidate for governor, secessionist members of the legislature were placed under arrest, soldiers were furloughed home to vote, and provost marshals kept anti-Unionists from the polls. By a result of 57,502 to 26,070 the Unionist Augustus W. Bradford won the governorship in November. The state rights party virtually succumbed, many pro-Confederate sympathizers fled from Maryland, and the state was thereafter loyal.[55]

The establishment of a Unionist government in western Virginia had contributed to the growth of loyalism in Maryland. In June the

[53] Robertson, "Sectionalism in Kentucky," p. 60.

[54] Phisterer, *Statistical Record*, p. 10.

[55] Randall and Donald, *Civil War*, pp. 231–233.

Wheeling convention, representing most of the western counties, had nullified the Virginia ordinance of secession and named Francis Pierpoint governor of "restored" Virginia. A convention that met in November drafted a constitution for West Virginia that was silent on slavery. The voters ratified the document in April, 1862, by a resounding majority. After a delay because of various complications, including slavery, West Virginia was admitted to the Union in June, 1863. A new state had been born out of the Borderland during the war.[56]

With Missouri's duly elected government expelled by force, a new one was needed. The convention reassembled on July 22; its former president, Sterling Price, was in exile, and fifteen other pro-Confederates were absent. Originally convened in the apparent interest of secession, in a sharply ironic twist it now deposed the governor, vacated other offices—including the legislature—and abrogated several "odious laws." In its sovereign capacity, it named Hamilton R. Gamble, an old-line Whig and brother-in-law of Attorney General Edward Bates, as governor.

The provisional government remained in power in Missouri throughout the war. Its members were somewhat embarrassed by the arrival, in late July, of Major General John C. Frémont to assume command of a new Department of the West. He proved uncooperative, both with the provisional government and the Blairs, and he was blamed for failing to provide support for Lyon's forces, which were defeated at the battle of Wilson's Creek (where Lyon lost his life). Fremont incurred charges of being inaccessible, extravagant, incompetent, and tyrannical. It was he who instituted martial law in the state and at the same time freed rebels' slaves. As we have seen, portions of his decree had to be overruled, but friction persisted between Frémont on one side and Gamble and Frank Blair on the other. One hundred days after he had taken command he was relieved, but Missouri remained under martial law, partly as a result of the bitter divisions Frémont had unwittingly promoted. Missouri suffered internal strife—a war of neighbors—but the battle of Pea Ridge (fought in Arkansas, March 6–8, 1862)—the only major engagement west of the Mississippi River—placed most of the state

[56] Curry, "A Reappraisal of Statehood Politics," *passim.*

under Union control. Military superiority held Missouri for the Federal government throughout the war.[57]

During the great severance of 1861, the Bluegrass State, rent in spirit even as the nation, expressed its temper in neutralism. A fascinating speculation is what might have been if Virginia or the border slave states, as an entity, had pursued the same course. Be that as it may, one party to the conflict dealt more dexterously than the other with a most delicate political problem. The Union by its forbearance, by its reluctance to send troops into a state that set at naught national supremacy, by its restraint from the kind of rashness Blair and Lyon were guilty of in Missouri, by the adroit statements of its Chief Executive to Kentucky leaders, by lenient policing of the state's commerce, by keeping recruiting just apace of developing loyalism, and by realistically if quietly placing guns in friendly hands manifested high political capacity.

The Confederacy was less forbearing. Jefferson Davis regarded the unseceded state as an ally. The Confederate secretary of war, L. P. Walker, made the incredibly inept remark, on the eve of the legislative election in Kentucky, that the Confederacy did not want Kentucky as an ally but as a battleground. After Camp Dick Robinson had been established by the Unionists, Davis declared he would respect Kentucky's neutrality so long as the people of Kentucky maintained it; in effect, Kentuckians might have to drive the Unionists out, thereby abandoning neutrality by fighting against the North. Also, the Confederacy placed the state's commerce under rigid surveillance. Finally, it was the Confederate invasion of the state that shattered neutrality, to the Union's immense gain.[58]

The forces were delicately but unevenly balanced in Kentucky, and historians who have portrayed an equilibrium among Kentuckians misread or confuse the situation. Kentucky had been historically Whig—its *beau idéal* was Henry Clay, the Great Compromiser. Governor Magoffin and the lower house of the legislature, with their

[57] Parrish, *Turbulent Partnership*, chs. 3–4.

[58] Coulter, *Civil War*, pp. 104–115; Arndt M. Stickles, *Simon Bolivar Buckner, Borderland Knight* (Chapel Hill: University of North Carolina Press, 1940), pp. 75–86.

secessionist susceptibilities, did not represent the bulk of opinion in the state. They had been elected in 1859, at the end of a decade that had destroyed the Whig party and had raised up a sectional anti-slavery party, and that by recurring crises and sensation had deepened Kentuckians' awareness of their Southernism. In this same context, John Breckinridge had been elected U.S. senator in 1859— two years beforehand—by the legislature.

The elections of 1860–61 are a better index of popular sentiment than the political leanings of executive and legislature in early 1861. By their election of state officials and presidential electors in 1860, the voters had shown their Unionism. The three elections of 1861 uniformly attested an overwhelming preference for Union candidates over Southern Rights men. Moreover, Kentucky resisted secession under a series of provocative events: the election of Lincoln (to whom the state gave less than 1 per cent of its popular vote), Lincoln's call to arms of April 15, and the secession of Virginia—not to speak of events in neighboring Tennessee and nearby Arkansas.

Nevertheless, the danger of Kentucky's transfer of allegiance was real—very real. To say that the governor and legislature were more prone to secession than the majority of people is not to erase the menace of secessionist action by those holding power. The danger, to be explicit, was threefold: internal dissension, as in Missouri and briefly in Maryland; external invasion, which President Lincoln in Washington and General George B. McClellan in Cincinnati did not sanction; and external interference with slavery, which Frémont's proclamation presaged and which, again, Lincoln did not sanction.

It is also necessary to say a word about the nature of Unionism in Kentucky. It was, persistently throughout the war, moderate, reluctant, and disfavorable to the extreme nationalistic measures employed in the realms of civil liberties and emancipation. It was never imbued with a perfervid nationalism, and it was often openly hostile to the Lincoln administration. For the first six months of the war, which encompassed the shock of Bull Run, neutrality was an acceptable posture to Unionists.

We will return to a consideration of Kentucky when we examine other turning points: Antietam and its western counterpart, Perryville; the policy of emancipation; and the reelection of Lincoln. But with its decision to adhere to the Union—and the decision was Kentucky's—the possibility that the slaveholding Borderland might defect to the slaveholding Confederate States of America had been closed out. When Congress assembled in December for its regular session, Lincoln welcomed the verdict of his native state: "Kentucky ...for some time in doubt, is now decidedly, and, I think, unchangeably, ranged on the side of the Union."[59]

[59] Basler (ed.), *Collected Works*, V, 50.

Bull Run

We now begin to see the magnitude
of the contest.

Senator John Sherman

While Kentucky was in travail, the nation suffered the first massive shock of civil war. From April to September, Kentucky was a grave Union concern; meanwhile the Union hoped to take Richmond, which became the enemy capital May 21, and to deliver a knockout blow to the upstart government. Bull Run was both a repulse to Union armies and a rebuke to Northern expectations. It was nearly a home thrust, for it took place but a few miles from the Union capital, whose inhabitants from the time of the Baltimore riots of April, 1861, through Jubal Early's raid of July, 1864, dwelt in intermittent fear of being captured.

Bull Run was the first test of strength. By all odds, the North should have won, it was thought, but the capacity of the North to win was deeply flawed by a distinctive national outlook. The Americans, in contrast to the Spartans or the Prussians, were not a military people. To be sure, they had fought and won two wars against Great Britain (putting the more favorable interpretation on the War of 1812) and one against Mexico, but these wars had not served to educate the Americans to think realistically about arms and men. Vast political results flowed from the wars, and American history was full of romance about heroes and victories, but the nation preferred a citizen militia to a large standing army as an instrument of national policy.

The tribulations of entering these past wars unprepared, and the humiliation of having the nation's capitol burned by the British, were memories that had been overwhelmed by a democratic ideology of antiCaesarism, pacifism, and low taxation. Jefferson in his first inaugural had put it down as part of "the creed of our political faith" to have "a well-disciplined militia, our best reliance in peace and for the first moments of war."

At the outbreak of the Civil War, the United States army mustered 16,367 men—about the number President Kennedy sent into a southern state in 1962 to maintain order in a school desegregation incident. The deficiencies of this small standing army may be enumerated. There were too few trained officers to lead the giant citizens' army that bodied forth during the war. Despite what some historians have said about the Mexican War as a rehearsal for the great conflict of 1861–65, there were few officers who had experience in fighting, and none at all who had experience in commanding a large army. Small numbers and limited field experience do not end the enumeration. The United States did not have a staff school for its officers, and few, if any, were by training or experience equipped to deal with the staff demands of a new kind of war. American officers were not taught strategy or the history of war at West Point, nor were they familiar with military literature (much of it was foreign)— except for an obsession with the writings of Baron Henri Jomini, who had formulated rules about how to fight in the pre-industrial age of Napoleon.

Employed principally to fight the plains Indians, the army had no war plans for fighting Southern Americans, little technical information, and few military maps. There was no modern system of command, and one would not fully evolve until the spring of 1864, when the team of Lincoln, Grant, and Halleck was formed. President Lincoln, the civilian Commander-in-chief, knew little about waging war, but his instincts were often right; he educated himself, and he evidenced here—as in politics and diplomacy—a large capacity for personal growth. The General-in-chief was Winfield Scott, born in Virginia two years before the Republic was established. He was not a West Pointer, but was so punctilious about military decorum that he was called "Fuss and Feathers"; he was a veteran of both the War of 1812 and the Mexican War, and had been the Whig candidate for the presidency in 1852. In the war with Mexico, where he had won popular fame, he had commanded an army of only 14,000 men. Now ill with dropsy and vertigo, unequipped to run a modern war, the old patriot—sagacious but senescent—soon betrayed his inadequacies.[1]

[1] Kenneth P. Williams, *Lincoln Finds a General: A Military Study of the Civil War* (5 vols.; New York: The Macmillan Co., 1949–59), I, 67, 75–76; Emory Upton, *The Military Policy of the United States* (Washington: Government Printing Office, 1917), p. 243; T. Harry Williams, *Lincoln and His Generals* (New York: Alfred A. Knopf, Inc., 1952); Charles W. Elliott, *Winfield Scott, The Soldier and the Man* (New York: The Macmillan Co., 1937), especially pp. 724, 728, 739.

Such were the broad contours of the military organization now challenged to subdue a large section of the nation. On April 15 Lincoln published a proclamation that commanded treasonable combinations to disperse within twenty days, that called up 75,000 militiamen for three months, and that convened Congress in special session on July 4. The short term of militia service did not mean he thought the need would be over that soon, but was dictated by an act of Congress passed in 1795. Within three weeks, during which four states seceded, various slave state governors refused to meet their quotas, and Baltimoreans rioted, Lincoln—by mere executive fiat—increased the regular army by 22,714 men and the navy by 18,000.

The new government below the Potomac was beforehand in raising an army. The Confederate Congress on February 28 authorized as many volunteers for one year as President Davis wished; and on March 6 he called for 100,000 men for one year.[2] The Confederacy was compelled to build an army *de novo*. Contrary to legend, the vast bulk of the U.S. Army officers remained loyal to the Union. There were 821 graduates of West Point in the army at the start of secession, of whom 78 per cent stayed with the North; 115 graduates reentered service from civilian life on the side of the North, and 99 reentered on the side of the South. Only 26 enlisted men joined the Confederate armies, and when they are added to the figure for officers the total is 339—or less than 3 per cent of the whole army. Mere numbers mislead, however, for fine quality in military leadership became more quickly evident in the South than in the North. Discrepancy in firepower was not a factor at Bull Run, for both sides were improvising weapons and scurrying abroad for arms, and the Confederacy had seized about 190,000 small arms from Federal arsenals. The famous Springfield arsenal was as yet machining enough guns each month to outfit only one Union regiment.

Commanded by the hero of Fort Sumter, P. G. T. Beauregard, the Confederate forces stood at Manassas Junction, about twenty-six miles southwest of Washington, where the Orange and Alexandria

[2] K. P. Williams, *Lincoln Finds a General*, I, 86; Upton, *Military Policy*, pp. 225, 229; James K. Hosmer, *The Appeal to Arms* (New York: Harper & Brothers, 1907), pp. 31, 44–45.

Railroad intersected the Manassas Gap Railroad. Below Manassas lay Richmond, the seat of rebellion. It all seemed so easy—to hurl the superior Federal armies against the perpetrator of the Sumter outrage, and to stamp out the foul blot of secession in Richmond. Few grasped the magnitude of subjugating the South by arms. On May 4 the editor of *Harper's Weekly* wrote: "With such support, and such resources, if this war is not brought to a speedy close, and the supremacy of the Government asserted throughout the country, it will be the fault of ABRAHAM LINCOLN."[3]

Such rashness was however a reason—and not a bad one—for engaging the enemy at Manassas. Sumter had inspired a rising in the free states that demonstrated a unanimity of opinion and a high morale, and that offered the government more troops than it could provide for. Should all this melt away, the Union would have been hard put to it to fight at a later day. Congressmen, the press, and the public were demanding an offensive. From June 26 on, the *New York Tribune* daily exhorted: " Forward to Richmond! The Rebel Congress must not be allowed to meet there on the 20th of July!" And a poet of the day clamored:

> A hundred thousand Northmen,
>   In glittering war array,
> Shout, "Onward now to Richmond!
>   We'll brook no more delay;
> Why give the traitors time and means
>   To fortify the way
> With stolen guns, in ambuscades?
>   Oh! answer us, we pray."[4]

There was a very practical, urgent reason for using the volunteer army: enlistments of the three-month men were expiring. General Robert Patterson, commanding the Army of the Shenandoah, wrote from Charlestown on July 18:

Before marching from Martinsburg I heard of the mutterings of many of the volunteer regiments and their expressed determination not to serve one hour after their term of service should expire....

[3] Quoted in K. P. Williams, *Lincoln Finds a General*, I, 62.
[4] Burton Stevenson, *Poems of American History* (Boston: Houghton Mifflin Co., 1908), pp. 419–420.

I am, therefore, now here with a force which will be dwindling away very rapidly. I to-day appealed almost in vain to the regiments to stand by the country for a week or ten days.[5]

On the very morning of Bull Run, as Federal troops moved forward to engage the enemy, they passed an infantry regiment and an artillery battery whose enlistments had expired, and which were returning to Washington.

Beyond all this lay the fundamental fact that the North had to wage an offensive war in order to bring the South back into the Union. Stalemate meant survival of the Confederacy. And a final reason favoring an engagement at this early season was the need to impress European governments of Northern strength, and to evoke their sympathy. So preparations went forward.

On June 24 General Scott received a plan and estimate of men from General Irvin McDowell, commander of the forces at Alexandria.[6] Five days later Scott met with Lincoln, the cabinet, and leading military officers to discuss a movement upon Manassas. The aged general announced disapproval of the movement. "He did not believe in a little war by piecemeal." He favored constriction, the "anaconda" policy, and a movement down the Mississippi in the fall and winter. With this advice the responsibility of the military ended, having reached its limits under the American Constitutional system. A political decision was made by the President and cabinet. The public temper required an offensive *now*. Many authorities endorse the political decision, given the historical context.

It has been said that because Scott was too old to mount a horse he was thought too old to give advice. On being overruled, he produced McDowell's plan, which he had approved, and now graciously gave his counsel about how to carry it out. There was surprisingly little discussion, either of the grand policy question whether to attack now or wait, or of the details for an onslaught against Beauregard.[7]

[5] Upton, *Military Policy*, p. 244; K. P. Williams, *Lincoln Finds a General*, I, 75.

[6] *War of the Rebellion: . . . Official Records of the Union and Confederate Armies* (128 vols.; Washington: 1880–1901), Ser. I, Vol. II, 719–721, for McDowell's plan. (This work will hereafter be cited as *OR*.)

[7] Allan Nevins, *The War for the Union*, I, 214–216; K. P. Williams, *Lincoln Finds a General*, I, 96.

McDowell was to lead the first great field action of the war. He had just been promoted from major to brigadier general in the regular army; he had never had a large command. He later testified before the Committee on the Conduct of the War:

> There was not a man there who had ever maneuvered troops in large bodies. There was not one in the Army. I did not believe there was one in the whole country.... I had seen them handled abroad in reviews and marches, but I had never handled that number, and no one here had. I wanted very much a little time all of us wanted it. We did not have a bit of it.[8]

When he testified that his troops were green and untrained, a committee member shot back: "You are green, it is true; but they are green also; you are all green alike."

And so it was that a Commander-in-chief, innocent of military affairs, a General-in-chief, archaic in his knowledge of staff, and a field commander, inexperienced in handling large bodies of troops, launched a great offensive to end the war in one mighty swoop.

Beauregard moved north to Bull Run Creek to await attack. His 22,000 men were outnumbered by the 30,000 under McDowell. Notwithstanding his committee testimony, McDowell had not advantageously used the short time available for instructing and conditioning his men. He now compounded his difficulties by issuing a march order, on July 16, that failed to assign a mission to his cavalry and that threatened disciplinary action against commanders surprised by the enemy—thereby slowing down the movement. The march order further warned: "There is on many of our regiments nothing to distinguish them from those of the enemy, and great care must be taken to avoid firing into each other."[9]

Much depended upon preventing the 9,000 Confederate troops under General Joseph E. Johnston at Winchester from joining Beauregard—a mission that was assigned to General Robert Patterson, a seventy-year-old veteran of the War of 1812 and the Mexican War, who had reentered service with the call of April 15.

---

[8] K. P. Williams, *Lincoln Finds a General*, I, 66–68.

[9] *OR*, Ser. I, Vol. II, 303–305; Robert U. Johnson and Clarence C. Buel (eds.), *Battles and Leaders of the Civil War* (4 vols.; New York: Thomas Yoseloff, Inc., 1956), I, 167–261, for firsthand accounts.

No great soldier, he failed to give battle, and Johnston slipped out of the Shenandoah Valley with the bulk of his army—6,000 men— and arrived by rail at Manassas on Saturday, July 20.[10]

McDowell's men marched slowly (it was said they picked berries on the way), using excessive time in reconnaissance and in cooking rations, hamstrung by the commander's inexperience. They confronted the now united Confederate forces on Sunday morning, July 21. The military authority, Kenneth P. Williams, entitled his chapter on Bull Run "A Day Too Late." McDowell would have agreed, for he had written in his report: "...and could we have fought a day— yes, a few hours—sooner, there is everything to show that we should have continued successful, even against the odds with which we contended." Unusual candor, for the fault was McDowell's!

At first the Federals prevailed, pushing the Confederates back to the plateau around the Henry House. But a series of misfortunes transpired. McDowell, without a staff organization, lost control of the fighting. Two Union batteries were lost, surprised by the appearance of blueclad Confederate troops. The Confederacy now discovered a source of strength in Thomas J. Jackson, who stood like a stonewall against a Federal attack. In mid-afternoon, fresh troops were thrown into the battle by the Confederacy, thanks in part to the seasonable arrival of the remainder of Johnston's division. Federals began to retire in the face of a new forward movement ordered by Beauregard, and, without the benefit of discipline, they were shortly in disorderly retreat.[11]

> Yankee Doodle, near Bull Run,
>   Met his adversary,
> First he thought the fight he'd won,
>   Fact proved quite contrary.

[10] "Robert Patterson," *Dictionary of American Biography*, XIV, 306– 307; *OR*, Ser. I, Vol. II, 470–478, for Johnston's report of the battle; Lenoir Chambers, *Stonewall Jackson* (2 vols.; New York: William Morrow & Co., 1959), I, 364 ff.

[11] The best book on the battle is R. M. Johnston's *Bull Run, Its Strategy and Tactics* (Boston: Houghton Mifflin Co., 1913); see especially pp. 228 ff. K. P. Williams, *Lincoln Finds a General*, I, ch. III; *OR*, Ser. I, Vol. II, 325, for McDowell quotation.

Panic-struck he fled, with speed
Of lightning glib with unction,
Of slippery grease, in full stampede
From famed Manassas Junction.[12]

Early dispatches had augured success, and Lincoln had gone out for his Sunday drive. On hearing the bad news, Scott wired McDowell that he supposed McDowell would rally his men at Centreville, "or at the worst, you will rally at Fairfax Court-House and Fairfax Station." But the greenhorn armies were intent on returning to Washington. Footsore, dusty citizen soldiers recrossed the Potomac in the moonlight and made their camps in the capital.[13]

"Never on the Western Hemisphere had so many men fallen on a field of battle"; 481 Union lives had been lost, and 387 Confederate. The Union reported 1,011 wounded and 1,216 missing, and the Confederacy 1,582 wounded and a small number missing.[14] A series of factors had contributed to the miscarriage of Union plans, but the root cause was—in a broad, historic sense—the military policy of the United States. The Northern democracy, not without some justice, found a scapegoat in General Patterson, whose discharge had been ordered two days before Bull Run, but public censure touched too lightly on Lincoln, Scott, and McDowell, as well as upon itself.

A more seasoned president, a younger, more sprightly general than Scott, a faster-moving general than McDowell, a less steadfast general than Jackson, a different color of Confederate uniforms— such contingencies might have turned Bull Run into a Union victory. In that event, it has been conjectured, a temporary peace might have resulted, with slavery unassailed. But Bull Run was a turning point in the American Civil War not so much in the sense that the North might have been the victor, and, backed by European opinion, imposed a truce, as in the sense that the battle struck with

[12] Stevenson, *Poems*, p. 425.

[13] Nevins, *War for the Union*, I, 216–222; K. P. Williams, *Lincoln Finds a General*, I, 95–97; Johnston, *Bull Run, loc. cit.*; *OR*, Ser. I, Vol. II, 748, for quotation.

[14] K. P. Williams, *Lincoln Finds a General*, I, 97; Thomas L. Livermore, *Numbers and Losses in the Civil War* (Boston: Houghton Mifflin Co., 1901), p. 77.

impelling force upon public opinion at home and abroad, upon Congress, and upon the Commander-in-chief. It framed new patterns of thought and led to far-reaching changes in the conduct of the war.

The failure at Bull Run inspired a second Northern rising. Volunteering accelerated, 90-day men reenlisted, states rushed fresh regiments forward in plenitude. Governor Edwin D. Morgan of New York, already distinguished by the vigor with which he had been furnishing troops, was in Washington to see Lincoln the day of Bull Run. On getting a note from the President, he hastened back to Albany and issued a call for 25,000 men to serve for three years, or the duration of the war.[15]

As they realized victory would not come readily, a new mood fastened upon Northerners. An iron resolve entered the Northern soul, and Lincoln, having perhaps overestimated the strength of Unionism in the South in shaping his Sumter policy, now placed his reliance in the plain people of the North.

An anonymous poet contributed inspiriting lines to the New York *Evening Post* of July 26, 1861:

> *"Cast Down, But Not Destroyed"*
>
> Oh, Northern men—true hearts and bold—
>   Unflinching to the conflict press!
> Firmly our country's flag uphold,
>   Till traitorous foes its sway confess!
>
> Firmly resolved to win success,
>   We'll tread the path our fathers trod,
> Unflinching to the conflict press,
>   And, fearless, trust our cause to God![16]

Congress met on the day after Bull Run, not visibly shaken by the disaster but certainly conscious of it. The lawmakers cannot be accused of having been unalert before Bull Run, for they had already unloosed the floodgates to the immense manpower reservoir possessed

---

[15] Johnston, *Bull Run*, pp. 269–270; Nevins, *War for the Union*, I, 223 ff., for effects of Bull Run on the North; James A. Rawley, *Edwin D. Morgan, 1811–1883* (New York: Columbia University Press, 1955), p. 161.

[16] Frank Moore (ed.), *The Rebellion Record: A Diary of American Events* . . . (11 vols.; New York: G. P. Putnam's Sons, 1861–64), II, sec. III, 5.

by the North. On July 18—three days before the battle—both houses had approved, over the objections of the senators from Kentucky, a measure to provide the largest citizens' army yet known to history. The Army Bill authorized enlistment for service up to three years of half a million men—100,000 more than the Commander-in-chief had asked for. Lincoln signed the bill on July 22; and that same day a supplemental measure was introduced in the Senate, which when it became law four days later provided that the volunteers be mustered into service for the duration of the war.

On July 24 Senator Henry Wilson of Massachusetts, chairman of the military affairs committee, introduced a bill to empower the President to remove officers for incompetency, incapacity, or neglect of duty—even though the officers had been appointed by state governors. Debate on the bill disclosed something of Bull Run's impact on the lawmakers. Wilson argued in behalf of his bill: "The utter rout the other day is only the legitimate fruit of the incapacity of many of the field and company officers connected with the volunteers."

Ohio's Senator John Sherman, younger brother of the general, regretted Wilson's line of argument, and said this was not the time for faultfinding.

> There never was a braver army. I believe the repulse—not the rout, the repulse—of last Sunday will do good. It has stirred up all over this country but one responsive feeling. We now begin to see the magnitude of the contest in which we are involved; and I believe every American citizen felt, when he read the account of the achievements of our Army on last Sunday, and their repulse, only a deeper and a stronger determination that, whatever might come, this rebellion should be put down, and with force of arms; and I have no doubt that it will be done.

Western Senator Henry M. Rice of Minnesota made the colloquially phrased plea: "This is no time for us to be fiddling; it is no time for us to be swapping jack-knives when the ship is sinking. Give the Administration the power it asks for."[17]

"The North had been taught a lesson" by Bull Run, James G. Blaine wrote. "The doubting were at last convinced that the

[17] *Congressional Globe*, 37th Cong., 1st sess., pp. 239–242.

Confederates were equipped for a desperate fight, and intended to make it. If the Union was to be saved, it must be saved by the united loyalty and the unflinching resolution of the people."

"The special and immediate danger," Blaine continued, "was an outbreak in the Border slave States."[18] Two days before Bull Run, Crittenden had given notice in the House of Representatives of a proposed resolution to define the war's aims. The day after the battle he called up his noted congressional statement, which declared that the war was the work of Southern disunionists and that the resolution's purposes were solely to maintain the supremacy of the Constitution and to preserve the Union without interfering with the rights or institutions of the states. Kentucky's one Southern Rights representative, Henry C. Burnett, who later sat in the Confederate Congress, asked that the resolution be divided, and it was agreed to. He found one other dissident who joined him in voting against blaming the war on Southern disunionists. Only two persons voted in the negative on the second part of the resolution.

Senator Andrew Johnson of Tennessee, the only Southern senator who supported the Union during the war, offered the resolution to his Senate colleagues two days later. It was heatedly denounced by Breckinridge, as we saw earlier, and Wisconsin Senators Sherman and Doolittle answered him. But when the resolution was brought to a vote, only five senators opposed it: the four from Kentucky and Missouri strangely combined with Trumbull of Illinois, who asserted he thought the war *was* for the purpose of subjugation of traitors and rebels.[19] Before the session had completed its work, Congress had violated the spirit of the Crittenden Resolution and had yielded to the spirit of Trumbull by passing a confiscation act.

Lyman Trumbull—a Republican of Democratic antecedents, who would later sponsor the Freedmen's Bureau Bill of 1865 and write the Civil Rights Bill of 1866, but refuse to vote to convict President

[18] James G. Blaine, *Twenty Years of Congress* ... (2 vols.; Norwich, Conn.: 1884–86), I, 338–339.

[19] *Congressional Globe*, 37th Cong., 1st sess., pp. 222 ff.; Albert D. Kirwan, *John J. Crittenden, The Struggle for the Union* (Lexington, University of Kentucky Press, 1962); *American Annual Cyclopaedia* ... *1861* (New York: D. Appleton & Co., 1866), pp. 241–244.

Andrew Johnson—had gone to witness the battle of Bull Run with other senators. "It was the most shameful rout you can conceive of," he wrote his wife in a long, vivid description. "God's ways are inscrutable. I am dreadfully disappointed and mortified."[20]

On the day after Bull Run the judiciary committee of the Senate reported a bill to confiscate the property of rebels. To this extraordinary measure—waging war by legislation—Trumbull moved an extraordinary amendment, and explained the effect and motivation of his proposal.

> The amendment provides that if any person held to service or labor in any state, under the laws thereof (by which, of course, is meant a slave in any of these states), is employed in aid of this rebellion, in digging ditches or intrenchments, or in any other way, or if used for carrying guns, or if used to destroy this Government, by the consent of his master, his master shall forfeit all right to him, and he shall be forever discharged.

Why should this group of slaves be freed? "I understand that negroes were in the fight which has recently occurred," he went on. "I take it that negroes who are used to destroy the Union, and to shoot down the Union men by the consent of traitorous masters, ought not to be restored to them." The six senators from the border slave states of Maryland, Kentucky, and Missouri voted against the amendment, the senators from Delaware abstained. The Senate accepted Trumbull's amendment 33 to 6, and then passed the bill without a division.[21]

The confiscation bill evidenced a radicalism developing under the shadow of the Union reversal. When it came to the House on August 2, it encountered opposition from Crittenden. The Kentuckian pointed out that the bill contradicted his resolution, approved by the House ten days before. The bill, he argued, was both unconstitutional, for Congress did not have the power to legislate on slavery in a state, and impolitic, for partisans would charge "we are making an anti-slavery war." Crittenden won support from forty-seven other representatives when the measure came to a vote, but a majority of

[20] Horace White, *The Life of Lyman Trumbull* (Boston, Houghton Mifflin Co., 1913), pp. 165–167.

[21] John G. Nicolay and John Hay, *Abraham Lincoln, A History* (10 vols.; New York: The Century Co., 1909), IV, 380–381.

sixty carried it. The Confiscation Act of 1861 was the thin entering wedge of emancipation by legislation.[22]

The disaster in Virginia impelled the *New York Times* to see the need for army reorganization and careful planning. "The people have required precipitancy, and they have it, with all its consequences.... We can now reorganize and reconstruct an army which has been too suddenly improvised and led into the field." The defeat, it continued, "should arouse us to a proper sense of the magnitude of the crisis, and of the steps to be taken for a vigorous, methodical and successful prosecution of the war."

In a departure from its normally moderate tone, this Republican organ hinted at the possibility of emancipation as an outcome of the strife. "There is one thing, and only one, at the bottom of the fight,—and that is the negro.... Would anything short of our unexpected repulse at Manassas have quickened the conscience and judgment of twenty millions of people in regard to this conflict?... Shall we 'fight the devil with fire,' according to the wisdom of the ancients? Let a paralyzed Army and a reeling Nation answer."[23]

Walt Whitman wrote of the Washington scene after Bull Run:

> But the hour, the day, the night pass'd, and whatever returns, an hour, a day, a night like that can never again return. The President, recovering himself, begins that very night—sternly, rapidly sets about the task of reorganizing his forces, and placing himself in positions for future and surer work. If there were nothing else of Abraham Lincoln for history to stamp him with, it is enough to send him with his wreath to the memory of all future time, that he endured that hour, that day, bitterer than gall—indeed a crucifixion day—that it did not conquer him—that he unflinchingly stemm'd it, and resolv'd to lift himself and the Union out of it.[24]

If congressmen, journalists, and poets had begun to see the dimensions of the contest, it was the Commander-in-chief who took the more decisive steps in the aftermath of defeat. On returning from

[22] Kirwan, *Crittenden*, p. 442; Edward McPherson, *Political History of the United States during the Rebellion* (Washington, 1865), pp. 195–196; James G. Randall, "Some Legal Aspects of the Confiscation Acts of the Civil War," *American Historical Review*, XVIII (October, 1912), 79–96.

[23] *New York Times*, July 22 and 24, 1861.

[24] Quoted by K. P. Williams, *Lincoln Finds a General*, I, 202.

his drive at 6:30 P.M. on the day of the battle, he listened to the adverse news "without the slightest change in feature or expression," and then went to army headquarters to see the reports.

"From this time onward to the end of the war," his private secretaries have recorded, "his touch was daily and hourly amidst the vast machinery of command and coordination in Cabinet, Congress, army, navy, and the hosts of national politics."[25] That night, lying on a sofa in his office, he began to outline (in pencil) a fresh military program, and two days later he had produced a nine-point memorandum. Among other matters it called for the rapid forwarding of troops to Washington, strengthening the forces in the Shenandoah Valley and at Fort Monroe, tightening the blockade, and reorganizing McDowell's army without the three-month men.

But above all—to restore morale in the army and among the public, and to give the North victories—a new military commander must be named. Although McDowell was suffering unfairly for his reversal, he must be replaced. While Bull Run had brought to the fore two preeminent Confederate commanders, Joseph E. Johnston and Stonewall Jackson, it had only begun Lincoln's long search for a successful general.

One name was on people's lips—George B. McClellan—who had given the Union victories in western Virginia, not without inviting notice to them and himself. On July 26, McClellan, young, handsome, short of stature, full of self-confidence, and endowed with a fresh and unusually winning manner, arrived in Washington. A Philadelphia aristocrat, he had graduated from West Point in 1846 while under twenty years of age, second in his class. He quickly established for himself a reputation for brilliance, ambition, and flamboyance. Receiving a commission in the engineers, he served in the Mexican War, was a military observer in Europe, and had left the army to become a railroad executive. He did not vote until 1860—and then for Stephen A. Douglas—but he held definite political views. He favored a federal type of government, with respect for state rights; he opposed slavery, but disfavored sudden emancipation; and he believed the South's desertion of Douglas in 1860 made the South accountable for bringing on war. In 1860 he had married Ellen

[25] Nicolay and Hay, *Abraham Lincoln*, IV, 367.

Marcy, young and comely daughter of the Indian fighter and army explorer, R. B. Marcy; and in the same year he had taken up residence in Cincinnati as president of the Ohio and Mississippi Railroad.[26]

When war came, McClellan moved with alacrity, and eight days after Lincoln's proclamation he accepted command of all the Ohio forces. On May 13 he was appointed major general in the regular army, commanding the Department of the Ohio, which included Ohio, Indiana, and Illinois, and later embraced parts of Pennsylvania and Virginia. He made his headquarters in Cincinnati, a border city of about 160,000, across from which stood Covington, Kentucky, at the mouth of the Licking River. The mere presence of the esteemed young general and his army at this key point doubtless had a steadying effect on the Borderland, in particular Kentucky and western Virginia.

On June 5 McClellan informed General Scott: "I feel so keenly the vital importance of keeping Kentucky in the Union, that I must urge delay until we know exactly what we are doing."[27] Simon B. Buckner, head of the Kentucky state guard and an old friend, came to see him three days later, and in an interview at ten at night in McClellan's home inquired what the Northerner would do if Confederate forces in Tennessee under General Gideon J. Pillow should invade Kentucky.

Buckner was uneasy that McClellan might not respect Kentucky's neutrality, and was relieved by an assurance that McClellan would prefer to see Kentucky deal with invaders. The Union commander appended, however: "You had better be quick about it, Simon, for if I learn that the rebels are in Kentucky I will, with or without orders, drive them out without delay." McClellan thought he had made it clear, so he later said, that he had no authority to guarantee the neutrality of Kentucky.[28]

Two days after the interview, however, Buckner wrote Magoffin

[26] William S. Myers, *A Study in Personality, General George Brinton McClellan* (New York: D. Appleton-Century, 1934); H. J. Eckenrode and Bryan Conrad, *George B. McClellan: The Man Who Saved the Union* (Chapel Hill: University of North Carolina Press, 1941); Warren W. Hassler, *General George B. McClellan, Shield of the Union* (Baton Rouge: Louisiana State University Press, 1957).

[27] Quoted in Myers, *McClellan*, p. 177.

[28] *OR*, Ser. I, Vol. II, 674–675; Myers, *McClellan*, pp. 177 ff.

that McClellan had promised to respect Kentucky's neutrality, unless Kentucky called on him to dislodge Southern forces. Magoffin then sent Buckner to advise Governor Isham Harris of Tennessee of the agreement and of Kentucky's determination to maintain neutrality, with force if necessary. "He gave me every assurance that the territory of Kentucky would be respected by Tennessee and the Southern States," Buckner reported to Magoffin.

On his way home the emissary learned that General Pillow was preparing to enter Columbus, Kentucky, on invitation of the mayor, who had represented to Pillow that his town was under occupation by Federal forces from Cairo (actually, some troops had entered to haul down a Confederate flag). Buckner told Pillow of the stand taken by Kentucky, and said if the Tennessean entered Kentucky McClellan would come after him. Pillow answered belligerently: "He is the very person I want to meet"; but he "at once suspended his preparations for the advance movement of his troops," Buckner told Magoffin. The next day Harris wrote the restive Pillow: "Both Governor Magoffin and General Buckner have entire confidence in the pledges of General McClelland [*sic*]. . . . I would not violate her neutrality."

Buckner's confidence in McClellan had wavered, though, and he hurried to see the Union general, then in Cairo. He took three friends with him as witnesses and secured what he considered confirmation of the agreement. When, however, Magoffin subsequently published Buckner's account of the Cincinnati agreement, he brought on a bitter controversy between McClellan and Buckner over the exact nature of the arrangement. Much of the self-justifying exchange appeared in the press, to the disadvantage of McClellan. The alleged pact seems to have served momentarily to dampen the ardor of General Pillow and of Kentucky secessionists. But after McClellan denied having promised to respect neutrality, Harris grew fearful of Union invasion through Kentucky and offered Magoffin aid to effect secession as a means to enhance the security of Tennessee.[29]

[29] E. Merton Coulter, *The Civil War and Readjustment in Kentucky* (Chapel Hill: University of North Carolina Press, 1926), p. 99; Moore, *Rebellion Record*, II, 163–164; Arndt M. Stickles, *Simon Bolivar Buckner, Borderland Knight* (Chapel Hill: University of North Carolina Press, 1940), pp. 58–64.

The Buckner-McClellan contretemps was but the beginning of controversies that were to encircle McClellan's public life. Whatever discredit his probably careless language to Buckner, once a friend of West Point days, may have brought him, it was overshadowed by his military victories in western Virginia. After the Virginia convention had passed the ordinance of secession, with 55 votes opposing the majority of 88, citizens of western counties met in Wheeling and repudiated the ordinance. Soon Virginia volunteers, numbering less than 1,000, under Colonel G. A. Porterfield, had interrupted communication with Washington, D.C., from the west by cutting the Baltimore and Ohio Railroad in portions of the western counties.

McClellan recognized the significance of this section of the Borderland fully as much as he had the significance of Kentucky. On May 26 he issued a flamboyant address "To the Union Men of Virginia," which in part pronounced:

> I have ordered troops to cross the Ohio River. They come as your friends and brothers.... Now that we are in your midst, I call upon you to fly to arms and support the general government. Sever the connection that binds you to traitors.[30]

He presented his troops with a similar piece of bombast, and sent both proclamations to President Lincoln. Without authorization, McClellan sent a small force into Virginia, and on June 3, at Philippi, Porterfield was routed. Fearful that McClellan might advance upon the armies of Johnston and Beauregard, the Confederacy sent some 4,000 men to join Porterfield. Aroused, McClellan put himself at the head of 20,000 men, marched to engage the Confederates, and on July 11 and 13—a few days before Bull Run—his forces decisively defeated the enemy. General Scott wired that he, and the cabinet, and the President "are charmed with your activity, valor, and consequent success," and the House of Representatives voted McClellan its thanks.[31]

The western Virginia campaign, small as it was, had two grand outcomes. One of these was to preserve the loyalty of western Virginia, with all its advantages of geography, population, and

---

[30] *OR*, Ser. I, Vol. II, 48–49.

[31] *OR*, Ser. I, Vol. II, 204; *Cong. Globe*, 37th Cong., 1st sess., p. 148.

communication, and thereby to create another state for the Federal union. Of more immediate importance, it gave the Union a conquering hero (albeit not a self-effacing one), which it sorely needed in the dark sequel to the movement against Manassas.

When in the late afternoon of Friday, July 26, the young general, confident in step, powerful in build, red of hair and mustache, appeared in Washington to take command of McDowell's troops, he was the tonic the capital and the North needed. The best of his qualities soon were manifest, as he energetically addressed himself to organizing, planning, disciplining, and inspiring the Army of the Potomac. He looked and acted the part of a future Napoleon. Washington breathed secure behind the defenses he erected; the troops lavished their loyalty and devotion on their enthusiastic commander. Congress, the cabinet, and the President deferred to him. Bull Run had turned the Union toward a leader who comprehended the meaning of organization and training.

His propensity to herald his achievements and his self-vindicatory reflex to criticism (as in the Buckner affair) were shortcomings that were apparent from the start of his meteoric rise. Other faults soon became evident: naiveté, insensitivity to public opinion, a tendency to exaggerate the enemy's strength and underestimate his own, slowness to move (which Lincoln once said was the only fault he had to find in him), and above all—as Bruce Catton phrased it—a lack of a "ruthless, driving insistence on victory."[32]

With this mixture of merit and defect yet to be fully revealed, McClellan had played a small role in the drama of Kentucky's trials as a neutral, and had been whirled to the center of high command in the vortex of Bull Run. He would go on to lead the Northern armies in two grand campaigns, and the Democratic party in the election campaign of 1864. In all he did, he provoked—indeed, ingenuously invited—controversy—the "Little Napoleon," "Tardy George." He suffered defeat in the Peninsula, won at Antietam, and lost the election. Two of these campaigns, Antietam and the presidential

[32] McClellan's description of his work in organizing the Army of the Potomac is in *OR*, Ser. I, Vol. V, 5–32; Nevins, *War for the Union*, I, 266–305; Bruce Catton, "Sheridan at Five Forks," *Journal of Southern History*, XXI (August 1955), 315.

election, were turning points of the Civil War. Still, in any assessment, we should be mindful of the reputed testimony of Robert E. Lee on the famous Union commander: "He was the ablest soldier they [the union army] had." Let McClellan have the last rueful word on his career: "It would probably have been better for me personally had my promotion been delayed a year or more."[33]

At Bull Run the Union was given its baptism in blood and fire. The battle in its aftermath opened Northern eyes to the magnitude of the work of subduing a vast area in determined revolt. It prompted a reordering of Federal military affairs and it drove Northern opinion toward more extreme views on the Negro. It deepened the new President's sense of responsibility as Commander-in-chief. It caused the Union to turn toward a youthful commander—prematurely hailed after Philippi as a new Napoleon—who would play a leading role for the next three years. It presented the Confederacy with its first true military hero—Stonewall Jackson—and at the same time lulled the South into a false confidence. "Universal gratulation at our success inspired an overweening confidence," President Jefferson Davis later observed.[34] And not the least result of the first battle of Bull Run was the fall of Union prestige in Europe, which we will examine in connection with the *Trent* Affair, a crisis in Anglo-Union relations.

[33] Quoted in Myers, *McClellan*, pp. 513, 197–198.

[34] Jefferson Davis, *The Rise and Fall of the Confederate Government* (2 vols.; London: Longmans, Green & Co., 1881), I, 384; also see T. Harry Williams, *P. G. T. Beauregard: Napoleon in Gray* (Baton Rouge: Louisiana University Press, 1955), pp. 91–93.

The *Trent* Affair

The people are frantic with rage.
A Journalist in London

Lord Palmerston, the prime minister of Great Britain, noted—and remarked upon—the Southern victory at Bull Run—"or rather at Yankee's Run," as he put it with his sardonic wit. In a private minute he wrote:

[It] proves two things. First, that to bring together many thousand men and put uniforms upon their backs and muskets in their hands is not to make an army.... The Truth is, the North are fighting for an Idea chiefly entertained by professional politicians, while the South are fighting for what they consider rightly or wrongly vital interests.

In a public address at Dover, he spoke of the "fast running which signalized the battle of Bull Run."[1]

Lord John Russell, the foreign secretary, observed in a letter to Lord Lyons, British minister to the United States: "The defeat of Manassas or Bull's Run seems to me to show a great want of zeal." Charles Francis Adams, the American minister to the Court of St. James's, gloomily reported to Seward on August 8: "The ill news of last week has had the effect of bringing to light the prevailing feeling in Great Britain.... The division of the Union is now regarded as a *fait accompli*."[2]

The impression of Northern weakness in military capacity and moral idealism was broadcast throughout Britain by the dispatches from America of W. H. Russell of the London *Times*. He missed seeing the battle, but he met returning troops as he drove out from Washington; and in his dispatch of July 22 he wrote of "a cowardly rout," "scandalous behavior on the part of Soldiers," and "the

[1] Quoted in T. W. L. Newton, *Lord Lyons* (2 vols.; London: Longmans, Green, 1913), I, 48; Thomas L. Harris, *The Trent Affair* (Indianapolis and Kansas City: Bowen-Merrill Co., 1896).

[2] Quoted in Ephraim D. Adams, *Great Britain and the American Civil War* (2 vols. in one; New York: Russell & Russell, n.d.), I, 179, n. 1; James Ford Rhodes, *History of the United States* . . . (7 vols.; New York: The Macmillan Co., 1895–1900), III, 344.

state of arrogance and supercilious confidence" of the North. So great was the prestige of the *Times* that Northerners had been asking, What will Russell say? Now that his biting criticism was published, "Bull Run Russell," as he came to be called, was subjected to a storm of vilification that increased the tension between the Union and Britain.[3]

If Bull Run moved Britons in high places to think ill of the Union's prospects and purpose, it did not move the British government to alter its policy toward the American Civil War. That policy had been determined within a month after Lincoln's call for troops, and it was an occasion for disappointment North and South. Queen Victoria on May 13 proclaimed Britain a neutral in the war.

The Confederacy at first hailed the Queen's proclamation hopefully, thinking it presaged diplomatic recognition. Just as the Deep South had expected the border slave states to cleave to it, the Confederacy had expected Britain to support the "Cotton Kingdom." In 1858, Senator James H. Hammond of South Carolina had boasted of the supremacy of cotton in Anglo-American relations. And Senator John Slidell of Louisiana, in addressing the U.S. Senate just after his state had seceded, asked:

> How long, think you, will the great powers of Europe permit you to impede their free intercourse with their best customers for their various fabrics and to stop the supplies of the great staple which is the most important basis of their manufacturing industry, by a mere paper blockade?[4]

Northerners feared the South might be correct in expecting English support, but they hoped the South was wrong, for surely Britons would recognize the righteousness of the Northern cause. James Russell Lowell phrased it colloquially in "Jonathan to John":

> We know we've got a cause, John,
> Thet's honest, just, and true;
> We thought't would win applause, John,
> If nowheres else, from you.

[3] W. H. Russell, quoted in Frank Moore (ed.), *The Rebellion Record: A Diary of American Events* ... (11 Vols.; New York: G. P. Putnam, 1861–64), II, Sec. II, 52; Adams, *op. cit.*, I, 177–178.

[4] *Congressional Globe*, 36th Cong., 2d sess., part 1, p. 721.

Ole Uncle S. sez he, "I guess
His love of right," sez he,
"Hangs by a rotten fibre o' cotton:
There's natur' in J. B.,
Ez wal ez in you an' me!

Just before the outbreak of the war, Anglo-American relations were in a healthy state. The war of the Revolution and of 1812 had receded into the past, and more recent instances of friction over Central America, the Caribbean, and Canada had been resolved by diplomacy. President Buchanan in his final message on the state of the Union had informed Congress: "Our relations with Great Britain are of the most friendly character."

Neutrality was the official position of Her Majesty's government, but the real sentiments of Britons covered a wide spectrum, extending through class and other group interests. Contrary to legend, there was no party division on the American question. Many upper-class Britons entertained favorable sentiments toward the Confederacy out of a compound of considerations: a feeling of kinship toward a landed aristocracy and fellow Anglo-Saxons, and a feeling of aversion toward the Yankee democracy. The middle class was divided by differing feelings over the new protective tariff of the North, the Southern market, the Southern right of revolution against the Yankee empire, the principle of majority rule, and by emancipation—which the North *seemed* to favor but which the President persistently declared was not an issue. The lower class, unenfranchised and threatened with unemployment if the cotton mills should shut down for want of raw material, looked to the Union to vindicate free labor, majority rule, and manhood suffrage—cost what it might in idleness in Lancashire.

The English liberal, Richard Cobden, at first disfavored the North because of its protectionism and its coercion of a people striving for independence. He was brought over to the side of the North by John Bright's persuasive representations of the section's hostility to slavery.

Whatever Englishmen felt about the distant war in America, they were British to the backbone, loyal to queen and country, and accustomed to ruling the waves. Moreover, they were almost one as well in sharing a loathing of slavery—perhaps beyond any other people in the Western world. Her Majesty's government had followed the national interest, not private conviction or public opinion, in announcing neutrality. The Liberal government, so often described by historians as pro-Southern, was in fact a coalition headed by an ancient statesman who did not wish to see his delicately balanced ministry topple. The Conservative party, headed by Lord Derby, which might be expected to be the more sympathetic of the two toward the Southern cause, was not only out of power but traditionally a supporter of neutrality.[5]

Her Majesty's first minister, Lord Palmerston, was a jaunty survival of the eighteenth century. He had spent his life in politics, and as foreign secretary for many years he had become familiar with American affairs. His inflexibility and truculence had figured in the Oregon crisis and in Central American negotiations. A staunch imperialist, who often had shown a belligerent attitude toward foreign powers, he had manifested his liberalism by friendliness to revolution outside the empire and by his inveterate antipathy toward the slave trade. His famous *Civis Romanus Sum* speech in 1850, upholding England's duty to protect British subjects abroad, had underscored his traits of aggressiveness in foreign relations and of meddling in the internal affairs of other nations. In his seventy-seventh year at the time of Fort Sumter, he was conservative about English domestic issues, and though tempted to rattle the sword as of old, he was mindful that in leading Britain to the brink of war he might end his ministry.

Lord John Russell, the foreign secretary, had formerly been Palmerston's superior. He too was an old hand in American affairs, and had once been prevented from forming a government because he had proposed to give the Foreign Office to the bellicose Palmerston. More intellectual, if less agile in politics, than Palmerston, Russell had privately told Lyons as early as January 10, 1861: "I do not see how the United States can be cobbled together again by any compromise"; but he had advised Parliament as early as May 2

[5] Rhodes, *op. cit.*, pp. 313-321, 389-406; Adams, *op. cit.*, *passim*; W. D. Jones, "The British Conservatives and the American Civil War," *American Historical Review*, LVIII (April, 1953), 527-543.

about the American war: "For God's sake, let us if possible keep out of it."[6]

The British policy of neutrality was intended neither as an affront to the North nor as an augury of aid to the South; it was a reflex to American developments. On April 17, President Davis had announced plans to license privateers, and two days later President Lincoln had proclaimed a blockade; on May 3, two Southern commissioners sent by Davis had confronted Russell. Russell later explained the British dilemma about the privateers to an American correspondent: "Unless we meant to treat them as pirates and to hang them we could not deny them belligerent rights."[7]

The neutrality proclamation, which accorded belligerent rights to the Confederates, was at variance with the official Union view that they were mere rebels—but not with the Union practice, for it grew clear that if the Union treated Southern captives as rebels and pirates, the South might retaliate in kind. The proclamation, then, in recognizing the belligerency of the Confederacy, assigned privileges and responsibilities to an insurgent government. Under international law, it affirmed the right of the South to send out privateers and denied the North the right to treat Confederate sailors as pirates. It prohibited Britons from enlisting on either side and from equipping ships of war. Lastly, it decreed that the Union blockade, in order to be respected, must be effective—must be able to block the passage of ships.

The proclamation appeared on the very day the new American minister arrived in England, and Adams lost little time in protesting what he described as "precipitous" recognition of belligerency. When he represented to Russell his fear that Britain's next step might be formal recognition, Russell denied any such purpose, but would not bind himself for the future. Soon the British government allayed Adams's apprehensions by three actions. After a member of Parliament had exulted in the House of Commons over the bursting of "the great Republican bubble," Lord John Russell, together with

[6] Evelyn Ashley, *The Life and Correspondence of Henry John Temple, Viscount Palmerston* (2 vols.; London: Richard Bentley & Son, 1879); A. Wyatt Tilby, *Lord John Russell, A Study in Civil and Religious Liberty* (London: Cassell & Co., Ltd., 1930); quoted in Adams, *op. cit.*, I, 52, 90.

[7] Adams, *op. cit.*, I, 83 ff., quotation on 106, n. 1.

William E. Gladstone, chancellor of the exchequer, rebuked the M.P., and the Commons signified approval. More helpfully in a positive sense, the government on June 1 forbade privateers of either side to carry prize ships into British ports—a blow to the Confederacy, the only side dependent upon privateers. And, after Adams objected —on belligerently worded instructions from Secretary of State Seward (which he watered down)—to further intercourse between the Confederate commissioners (Yancey and Rost, whom Russell had seen twice) and the British government, Russell answered he did not intend to see the men again.

Adams, in truth, found much sympathy for the North. He was honored at five dinners, given by as many cabinet members. He discovered that the Earl of Derby, leader of the Tories, was friendly; and he saw a motion in Parliament, offered by Sir William Gregory, a pro-Southern M.P., fail to command support. Throughout the summer and fall of 1861, an Anglo-American equilibrium was maintained. There were strains and stresses over negotiations about the principles of international law contained in the Declaration of Paris of 1856, Confederate ships in British ports, and the threatened intervention of Britain, France, and Spain in Mexico. Bull Run dampened Adams's spirits, for he saw plainly not only the need for a Northern victory to bolster his diplomacy but that the defeat had deepened a British conviction that Northern coercion would never conquer the Confederacy.[8]

Yet he was impressed by a dutiful maintenance of neutrality and the growing cordiality of Lord and Lady Palmerston. At the lord mayor's dinner in November, Palmerston spoke—Adams noted in his diary—touching "gently on our difficulties and at the same time gave it clearly to be understood that there is to be no interference for the sake of cotton." Another diary entry, soon after, recorded that he and Mrs. Adams had gone to Lady Palmerston's: "We had been invited to dine ourselves, last Saturday, and are again invited for next Saturday evening. This civility is so significant that it must by no means be declined."

On November 12, at one in the afternoon, Adams drove to

[8] Martin B. Duberman, *Charles Francis Adams, 1807–1886* (Boston: Houghton Mifflin Co., 1961), pp. 258 ff.

Cambridge House, where he was cordially greeted by the prime minister. Palmerston expressed concern over the American armed ship that had put into Southampton, fearing it might intercept the British ship bringing two new agents of the Confederacy, Mason and Slidell. The elderly statesman appeared anxious to avoid an international incident, and was reassured by Adams that the American cruiser had come to intercept a Confederate ship, and that he had advised the captain to go home.

Adams did not know that the day before this Lord Palmerston, at a meeting with the chancellor and three law officers, had been advised, or thought he had, that under international law the captain of the American cruiser did have the right to stop the British ship, search her, and either remove the men and their dispatches or carry the ship to a prize port in New York. If Palmerston had waited a day, he would have been in receipt of a written, official opinion from the law officers denying the right of removal. Nor could Adams or Palmerston know that, four days before their pleasant interview, a Union naval captain had halted the British mail packet, *Trent*, and had removed Mason and Slidell. In the absence of an Atlantic cable, this news was delayed a fortnight more, and then it burst over Britain like a bombshell. The threat of war had come not because of English interference on behalf of the Confederacy but because of American interference with neutral rights.[9]

Captain Charles Wilkes, U.S.N., commander of the *U.S.S. San Jacinto*, was the author of this crisis. His grandfather's brother, the English radical John Wilkes, had given pain to the Crown in the days of George III. The American captain, at sixty-three, was a redoubtable figure. In his long naval service he had explored the South Polar Ocean, where Wilkes Land attests to one of his discoveries, and he had written voluminously about his scientific investigations. Able in his seamanship, he was independent of mind and temperamental in character; and his excellent naval record had been marred in 1842 when a court-martial adjudged him guilty of severely punishing some of his men and decreed that he be publicly reprimanded.

[9] Charles Francis Adams, "The Trent Affair," *American Historical Review*, XVII (April, 1912), 540–562, quotation on 550; Palmerston's speech is in Moore (ed.), *Rebellion Record*, III, Sec. II, 347–348.

The *San Jacinto*, an American war steamer that mounted fifteen guns, was returning to American waters after twenty months of service (patrolling the African slave trade) when Captain Wilkes learned that Confederate agents were about to sail from Havana for Southampton. He had not communicated with Washington in months, and had learned of the envoys through newspapers he had read in Cuba.[10]

"I determined to intercept them," he later said, "and carefully examined all the authorities on international law to which I had access." Did he have the right to capture persons from a neutral ship? There was no doubt, according to his authorities, that he could capture vessels with written dispatches, but—as Wilkes himself declared—"these gentlemen were not dispatches in the literal sense." Captain Wilkes jumped to an audacious conclusion: "I then considered them as the embodiment of dispatches."[11]

He informed his executive officer, Lieutenant Fairfax, from whom he had recently taken command of the ship, that he intended to seize the "live dispatches." The prudent junior officer is said to have protested, strenuously recommending consultation with the American judge at Key West, and suggesting that international difficulties might result. But the old sea dog had made up his mind, and he ordered his ship to take a position where the Bahama Channel narrows to about fifteen miles.[12]

James M. Mason and John Slidell were being sent by Jefferson Davis to Britain and France (respectively) to represent the Confederacy. The earlier mission of Yancey, Rost, and Mann had failed, and two of the South's most eminent statesmen were now to try to assert the supremacy of King Cotton. Designation of Slidell and Mason, one a Louisiana Democratic boss with a reputation for intrigue and filibustering and the other a former Virginia senator— of ability, but also the author of the Fugitive Slave Law—did not

[10] Harris, *Trent Affair, passim*; "Charles Wilkes," Allen Johnson and Dumas Malone (eds.), *Dictionary of American Biography* (22 vols. and supplements; New York: Charles Scribner's Sons, 1928–36), XX, 216–217.

[11] *War of the Rebellion: . . . Official Records of the Union and Confederate Armies* (128 vols.; Washington: 1880–1901), Ser. II, Vol. II, 1098. (Hereafter cited as *OR*.)

[12] Harris, *op. cit.*, p. 100.

present the South's most pleasing face to Europe. Nor could the two men fail to be hated in the North.

They had easily slipped through the blockade at Charleston harbor one rainy night in October, aboard a Confederate steamer. On November 7, with their secretaries and families, they embarked at Havana on the British mail packet *Trent*, commanded by Captain Moir. The *Trent* was a ship of a neutral nation, and it was plying a regular schedule between neutral ports. It was not a blockade-runner. About noon the next day she was sighted by the *San Jacinto*, and as she drew near the cruiser fired a shot across her bow and hoisted the American flag. Plainly displaying the Union Jack, the *Trent* continued her course under a full head of steam. Ten minutes later a second shot exploded, and the *Trent* hove to. Lieutenant Fairfax, at the head of armed marines, proceeded forcibly to remove Mason, Slidell, and their secretaries.

"This is the best thing in the world for the South; England will open the blockade," rejoiced a Southern passenger. Mrs. Slidell expressed surprise that Captain Wilkes would play into Confederate hands by stirring up British wrath. Captain Moir said little, but Commander Williams, in charge of the mails, denounced the action as "wanton piracy." Almost incredibly, Fairfax failed to seize the dispatches, and apparently did not even think about them.[13]

As an act of deliberation, however, he ignored his instructions to seize the ship. On returning to the *San Jacinto*, he gave Captain Wilkes two reasons for not taking the ship as prize. He argued that the *San Jacinto* would be weakened by the loss of a prize crew at a time when she was expecting to join a naval attack on Port Royal. He also spoke of the inconvenience and loss to the *Trent*'s passengers if the ship should be taken into a port for adjudication. It is ironic that the officer who had at first disfavored the whole enterprise, and had suggested inquiry into international law, was now committing a crucial oversight in the realm of law. Wilkes listened to Fairfax's statement and approved letting the *Trent* go free. The American officers had violated the very rights that in 1812 their country had gone to war with Britain to uphold—the rights of neutrals.

[13] *Idem*, pp. 105–106. For Captain Moir's account, see *OR*, Ser. II, Vol. II, 1156–1157.

Doubtless moved by his fervent patriotism, Captain Wilkes had created an international affair, whose dimensions he did not foresee. The rash officer had brought the sorely beset Union to the brink of foreign war against the foremost naval power in the world. He had precipitated "perhaps the most perilous moment of the Civil War," Allan Nevins has judged.[14]

News of the incident electrified the Northern people, who exulted in the capture of two secessionist conspirators and in the slap at Britain, once the proud asserter of the right of search, and now the suspected friend of the South. What was more, after Bull Run the public cried out for a hero, for a valorous deed amidst the quiet along the Potomac maintained by General McClellan. Wilkes arrived at Fort Monroe, Virginia, on November 15; and the next day the telegraph flashed the news throughout the country. The *New York Times* observed:

> We do not believe the American heart ever thrilled with more genuine delight than it did yesterday, at the intelligence of the capture of Messrs. Slidell and Mason.... as for Commodore Wilkes and his command, let the handsome thing be done, consecrate another *Fourth* of July to him. Load him down with services of plate and swords of the cunningest and costliest art.[15]

The handsome thing was done for Wilkes. His superior, the secretary of the navy, congratulated him and gave the "emphatic approval of this department," carefully adding that the failure to take the *Trent* to a prize court must not be a precedent. The *San Jacinto* steamed on to Boston, where a public banquet was given the captain and his officers. Speaking at the affair, Governor John A. Andrew exulted that the heroic Wilkes had "fired a shot across the bows of the ship that bore the English lion's head." On the opening of Congress, the House of Representatives tendered the thanks of Congress to Captain Charles Wilkes "for his brave, adroit and patriotic conduct in the arrest and detention of the traitors."[16]

---

[14] Allan Nevins, *The War for the Union* (2 vols.; New York: Charles Scribner's Sons, 1960), II, 394.

[15] *New York Times*, November 19, 1861.

[16] *OR*, Ser. II, Vol. II, 1109, for Welles; Edward McPherson, *Political History*, p. 343; *Cong. Globe*, 37th Cong., 2d sess., part I, p. 5.

The furies of public opinion had been unleashed in the United States—a nation peculiarly governed by popular will. Few Americans probably understood the niceties of international law, but if they thought of this side of the matter they could have the reassuring, if erroneous, opinion of the former secretary of state, Edward Everett, who affirmed "the capture was perfectly lawful." True, a former Supreme Court justice, George T. Curtis, thought Wilkes should have taken the *Trent* to a prize court for adjudication, and the Baltimore *American* branded the act "a violation of the laws of neutrality strictly considered." But if any Yankee doubted that the gallant captain had dealt a blow to secession, he had only to read the condemnatory words Jefferson Davis addressed to the Confederate Congress, charging the United States had violated rights "for the most part held sacred even among barbarians."[17]

However, Davis's words were probably intended to be read abroad, for conceivably Mason and Slidell could be more effective instruments of Confederate diplomacy in a Yankee prison than in the courts of Europe. Such was nearly the case.

Intelligence of the *Trent* outrage arrived in England on November 27. A journalist familiar with the English scene wrote from London to Secretary Seward: "There never was within memory such a burst of feeling as has been created by the news of the boarding.... The people are frantic with rage, and were the country polled, I fear that 999 men out of a thousand would declare for immediate war. Lord Palmerston cannot resist the impulse if he would." "Bear this, bear all," was the prevailing spirit.[18] It had now become the task of British as well as Union statesmanship to settle the *Trent* affair to the satisfaction of public opinion in both countries.

What would the British government do? The Union's staunchest friend in the cabinet, the Duke of Argyll, at first flared out to Gladstone about "this wretched piece of American folly.... I am all against submitting to any clean breach of International Law, such as

[17] Harris, *op. cit.*, pp. 129, 127.
[18] *OR*, Ser. II, Vol. II, 1107; Theodore Martin, *The Life of His Royal Highness the Prince Consort* (5 vols.; London: Smith, Elder & Co., 1875–80), V, 347.

I can hardly doubt this has been." The foreign secretary, Russell, in a speech in October, after noting that slavery was not at stake in the American war, had declared that separation of the two sections was the only logical and permanent settlement of the strife. Palmerston hastily summoned the cabinet to meet the day following receipt of the news; to his assembled colleagues he ripped out, "You may stand for this but damned if I will!" The law officers advised that the Queen's government would "be justified in requiring reparation for the international wrong which has been on this occasion committed."[19]

The cabinet met again the next day and directed Russell to instruct Lord Lyons

> ...that the Washington Government should be told that what has been done is a violation of international law, and of the rights of Great Britain, and that [Her] Majesty's Government trust that the act will be disavowed and the prisoners set free and restored to British protection; and that ... if this demand is refused he [Lord Lyons] should retire from the United States.[20]

The cabinet met a third time, on November 30. At the urging of Gladstone, who had dined with the Queen and the Prince Consort the night before, the ministers moderated somewhat the draft Russell had prepared. The tone was still firm, not alone because the affront to maritime right had touched Britannia's sensitive nerve, but also because of the belief that the American secretary of state was spoiling for a war with Britain. The colonial secretary, the Duke of Newcastle, had a story to tell the cabinet, which was later widely circulated. At a dinner given in 1860 by Governor E. D. Morgan of New York, Seward had remarked to the duke that he expected to occupy a high office in the next administration, and that "it would become his duty to insult England, and that he should insult her accordingly." In October, 1861, Seward had recommended to the Northern governors that they fortify their coast and lake frontiers, and it was believed that he would welcome a war with Britain to

[19] Rhodes, *History*, III, 391; Nevins, *War for the Union*, I, 388; Norman D. Ferris, "The Prince Consort, 'The Times,' and the 'Trent' Affair," *Civil War History*, VI (June, 1960), 152.

[20] Ferris, *op. cit.*, p. 152.

attain his well-known purpose—the annexation of Canada. Englishmen also believed—with better reason than they reckoned—that early in the administration he had proposed a foreign war to reunite South and North.[21]

The cabinet's dispatches were promptly sent to the Queen at Windsor Castle for her approval, with Russell's expression of hope she would return them in time for the evening mail packet sailing to America. The Queen was occupied with a dinner party, and there was a day's delay. Already mortally ill, the Prince Consort, after sleepless hours, rose in the early morning and pored over the stiffly worded drafts. He did not approve, and made some crucial corrections, drawing on editorial comment in the *Times*, it has been suggested. He then went to the Queen. "He could eat no breakfast," she entered in her diary, "and looked very wretched." He told her he could scarcely hold his pen while making the revision; it was his last political memorandum. Victoria accepted Albert's suggestions, and in her own hand made slight alterations of his wording.

To the twentieth-century mind the interlude in Windsor Castle seems strange: a prince consort, as private secretary, advising a limited monarch to moderate the popular point of view expressed by an elected government. In this instance monarchy had a surer grasp of reality than the prime minister. What royal intervention had done is worth examination.

In returning the drafts of December 1, the Queen said she felt the main draft was "somewhat meagre."

> She should have liked to have seen the expression of a hope [the royal memorandum continued] that the American captain did not act under instructions, or, if he did, that he misapprehended them,—that the United States Government must be fully aware that the British Government could not allow its flag to be insulted ...and Her Majesty's Government are unwilling to believe that the United States Government intended wantonly to put an insult upon this country ... and that we are therefore glad to believe that, upon a full consideration of the circumstances of the undoubted breach of International Law committed, they would

[21] John Morley, *The Life of William Ewart Gladstone* (2 vols.; New York: The Macmillan Co., 1903), II, 418–419.

spontaneously offer such redress as alone could satisfy this country, viz., the restoration of the unfortunate passengers and a suitable apology.[22]

The royal couple had acted with wisdom in the ways of diplomacy. They had not backed the United States into a corner, as the peremptory draft would have done, but had kept open a graceful exit from the perilous position Wilkes's excess of zeal had put it in. Proof of this is the response Seward made to Lord Lyons when the minister apprised him he had an official dispatch to deliver: "So much depended upon the wording of it."[23]

The royal suggestions went back to the cabinet. "Lord Palmerston thought them excellent," it was reported to the dying prince. The old statesman had been saved from his own recklessness. Cobden put it well: "Palmerston likes to drive the wheel close to the edge, and show how dexterously he can avoid falling over the precipice. Meantime he keeps people's attention employed, which suits him politically." The principal dispatch was rewritten in conformity with the prince's memorandum, and sent on its way. With regard to the issue of international law, Britain founded her case solely on the rights of neutrals. Would the Americans yield? Palmerston did not think so, and told Russell he feared they would not get what they asked for "without fighting for it."[24]

Even before the dispatch was sent, Britain began girding for war. On November 30 the fleet was ordered to stand by, preparations were commenced to send 8,000 troops to Canada, and the arsenals were busy. The Queen by proclamation prohibited export of arms and ammunition. In the interest of national unity, Lord Derby was

[22] Martin, *op. cit.*, V, 349–350. The Gladstone Papers, BM, Vol. CCCXLIII, Additional MSS 44,428, pp. 284–285, for "Draft to Lord Lyons as originally agreed upon by the Cabinet and sent to the Queen" and "Alteration in Lord Palmerston's handwriting marked 'Proposed Alteration from A. to B.' and endorsed by Mr. Hammond. 'N.B. The substance of this alteration was suggested by the Prince Consort.' E. H."

[23] Newton, *op. cit.*, I, 66.

[24] Martin, *loc. cit.*; John Morley, *The Life of Richard Cobden* (2 vols.; Boston: Roberts Brothers, 1881), II, 385; John Bassett Moore, *The Principles of American Diplomacy* (New York: Harper & Brothers, 1918), pp. 114–115; Duberman, *Adams*, p. 281.

consulted and Conservative support of the militant posture was secured.[25] A good part of the press, relishing the sensation, kept up a belligerent tone. Adams wrote Seward on December 6 that the critical state of British opinion could easily lead to war, and nearly a fortnight later the veteran Albany editor, Thurlow Weed, wrote Seward from London: "The purpose of this government is war, unless you give up S. & M."[26] News of congressional approval of Wilkes's deed arrived in England December 16 and deepened the crisis. And approval by high officials in Massachusetts "makes it very hard for Bright and me to contend against the 'British lion party' in this country," Cobden told Charles Sumner, chairman of the senate foreign relations committee.[27]

The United States would stand isolated if it upheld Captain Wilkes. Napoleon III was markedly hostile to the Union, and he was already scheming to exploit the American disruption to France's advantage in Mexico. For some time France, concerned about the cotton shortage, had urged a vigorous American policy, sounding out Britain about joint intervention to break the blockade. On the question of neutral rights raised in the Bahama Channel, all Europe supported the British view, not unmindful that Britain was usually the poacher on these rights. On December 3 the French foreign minister wrote a long communication to the French minister in Washington, upholding the immunity of the neutral flag, and expressing the opinion the Federal government should yield to Britain. These views, he wrote, were to be stated frankly to Seward. Vienna, Berlin, St. Petersburg, Turin—all pronounced London to be in the right on the question of international law.[28]

The British dispatches did not reach Washington until December 18, almost three weeks after they had left London. By that date, sober second thought was being taken on both sides of the Atlantic. The Union's fastest friend in Britain, John Bright, seized advantage of a

[25] Harris, *op. cit.*, pp. 142–143; Jones, "The British Conservatives," etc., *AHR*, LVIII, 420.

[26] *OR*, Ser. II, Vol. II, 1119–1120, for Adams's letter; Rhodes, *History*, III, 419.

[27] Morley, *Cobden*, II, 389.

[28] *OR*, Ser. II, Vol. II, 116–118, for Thouvenel's letter; also see pp. 1126–1127, 1158–1159; Harris, *op. cit.*, pp. 154–155.

public dinner in Rochdale on December 4 to oppose war with America, appealing to bonds of Anglo-Saxon blood and free institutions that connected the English-speaking peoples. Bright and another pro-American Liberal, Richard Cobden, corresponded with their friend, Senator Sumner, on behalf of conciliation. An ardent foe of slavery, learned and eloquent, if vituperative (a latter-day Puritan), Sumner had lived abroad for several years and had maintained an extensive correspondence with liberal leaders in England. A mollifying belief spread in England, which in time was confirmed by a letter from Seward to Adams that Wilkes had acted without instructions. General Winfield Scott, who had gone to Europe after his retirement in November, published a conciliatory letter in the European press stating he doubted the seizure had been authorized, and he was sure the United States would be happy to free the men if England would accept the historic American stand on neutral rights. He undermined his pacific effort, however, when a few days later he suddenly embarked for home, remarking that if there was to be war with England he could perhaps be of service to his country.[29]

The *Trent* affair was the first major challenge to Union diplomacy. Abraham Lincoln, "diplomat in carpet slippers," was in truth as little versed in international statecraft as he was in military craft. He was markedly endowed, though, with three qualities of statesmanship: common sense, realism, and pragmatism. When on April Fool's Day, and not in jest, Secretary of State Seward had offered him some thoughts for consideration, which embraced a foreign war to draw the seceded states back into a common cause with the North, he had quietly laid the memorandum aside, replying "I remark that if this must be done, *I* must do it."[30]

Here was the assignment of Abraham Lincoln, self-taught in law, politics, and rhetoric: In order to save a nation he must deepen his knowledge of these subjects, teach himself diplomacy and strategy, and in turn teach the people democratic values.

[29] Harris, *op. cit.*, pp. 155 ff.; Victor H. Cohen, "Charles Sumner and the Trent Affair," *Journal of Southern History*, XXII (May, 1956), 205–219; Charles W. Elliott, *Winfield Scott*, pp. 749 ff.

[30] Jay Monaghan, *Diplomat in Carpet Slippers* (Indianapolis: Bobbs-Merrill, 1945); Nicolay and Hay, *Abraham Lincoln*, III, 448.

Seward—brilliant, erratic, astute, schooled in the tortuous politics of New York state and the U.S. Senate—grew to respect the untried President, who masked his seriousness of purpose by endlessly telling stories with a Western twang. Both men perhaps lost the moment for a masterstroke when they failed immediately to disavow Wilkes's seizure and to hand the Southerners back to British protection. In the cabinet, only Montgomery Blair appears to have sanctioned such a bold course from the start. McClellan advocated freeing the prisoners, and Seward eventually came to believe the step was necessary.

But both the secretary of state and the President kept a public silence. Lincoln did not give official sanction to Wilkes's deed or rejoice over the detention of the prisoners, who he said might prove "white elephants." The President coveted peace without political disaster, while the secretary of state awaited an official British communication. The Congress that applauded Wilkes heard not a word from the President on the subject of the *Trent* in his annual message, December 3. A little over a month elapsed between first news of the affair and the arrival of the British diplomatic response, and about a fortnight more before the American stand was announced. The administration's dilemma—war with Britain or political ruin through flouting outraged public sentiment—became less painful with the passing of time.[31]

The Queen's messenger brought the royal dispatches to the British legation in Washington at midnight on December 18. Lord Lyons had been the paragon of tact throughout the tense weeks, keeping a correct reserve, while uncertain about the opinion the law officers of the Crown might render. He anxiously read through the papers, three in all. The main dispatch, revised by the Prince Consort in the hope of withdrawing Britain from the brink of war, Lyons was to hand to Seward. But a private letter from Russell read: "My wish would be that at your first interview with Mr. Seward you should not take my dispatch with you, but should prepare him for it, and ask

[31] Thomas A. Bailey, *A Diplomatic History of the American People* (7th ed.; New York: Appleton-Century-Crofts, 1964), pp. 327 ff.; Norman A. Graebner (ed.), *The Enduring Lincoln* (Urbana: University of Illinois Press, 1959), pp. 68–94.

him to settle with the President and his Cabinet what course they would propose." Another private communication instructed Lyons to allow Seward seven days to reply, if the American asked for delay. If the British minister received no reply in that time, or an unsatisfactory one, he was ordered to close his legation and return to London forthwith.[32]

At the Foreign Office the permanent under-secretary, Hammond, stated his opinion Messrs. Mason and Slidell would be immediately executed. A British warship was sent to New York to receive the legation staff, in the event of an unfavorable reply from Washington. Hammond predicted "the Americans will never give way."

In London, the British government had not consulted Adams; the first contact between representatives of the two proud nations occurred in Washington. On December 19, Lord Lyons called upon the secretary of state and described the general tenor of the principal dispatch. Both men acted with adroitness, soon moving sensibly beyond the formal limits of protocol. Seward, who was capable of rodomontade, listened seriously and with dignity. He asked to be given time to consider the subject and to talk with the President.

Before Lyons left, Seward remarked he had one question to put informally: Was any time fixed within which the United States must reply? Lyons said he did not like to answer that question; he wished to avoid seeming to threaten. The interview became an exchange of confidences between the two men. Seward gave the tactful Briton assurance his answer would be held private, and learned of the seven-day deadline. He then asked for a copy of the dispatch "unofficially and informally," pointing out much time would be lost otherwise and remarking that so much depended upon its wording that it was impossible to make a decision without reading it. Recognizing that Seward was a force for peace in the cabinet, and knowing that a packet would soon bring a supporting dispatch from the French government, Lyons wisely sent Seward the dispatch informally, with the understanding the term of seven days would begin with the formal presentation, postponed until December 23.

On receiving the dispatch in an envelope marked "Private and

[32] *OR*, Ser. II, Vol. II, 1110–1113, for Russell's dispatches and letter to Lyons; Newton, *Lyons*, I, 62.

Confidential," Seward almost immediately hurried to the British legation. He expressed his pleasure that the tone was courteous and friendly, without menace or dictation. But another question had occurred to him: What if he refused or proposed discussion, within the seven days? Lyons replied that if the answer was not satisfactory, and particularly if it did not include surrender of the prisoners, he could not accept it.

"I was not sorry to tell him this in the way I did," Lyons reported to Russell that same day. "I avoided all menace which could be an obstacle to the U.S. yielding, while I did the only thing which will make them yield if they ever do, let them know that we were really in earnest.... I don't think it likely they will give in, but I do not think it impossible."[33]

Seward shut himself in his office, where he consulted works on international law and began to draft a reply. Lincoln decided to try his hand, and set down on paper two courses of action: arbitration or release of the men in return for English acknowledgment that the principle be fixed as "the law for all future analogous cases."[34] But the British stand was exigent, leaving no margin for compromise or time for negotiation.

Lincoln's cabinet met at ten on the morning of Christmas Day to discuss the grave crisis of the Union. Lord Russell's dispatch was read. Seward presented his draft, explaining why international law required that the men must be given up. During the meeting the dispatch from France, which had seasonably arrived, was sent in; it supported Britain and urged the United States to yield. Senator Sumner, chairman of the foreign relations committee, was invited in, and he read letters from Bright and Cobden counseling release of the men and saying England did not want war, but that all England opposed the seizure.

Attorney General Edward Bates backed Seward's stand, waiving the question of law and urging that "to go to war with England now is to abandon all hope of suppressing the rebellion." It would sweep our ships from Southern waters, ruin our trade, and bankrupt our

---

[33] Newton, *ibid.*, 61 ff.; *OR*, Ser. II, Vol. II, 1134–1135, 1142.

[34] For draft of Lincoln's dispatch, see Basler *et al.*, *Collected Works of Lincoln*, V, 62–64; Monaghan, *Diplomat*, pp. 189–190.

treasury. "There was great reluctance," he noted, "on the part of some of the members of the cabinet—and even the President himself —to acknowledge these obvious truths.... The main fear I believe, was the displeasure of our own people—lest they should accuse us of timidly truckling to the power of England."

In the end, after full deliberation, Lincoln chose to risk Northern wrath in order to avoid the risk of war with Britain. Bates entered in his diary: "All yielded to the necessity, and unanimously concur[r]ed in Mr. Seward's letter to Lord Lyons."[35]

It became Seward's task to acquiesce in the British demand for release of the prisoners, and at the same time to placate Yankee pride. He must not offend the House of Representatives or humiliate the secretary of the navy. He was equal to the challenge. The letter he handed Lord Lyons December 26 met the crucial question with the declaration the prisoners would be "cheerfully liberated." But, before reaching that point, he had composed a lawyer's brief, rehearsing a set of adroit arguments in the realm of international law with a kind of masterly confusion. He conceded that Captain Wilkes had been at fault in failing to carry the *Trent* to a prize court. Wilkes had thereby violated cherished American principles and had fallen into the British way of dealing with neutrals. "We are asked to do to the British nation just what we have always insisted all nations ought to do to us," he wrote with blithe impudence. "Your lordship will please indicate a time and place for receiving" the prisoners, Seward ended his letter to Lyons.[36]

American resentment of British pugnacity at a time when the Union was taxed to the utmost with a war at home was expressed by Lowell in his "Jonathan to John":

> It don't seem hardly right, John,
>   When both my hands was full,
> To stump me to a fight, John,—
>   Your cousin tu, John Bull!

[35] J. G. Randall, *Lincoln the President* (4 vols.; New York: Dodd, Mead and Co., 1945–55), II, 37 ff.; Cohen, *loc. cit.*; Howard K. Beale (ed.), *The Diary of Edward Bates, 1859–1866* (Washington: Government Printing Office, 1933), p. 216.

[36] *OR*, Ser. II, Vol. II, 1145–1154; McPherson, *Political History*, pp. 338–342.

> We give the critters back, John,
>   Cos Abram thought 'twas right;
> It warn't your bullying clack, John,
>   Provokin' us to fight.

Lord Lyons, acting within his instructions, accepted Seward's reply, even though it did not contain an apology. He ordered an English sloop-of-war to receive Mason and Slidell, and they were carried to St. Thomas—the *Trent*'s destination—from where they sailed for Europe. It quickly became clear that the British interest had been British honor and not the Southern cause.[37]

The *Times*, "the Thunderer," usually belligerent during the crisis, now expressed the hope "that our countrymen will not give these fellows anything in the shape of an ovation. The civility that is due to a foe in distress is all that they can claim.... They must not suppose that because we have gone to the very verge of a great war to rescue them, that therefore they are precious in our eyes. We should have done just as much to rescue two of their own negroes."[38] Clearly, the North had overrated the influence abroad of the Mason and Slidell mission.

Mason was never officially received by the British government. He wrote home that Russell's sympathies were not with the South and that his policy was one of inaction. When Parliament opened in February, and debate began on American affairs, Lord John announced that the government intended to maintain its present policy. From the Conservative side, Derby asserted, "the time is not yet come when they [Her Majesty's Government] can be called on to recognize the Government representing the successful revolt of the Southern States."[39]

The *Trent* affair had flashed through the lowering skies like a thunderbolt. It had illuminated the national sensitivities of Americans and Britons—the thin-skinned chauvinism exhibited in Anglo-American relations from the War of 1812 through the Venezuelan boundary crisis of 1895. Once passed, it had cleared the air. The spasm of superpatriotism was a six weeks' sensation. Russell, on

[37] Harris, *Trent Affair*, p. 235.
[38] McPherson, *Political History*, pp. 342–343.
[39] Duberman, *Adams*, p. 285.

January 11, fully accepted Seward's saucy reply. What would have been a constructive sequel—a pact on neutral rights, as suggested by Russell, Sumner, and Lincoln—did not ensue. (There were, in fact, fifty-six impressments from American ships during World War I.)[40]

Not the least benefit was the light in which Britain now saw Seward, who clearly did not want to pick a quarrel with Britain— merely to twist the British lion's tail. "Ten months of office have dispelled many of his illusions," Lyons wrote Russell; and although Lyons could not say his general opinion of Seward had undergone any change, "I must allow him the merit of having worked very hard and exposed his popularity to very great danger."[41]

The war scare, further, had made plain to many Britons the difficulties and dangers of a war with the Northern states, especially in Canada—a hostage to the Union. It forced realization upon the peace-loving and anti-slavery masses that war with the Union would be "an unloosing of hell" in alliance with a "slaveholding oligarchy." Lastly, its passing called up a surge of relief that exceeded the anger of the first wave of outrage.

On the western side of the Atlantic, although the sting of resentment of England persisted in the North, the war fever quickly subsided. The Lincoln government made the official documents public, and Sumner delivered a widely quoted speech in the Senate chamber, emphasizing that in letting the rebels go the Union was conforming to the best American precedents. Anglo-Union relations were actually improved by the near-clash. South of the Potomac, hope had been keenly disappointed. The Richmond editor, E. A. Pollard, recalled: "The conclusion of the Trent [*sic*] affair gave a sharp check to the long cherished imagination of the interference of England in the war, at least to the extent of her disputing the blockade, which had begun to tell on the war-power and general condition of the Confederacy."[42]

[40] McPherson, *Political History*, p. 342; Thomas A. Bailey, "World War Analogues of the Trent Affair," *American Historical Review*, XXXVIII (January, 1933), 286–290.

[41] Newton, *Lyons*, I, 74, 72.

[42] E. A. Pollard, *The Lost Cause* (New York: E. B. Treat & Co., 1866), p. 197.

Lincoln, astonished at English passion and bad blood, had added reason to meditate upon a message to Congress proposing Federal purchase of slaves in the loyal border states. Within a little more than a month, the North had a more worthy hero to admire than Captain Wilkes, when General U. S. Grant moved south from Kentucky upon forts Henry and Donelson and forced unconditional surrender.

An act that was an accident had nearly catapulted two great nations into a war of momentous consequences. Contingency had played a dramatic part in the crisis. Had Lieutenant Fairfax remained in command of the *San Jacinto*, or had his initial advice been heeded, there would have been no *Trent* affair. Had Fairfax and Wilkes escorted the British ship to a prize court, the episode would have been appealed from public opinion drunk to legal opinion sober. Had Prince Albert died before the draft of the imperious Palmerston government was written (he died two weeks later), the Union might well have received an ultimatum that left no ground for retreat. Had a trans-Atlantic cable been in existence, the outcome might have been as Thomas A. Bailey has surmised: "If the British had known at once of Northern jubilation, they probably would have presented their demands in terms so vigorous as to make war the only alternative." Had Seward been prone to follow his "April Fool's Day" policy of a distracting foreign war, he might well have made impossible the understanding that was reached. Lastly, had Lyons been less skillful in his diplomatic methods, or Lincoln less realistic and pragmatic, the war might inadvertently have ended in a Southern victory.

The *Trent* affair was perhaps the most serious crisis in Anglo-American relations during the war. Only in recent years, however, have historians appreciated the gravity of the crisis of 1861. At no other time was Great Britain provoked to the point of waging war against the Union. At no other time did Great Britain prepare for war against the Union. There were two subsequent crises—in September, 1862, and September, 1863. The first involved a proposal of mediation, looking to recognition of Confederate independence. The second involved British construction of ironclads for the Confederacy. Neither crisis took the two nations quite as close to actual fighting as did the *Trent* affair. At neither time did either of the two nations gird for combat. In considering mediation, Britain did not intend to break the blockade by force. At neither time was public opinion so inflamed as in November and December of 1861.

No acts of aggression attended the two later episodes. Britain did not mean a war for Southern independence in contemplating recognition or in allowing the Laird shipbuilders to send their ships to sea. In September, 1862, Britain never went beyond *contemplation* of recognition—a move that was tied to Russian participation, which in turn was indeed dubious. In September, 1863, Britain hesitated over stopping the rams not because the government was pro-Confederate but because the legality of detention was questionable—a point that was solved by the government's purchase of them. Throughout the period 1862–63, in point of fact, Great Britain scrupulously pursued the policy of neutrality.

What would British intervention have meant? Through the month of December, Britain prepared for war, forwarding troops to Canada, strengthening her naval fleet in American waters, and despatching cruisers to the sea lanes most likely to be marauded by American privateers. Admiral David Milne, British commander of the North America and West Indies stations, stated in 1864 that if the *Trent* affair had issued in war, his "own idea at the time was to have secured our own bases, especially Bermuda and Halifax, raised the blockade of the Southern Ports ... and then to have immediately blockaded as effectually as my means admitted the chief Northern Ports, and to have acted in Chesapeake Bay in co-operation with the Southern Forces who would practically, if not in terms, have been our allies, and where our aid would have been invaluable."[43] Fleet bombardment could have rained destruction on Northern seaports; and Southern invasions of Maryland, Kentucky, and Pennsylvania

[43] J. P. Baxter, 3d, "The British Government and Neutral Rights, 1861–1865," *American Historical Review*, XXXIV (October, 1928), 17. The crucial importance of the *Trent* affair has only recently won the attention of historians. In addition to the Nevins judgment (n. 14, *supra*), see J. G. Randall, *Lincoln the President*, vol. I, ch. XVI; Robert Huhn Jones, "The American Civil War in the British Sessional Papers: Catalog and Commentary," *Proceedings of the American Philosophical Society*, 107 (October, 1963), 3; and W. D. Jones, *The Confederate Rams at Birkenhead* (Tuscaloosa, Ala.: Confederate Publishing Co., 1961), ch. V.

could have inflicted damage there as immense as the Confederacy suffered in Virginia, Georgia, and South Carolina later in the war.

Separation of North and South would have resulted from a war whose main theaters had been on the Atlantic and the Northern frontier. The balance of power in the western hemisphere would have profoundly shifted. The Confederate States of America would doubtless have become closely associated with Britain, selling cotton, buying English wares, and depending on the British fleet. The Confederacy would have had to liberate her slaves under the compulsions of British sentiment and the Northern haven for fugitives. Britain would have wielded vast influence in the New World, from which President Monroe had warned away the powers of the Old. Nor would it have been Britain alone that would have set aside the Monroe Doctrine, for France could have successfully established her empire in Mexico.

In an Anglo-Union war, though Britain would have enjoyed the advantage on the sea, the Union held Canada as a hostage. If it had fought well in Canada—better than during the American Revolution and the War of 1812—the Union might have annexed the Canadian provinces. The whole of this rearrangement of European and American strength would have radically altered the structure of world politics in the twentieth century.

Antietam

Its effects will be seen and felt in the destinies
of the Nation for centuries to come.

New York Times, September 21, 1862

"Eighteen Sixty-One"

Arm'd year—year of the struggle,
No dainty rhymes or sentimental love verses for you terrible year
.   .   .   .
Year that suddenly sang by the mouths of the round-lipp'd cannon.
I repeat you, hurrying, crashing, sad, distracted year.

(Walt Whitman)

Eighteen sixty-one—the first year of the war—had known only one major battle. By the opening of 1862, Kentucky had been nursed out of her neutrality, the Army of the Potomac had been turned into a splendid fighting machine by McClellan, and the danger of British intervention over the *Trent* affair had been averted.

In the early months of the new year, Federal fortunes prospered as Grant won control of the lower reaches of the Tennessee and Cumberland rivers and Nashville fell into Union hands. Grant's advance upon the Deep South, however, was checked at Shiloh and Corinth, and the summer was quiet in the West. In the East, McClellan, prodded by Lincoln, at length with great deliberation moved his army to the Peninsula, formed by the York and James rivers. Intricated with the administration over the defense of Washington, faced by Lee, and in time by Stonewall Jackson, whose Valley Campaign had deepened Lincoln's concern about the safety of the capital, McClellan failed to take Richmond.

Continuing his search for a winning general, Lincoln named Major General John Pope as head of a new Army of Virginia, and Major General Henry Halleck as General-in-chief at Washington. In late August, the second battle of Bull Run was waged, Lee striking a terrible blow upon Pope's army, sending it dispirited and in disarray back upon Washington. In the week ending September 2, Pope had lost in killed and wounded about 10,000, with another 6,000 missing, while the Confederate casualties were not as great—9,108 killed and wounded, with 89 missing. Pope, who had taken up his command with a boastful proclamation, had ended his usefulness as a campaigner against Lee. The Confederate army, in high spirits now, stood at Chantilly, not far from Washington; the Federal army, bruised and defeated, needed reorganizing and refitting. To Lincoln only one man seemed adequate to protect the capital and reinvigorate the Federal forces—the recently discredited McClellan. On September 5, without heed either to his cabinet or the critical press, he restored McClellan to command.

It was well that he did so, for perhaps the most acute crisis of the war was at hand. It was a multiple crisis—military, diplomatic, and political. The Confederacy was about to launch a triple offensive. General Lee had resolved upon an invasion of the North, while General Braxton Bragg was to invade Kentucky, and a third prong was to spear the Federals in northern Mississippi and recapture the rail center at Corinth. Lee's purposes were far-reaching: to win Maryland, where a pro-Southern rising was anticipated; to cut the rail bridge at Harrisburg, leaving the Northeast connected by rail with the Northwest only by way of northern New York; and to be in a position to threaten Washington. A successful thrust into the North, following Second Manassas, might influence Northern voters in the impending fall elections to declare themselves for peace. A Confederate victory might also bring foreign intervention to end a useless war.[1] Lee's purpose *was* far-reaching: to win independence for the Confederate States of America.

Meanwhile in the West, Braxton Bragg—in concert with Kirby Smith—was to win Kentucky for the Confederacy. Expectation that a border slave state would rise in welcome once a Confederate force was on Kentucky soil also figured in this western thrust.[2] Kentucky won, the northern frontier of the Confederacy would become the Ohio River, the states of Ohio and Indiana and Illinois would be vulnerable to raids, Missouri would be prone to join the Confederacy, and the Father of Waters in its middle span would pass under

[1] For Lee's aims in the Maryland campaign, see his report in Francis W. Palfrey, *The Antietam and Fredericksburg* (New York: Charles Scribner's Sons, 1882), pp. 15–16. The Antietam campaign is admirably described in Freeman, *Lee*, II, pp. 350 ff.

[2] Grady McWhiney, "Controversy in Kentucky: Braxton Bragg's Campaign of 1862," *Civil War History*, VI (March, 1960), 5–42.

Southern control. To the south, during this while, Generals Sterling Price and Earl Van Dorn were to fall upon Federal forces in Mississippi, prevent reinforcements from being sent to Kentucky, and retake Corinth—the rail section occupied by General W. S. Rosecrans. Perhaps at no other time during the war did the Confederacy so closely approach a coordinated military move.

Public discontent in the North was mounting because of the failure of Union arms to win victories in the field. Corruption in 1861 in the war department, the mounting costs of waging a prolonged war, abridgment of civil liberties (including *habeas corpus*), and the draft of men—all contributed to peace sentiment. Moderate Republicanism seemed on the wane, as an extremist or Radical spirit rose in the party, and as the Democrats experienced a resurgence. Elections were scheduled in October and November to choose a new House of Representatives and a substantial number of state officers. The middle-of-the-road Republican governor of New York, E. D. Morgan, troubled by the Radical spirit in his party, chose not to seek another term.

In Great Britain, the accounts of Second Bull Run made an impression more profound than First Bull Run. Prime Minister Palmerston wrote his foreign secretary in mid-September that the Federals "got a very complete smashing." If Washington or Baltimore should fall, he ventured, "would it not be time for us to consider whether ... England and France might not address the contending parties and recommend an arrangement upon the basis of separation?"[3]

Though the *Trent* affair had acted as a catharsis on Anglo-Union relations, pressures developed in 1862 to urge recognition of the Confederacy. Not the least of these was the belief that separation of North and South was inevitable. As early as January, 1862, Cobden had declared: "I don't believe the North and South can ever lie in the same bed again."[4] The inevitability of Southern

[3] Spencer Walpole, *The Life of Lord John Russell* (2 vols.; London and New York: Longmans, Green & Co., 1889), II, 349.

[4] John Morley, *Richard Cobden* (Boston: Roberts Brothers, 1881), p. 572.

independence seemed confirmed to many by the outcome of the Seven Days on the Peninsula and of Second Bull Run.

Lancashire, the heart of the British textile industry, was a second source of pressure. The cotton shortage—long delayed by a surplus on hand when the Americans went to war—now had caused mills to close down, had thrown half a million persons out of work, and had effected widespread distress. Though the unemployed bore their deprivations with unexampled fortitude, the government was nervously apprehensive of an outbreak. As for raw cotton, 80 per cent of which had previously come from the American South, lifting the blockade was a more direct approach than developing new sources in India and Egypt.

Southern supporters in Parliament were vocal, if not numerous, and Confederate propagandists were active. At the very time that the graycoats were moving into Maryland and Kentucky, the Confederate agent, George N. Sanders, arrived in London, and began to coordinate the invasions with a drive for British recognition. The *Times* reported (September 5) the grand strategy about to be implemented in Maryland and Kentucky, and even in Missouri. Sanders carried authorization to use cotton bonds in exchange for money to build ships for the Confederacy. British-built ships, the famous raiders *Florida* and *Alabama*, had already gone to sea to maraud Union shipping. In the Laird yards at Liverpool, formidable ironclads were under construction, intended for commerce-destroying under the Stars and Bars.[5]

The tone of much of the British press evidenced wide sympathy with the Southern cause. The conservative *Quarterly Review* discerned in American proceedings "the turning point of a political controversy of our own." It saw the American democracy, extolled by John Bright and his friends, fall prey to war, extravagance, corruption, class legislation and other Old World maladies. "The impression produced upon the majority of spectators in England has undoubtedly been that democratic institutions have failed," it exulted.[6]

Lord Palmerston, though relieved that there had been no war with the Union over the *Trent*, at the same time favored disunion,

[5] Nevins, *War for the Union*, II, 543.

[6] *The Quarterly Review*, 112 (October, 1862), 538.

writing Russell on January 19, 1862: "If the North and South are definitely disunited, and if at the same time Mexico could be turned into a prosperous monarchy, I do not know any arrangement that would be more advantageous for us."[7]

The establishment of a prosperous monarchy in Mexico was exactly the purpose of Napoleon III, emperor of France. Back in October, 1861, France, Britain, and Spain had signed a convention by which they agreed to occupy Mexican ports and collect customs duties in order to pay the suspended interest owed Europe by the Juarez government of Mexico. Spain and Britain subsequently withdrew, leaving Napoleon III in a position to go beyond instituting a financial receivership toward the fulfillment of his dream of reestablishing the French empire in North America, and promoting Catholicism and monarchy, while the republic of the United States was rent by war. "No more sinister project, in terms of American interest, American influence, and American ideas, has ever been conceived in the history of the Monroe Doctrine," Dexter Perkins, the authoritative historian of the doctrine has observed.[8]

The sword of Britain still hung over the Union. Seward had instructed Adams in early August 1862 that if Britain recognized the Confederacy he was to suspend his functions as minister. In response to Palmerston's query about Anglo-French mediation, Russell readily agreed; and he went on to state that he felt, in case of failure, Britain ought to recognize the Southern states as an independent nation. He proposed a cabinet meeting on August 23 or 30 to discuss the step, before taking it to France, and then it would be presented to other powers as a measure already decided upon by the two powers.

Palmerston skillfully began to refine the plan. It should be made to both sides simultaneously. "Might it not be well to ask Russia to join England and France in the offer of mediation?" As to the time of making the offer, he noted on September 23 that a great conflict [the battle of Antietam] was taking place northwest of Washington. "If the Federals sustain a great defeat, they may be at once ready for

[7] Nevins, *War for the Union*, I, 390, n. 41.

[8] Dexter Perkins, *A History of the Monroe Doctrine* (Boston: Little, Brown & Co., 1963), p. 118.

mediation.... If, on the other hand, they should have the best of it, we may wait awhile."[9]

Antietam might have become to the Confederacy what Saratoga was to the American states in 1778. It would not, to be sure, have forged an outright alliance, and Russia would probably not have joined in mediation or recognition, but recognition by Britain and France would have produced, as Seward once said, war between the United States and all of the recognizing powers.

Known but to a few, on a Northern victory hinged the reconstruction of the American social order. So immensely important a theme as emancipation must be reserved for a full chapter, yet we must note here that demands for executive action to free the slaves were sharply mounting. Military commanders, such as Frémont, exerted one form of pressure. Congress had passed a long series of abolitionist measures (as we shall see); and diplomatic ministers abroad—such as Adams, and Carl Schurz in Spain—represented to Washington that emancipation would enlist the sympathies of European liberals and make for difficulties in foreign governments' friendliness for the Confederacy.[10]

The North's most widely read newspaper editor, Horace Greeley, penned the famous editorial, "The Prayer of Twenty Millions," charging the President with remissness and entreating him to free the slaves. Religious groups visited the executive mansion and appealed to Lincoln to emancipate the blacks. With a wary regard for the border slave states, Lincoln refrained from committing himself. If the slaves were set free, millions "with one heart would join the foe," Congressman William Henry Wadsworth of Kentucky warned his colleagues.[11]

Privately, however, the President had resolved to adopt the emancipation policy in the late spring of 1862. He read a draft of a proclamation to his cabinet on July 22. What is notable in our

[9] Albert D. Kirwan (ed.), *The Confederacy* (Cleveland: World Publishing Co., 1959), pp. 237–239.

[10] Rhodes, *History*, III, 398, n. 1.

[11] John Hope Franklin, *The Emancipation Proclamation* (New York: Random House–Alfred A. Knopf, 1963), p. 19.

examination of Antietam as a turning point in the war was Seward's advice that the proclamation be postponed "until you can give it to the country supported by military success."[12] Lincoln felt the wisdom of Seward's suggestion and put the proclamation in his desk, where it lay for two months, awaiting military success—beyond Second Bull Run, beyond Greeley's importunate editorial, beyond the earnest solicitations of church delegations.

Between September 4 and 7, Lee's army forded the Potomac River above Washington, its bands playing "Maryland! My Maryland!"

> Come, for thy shield is bright and strong,
> Maryland, My Maryland!
> Come, for thy dalliance does thee wrong,
> Maryland! My Maryland!

Lee issued an address to the people of Maryland—"to aid you in throwing off this foreign yoke" was the object of this invasion—but the supposedly oppressed people gave no sign of rising.

News that "Little Mac" had been restored to command inspired the lines:

> Press on, young Chieftain, foremost in the van!
> The Hour of need has come—be thou the Man!

Rutherford B. Hayes wrote home, from an army camp eight miles from Washington, of the announcement about McClellan's reinstatement: "It was a happy army again. There is nothing of the defeated or disheartened among the men."[13] Lincoln, for his part, was deeply disturbed. Confederates had occupied Lexington, Kentucky, on September 2, and now their forces had carried the war close to the heart of the Northeast. On the sixth, the Southerners under Stonewall Jackson marched through Frederick, sighting the Union flag and giving Whittier occasion to write his stirring verse about Barbara Frietchie.

Lee had miscalculated in at least three respects: (1) The Marylanders did not want to be liberated. (2) McClellan reorganized his army, inspired it, and moved it with far greater celerity than Lee

---

[12] *Ibid.*, p. 43.
[13] Quoted in Myers, *McClellan*, p. 349, n. 19.

had anticipated, and on September 5 he was in pursuit. (3) The Federal troops at Harper's Ferry, now interdicted by the Confederates, failed to abandon their position, as the military textbooks said they should. Their retention of the garrison forced Lee, on September 10, to divide his invading forces by sending Jackson back to take Harper's Ferry.

Besides these miscalculations there was a stroke of bad luck, the intervention of contingency. On September 13, Private Mitchell of the Twenty-seventh Indiana found three cigars on the campground recently occupied by General D. H. Hill. The cigars were wrapped in Lee's order to Hill, revealing his whole plan—the division of forces and the scheme of march. Within a short time, Lee's Special Order No. 191 was in McClellan's hands, conclusively documenting reports made earlier by his cavalry. He now had the sure knowledge that could have been employed to crush Confederate striking power.[14]

Lee had not wholly misconstrued McClellan's qualities, however. The oft-repeated testimony of Lee that McClellan "was the ablest soldier they [the Union army] had" is perhaps true, but the military student, Kenneth P. Williams—no friend of McClellan, to be sure—has suggested that Lee's true estimate of his opponent is the record of how he dealt with him.[15] And now, during invasion, Lee boldly divided his forces, putting a river between them, and was vindicated in the event: victory at Harper's Ferry and reunion of his forces before McClellan undertook the major engagement.

Lee later wrote: "It had been supposed that the advance upon Frederick would lead to the evacuation of Martinsburg and Harper's Ferry, thus opening the line of communication through the Valley. This not having occurred, it became necessary to dislodge the enemy from those positions before concentrating the army west of the mountains." Jackson hastened to Harper's Ferry. Though it has

[14] *OR*, Ser. I, Vol. XIX, part 2, 281–282; Hal Bridges (ed.), "A Lee Letter on the 'Lost Dispatch' and the Maryland Campaign of 1862," *Virginia Magazine of History and Biography*, 66 (April, 1958), 161–166. The dispatch is in *OR*, Ser. I, Vol. XIX, part 2, 603–604, and McClellan's report to Lincoln about finding it is in *ibid.*, 281.

[15] Williams, *Lincoln Finds a General*, II, 479.

been estimated that a corps of Federals could have relieved the garrison at Harper's Ferry, McClellan did not send an adequate force for this purpose. Jackson and cooperating forces encircled the beleaguered Federals, and by 4:30 P.M. of September 13 had gained possession of Maryland Heights, which commanded the town. Making his dispositions with care, Jackson opened fire on the morning of the fifteenth. An hour later the Federals sent up the white flag.[16]

Panic clutched the hearts of Northerners on news of Lee's thrust. Women and children were sent away from the region north of Frederick, and the farmers remained behind to protect their homes against raiders. Governor Curtin of Pennsylvania called out 50,000 militia to defend the state. Boston cheered the Sixth Massachusetts as it went back to the front again. Baltimore fearfully prepared against the sack of its shops and warehouses.[17]

Lee's plan was to send his army under Longstreet north to Hagerstown by a route west of the Blue Ridge. Part of that range was South Mountain, twelve miles west of Frederick, and traversed by Crampton's Gap and Turner's Gap, six miles apart. McClellan's opportunity was to move his army through South Mountain, stand between Longstreet and Jackson, and dispatch his enemies piecemeal. At least thirty-eight hours elapsed between finding the lost order and the surrender of Harper's Ferry.

McClellan waited until the morning after he had received the lost order before he began moving his men.[18] If he had acted at once he could have won both passes by early morning of the fourteenth, for there were no Confederate forces to impede him (as he knew from the lost order). In possession of South Mountain, he could have dispatched relief to Harper's Ferry, assailed Longstreet and D. H. Hill, and interposed his troops between Jackson and Lee. (Before McClellan's march began, Lee had learned from a Southern sympathizer that the enemy knew his plan, but boldly he made no

[16] Palfrey, *Antietam and Fredericksburg*, p. 18.

[17] *OR*, Ser. I, Vol. XIX, part 2, 268, 279; Rhodes, *History*, IV, 143–144.

[18] Williams, *Lincoln Finds a General*, II, 375–376; Bruce Catton, "Crisis at the Antietam," *American Heritage*, IX (August, 1958), 54 ff.; James Longstreet, *From Manassas to Appomattox* (Philadelphia: Lippincott, 1896), p. 262.

change.) During the night's delay, the Confederates occupied the gaps, imposing on the Federals the work of clearing them out in the battle of South Mountain, September 14.

Two engagements were fought. At Crampton's Gap Brigadier General W. B. Franklin wielded a superior force that, after a three-hour action, permitted him to move into Pleasant Valley. At Turner's Gap—the larger of the two engagements—a Confederate force of fourteen brigades confronted a Federal force of eighteen. McClellan reported a loss of 1,568, in a struggle that continued until nine at night. When the actions at Crampton's Gap and Turner's Gap had ended, the Federals counted a tactical victory but a strategic loss. As General Hill observed: "We retreated that night to Sharpsburg, having accomplished all that was required, the delay of the Yankee army until Harper's Ferry could not be relieved." What Hill does not note, though, is that McClellan had wrested the initiative from Lee at South Mountain, and stood ready to attack.[19]

Lee took his stand at Sharpsburg, placing between himself and the Federal host Antietam Creek, not more than twenty yards wide. McClellan slowly brought up his forces, and allowed time to slip by. He lost an opportunity on the sixteenth to destroy half an army, for, after accepting the surrender of Harper's Ferry on September 15, Jackson had forthwith marched to join Lee. By the afternoon of the sixteenth, he was ready to meet McClellan's forces, portions of whom—under Hooker—had crossed Antietam Creek.[20]

The battle of Antietam, or Sharpsburg, fought September 17, was the bloodiest day of the Civil War. The Federals numbered 75,000, the Confederates 52,000. McClellan made his dispositions well, and then withdrew to watch the battle through a glass. Fighting opened in the morning, and early assaults on Lee's left were repulsed. In the afternoon, Burnside's corps crossed the Antietam over the bridge on Lee's right and drove the Confederates back; but A. P. Hill's

[19] Palfrey, *Antietam and Fredericksburg*, pp. 40–41; Hassler, *General George B. McClellan*, pp. 248–253.

[20] *OR*, Ser. I, Vol. XIX, part 2, 311. For criticism of McClellan's failure to attack on September 16, see G. F. R. Henderson, *Stonewall Jackson and the American Civil War* (2 Vols. in one; New York: Longmans, Green & Co., 1961), p. 518; and Nevins, *War for the Union*, II, 224.

division arrived from Harper's Ferry, having marched seventeen miles in seven hours, and repulsed the attack.

McClellan failed to use his full strength, and at the end of the day's fierce fighting Lee remained in possession of the field. Southern losses were 2,700 killed, 9,024 wounded, and 2,000 missing; Federal losses were 2,108 killed, 9,549 wounded, and 753 missing.[21] It is doubtful that Lee could have sustained a second day of battle, bruised as he was—and faced as he could have been by fresh troops. But we shall never know. The Virginian coolly held his ground through the next day, but McClellan did not attack. That night, undisturbed by the Federals, Lee recrossed the Potomac barrier and returned to the safety of Virginia.

McClellan had "missed the golden opportunity for a knockout punch to end the war," writes the historian Henry Commager.[22] But "Little Mac" saw it in another light. "Those in whose judgment I rely tell me that I fought the battle splendidly and that it was a masterpiece of art," he naively recorded in an intimate letter. And two days later he complacently wrote: "I feel that I have done all that can be done in twice saving the country."[23]

McClellan failed to pursue Lee, contending he lacked supplies.[24] The battle—the greatest battle to that time—had been a stalemate. Both men had failed: Lee to make good his thrust, McClellan to destroy Lee's army. Lincoln told a Washington official he had "great confidence" in McClellan, but went on to speak guardedly about the general.[25] While at first a sense of buoyancy coursed throughout the North, this feeling yielded to dissatisfaction with the realization that only the morsel of repulse had been nipped by the jaws of victory. McClellan suffered from outspoken criticism of his generalship and from a whispering campaign about his loyalty.

After Antietam, the portrait of General George B. McClellan was fairly drawn. He had again demonstrated his capacities of inspiring

[21] Livermore, *Numbers and Losses*, pp. 92–93.

[22] Morison and Commager, *Growth of the American Republic*, I, 734.

[23] McClellan, *Own Story*, pp. 612–613.

[24] *OR*, Ser. I, Vol. XIX, part 2, 342.

[25] Nevins, *War for the Union*, II, 230; Randall and Donald, *The Civil War and Reconstruction*, p. 224; Basler *et al.*, *Collected Works of Lincoln*, V, 442.

leadership, his organizing skill, his strategic excellence, and his thoroughness of preparation. But he had also disclosed his defects: his excessive caution, his habitual overestimation of enemy strength, his insatiable appetite for more troops and equipment, and (what seems fundamental) his lack of an overriding will to win. The month of September, 1862, was perhaps the most productive of his career. At Antietam he rendered his finest if not flawless service to the Union. What he had done was measurably great, but it may be observed he did not take the offensive and that battle was thrust upon him by Lee's invasion. Throughout the campaign he clung to a defensive psychology: to save the country—not to destroy the enemy.

He had assumed command of a beaten army at a moment when the Republic was imperiled by the first great Confederate invasion under Lee. He had frustrated the formidable aggression and had caused the aggressor to seek asylum on home soil. He had forced a reappraisal of British foreign policy, throwing Antietam into the delicate balance of diplomatic calculation. He had provided the occasion for the liberation of slaves in the Confederacy, unwittingly and indeed ironically, for, as he wrote his wife three days after the preliminary proclamation, "I cannot make up my mind to fight for such a cursed doctrine as that of servile insurrection—it is too infamous."[26] Lastly, he had stayed the hand of Northern peace advocates, who might well have swept into control of the House of Representatives as an aftermath of defeat at Antietam.

For these considerable results the North owed him much. Lincoln's use of Antietam to proclaim freedom for the slaves was an indirect tribute to McClellan's achievement, but the North thought it had the right to expect more in military results than an indecisive parrying of Lee's northern lunge. Lincoln went to visit McClellan in his camp, and soon issued an order "that you cross the Potomac and give battle to the enemy or drive him south." McClellan delayed, and at length—on November 5—he was relieved of his command.

His protracted inaction, an audacious Confederate raid all around his forces by Jeb Stuart, and a belief that he would never grasp his opportunities all told against him. He took leave of his troops—120,000 strong—in an affecting review and with the loyal

[26] Quoted in Myers, *McClellan*, p. 364.

pronouncement: "We shall ever be comrades in supporting the Constitution of our country and the nationality of its people."[27] His military career lay behind him; his political career lay ahead.

In the West, the Confederates (simultaneously with Antietam) were trying to redeem Kentucky. The principal Confederate commander was General Braxton Bragg, a dyspeptic martinet, esteemed by President Davis, and skilled in organizing and training soldiers, but never before the holder of high command. In rather loose association with General Kirby Smith, he hoped to inspire a rising in Kentucky, install the Confederate governor Richard Hawes, and place the Bluegrass State squarely in the Confederate camp.

Kirby Smith led the way, administering a defeat to Federal forces in late August and occupying Lexington on September 2. At the head of his liberating army of nearly 28,000, Bragg marched north from Chattanooga. On September 14 he issued a proclamation: "Kentuckians, I ... offer you an opportunity to free yourselves from the tyranny of a despotic ruler."[28] Federal forces—35,000 strong, under Don Carlos Buell—hastened from Nashville to counter the Confederate thrust. Both Bragg and Buell determined upon Louisville as their objective. That great commercial center on the Ohio River, the northern terminus of the Louisville and Nashville Railroad, was essential to Union logistics in the region.

Dwellers on the north bank of the Ohio had been alarmed earlier by General John Hunt Morgan's cavalry raid into Kentucky. Now scenes of consternation and fear were common. Governor Robinson of Kentucky, John J. Crittenden, and Senator Garrett Davis together telegraphed Washington: "The fate of Kentucky is hanging in the balance and the army of Buell is in imminent peril."[29] In a minor action at Munfordville, September 16, Bragg captured the small Union garrison. But Bragg delayed, and, to his discredit, allowed Buell to reach Louisville without a battle.

On the day the blueclad Army of the Ohio attained Louisville, Bragg reported in discouragement: "I regret to say we are sadly

[27] *Ibid.*, pp. 628–653; quotations on pp. 628, 653.
[28] *OR*, Ser. I, Vol. XVI, part 2, 822.
[29] *Ibid.*, 529.

disappointed at the want of action by our friends in Kentucky. We have so far received no accession to this army.... Unless a change occurs soon we must abandon the garden spot of Kentucky to its cupidity. The love of ease and fear of pecuniary loss are the fruitful sources of this evil."[30]

In a move often described as unwise, Bragg took possession of Frankfort instead of engaging the enemy. His purpose was to attend the inauguration of the Confederate governor, to talk with Kirby Smith, and to learn about conditions in central Kentucky. "The closing sentences of Gov. Hawes's inaugural address had not died upon the ear, when the roar of the guns of the Federal army, advancing under Gen. Buell, were heard, and his cavalry charged up to the bridge over the Kentucky river."[31]

Battle was given October 8, 1862, at Perryville—the "Western Antietam." Neither side used its full strength, but, handicapped by a divided command in the West for which President Davis was responsible, Bragg pulled back. Perryville was inconclusive in terms of victory or defeat, yet it was followed by Bragg's retreat into Tennessee, after he had found few supplies in the Bryantsville depot.[32] The abandonment of Kentucky threw the advantage to the Union. The Confederacy had lost its chance to redeem Kentucky and to establish its northern frontier on the Ohio River.

South of this action, the third salient of the Confederacy's multiple offensive was also parried. Victory for the Confederacy in the Lower South could lead to recovery of western Tennessee and juncture with the forces of Bragg. Victory for the Union could lead, with Bragg frustrated, to an advance from middle Tennessee to Chattanooga— gateway to Georgia—to occupation of the whole of Tennessee, and to an assault on Vicksburg, whose batteries blocked Union control of the Mississippi River.

Two days after Antietam, Confederate General Sterling Price was forced out of Iuka, Mississippi. He then joined forces with General Earl Van Dorn, and together the united Confederates struck at

[30] *Ibid.*, 876.

[31] Lewis Collins and Richard H. Collins, *History of Kentucky* (2 vols.; Covington, Ky.: Collins & Co., 1874), I, 345.

[32] McWhiney, "Controversy in Kentucky," p. 35.

Corinth, the heavily fortified rail and supply center defended by Rosecrans. The battle of Corinth lasted two days (October 3–4) and was marked by bitter, stand-up fighting. Rosecrans held firm, and the Confederates, with Van Dorn in command—their losses slightly heavier than the Union's—retreated.[33]

The grand design of the autumn of 1862 had been shattered. The Confederacy had failed in its ominous offensive, but in no theater had it suffered a decisive military defeat. The war would endure two and a half years more, but the hope of foreign help burned dimmer after Antietam and its western counterparts.

Palmerston's plan to mediate in the American war met favor with Gladstone, who in a letter of September 25 gave two special reasons for ending the struggle. He feared that if Maryland and Kentucky were to manifest powerful Southern feeling because of Confederate successes, the South would claim the Borderland as a condition of peace, erecting a new obstacle to settlement. Secondly, he believed the English government should act before a possible outbreak in Lancashire might make it appear that England was moved by self-interest.[34]

Friends of the Union were confounded when on October 7 Gladstone in a public speech asserted:

> There is no doubt that Jefferson Davis and other leaders of the South have made an army; they are making, it appears, a navy; and they have made, what is more than either—they have made a nation.... We may anticipate with certainty the success of the Southern States so far as their separation from the North is concerned.[35]

Three days before this speech by the chancellor of the exchequer, Lord John Russell had written Palmerston: "I think unless some miracle takes place this will be the very time for offering mediation, or as you suggest, proposing to the North and South to come to terms." October was the month (named in August) for a cabinet meeting, and the twenty-third was fixed as the date.

[33] Williams, *Lincoln Finds a General*, IV, 72–106.

[34] Philip Guedalla, *Gladstone and Palmerston* (New York: Harper & Brothers, 1928), pp. 233–236.

[35] Rhodes, *History*, IV, 339.

But the prospect of English mediation was not as probable as it had seemed in the first week in October. Actually by October 2 Palmerston had learned of a check to the Southern advance, and thought ten days or a fortnight might "throw a clearer light upon future prospects." Gladstone's speech expressed personal opinion, with which some members of the cabinet disagreed, and one of that number, Cornewall Lewis, replied in a speech that made it clear no cabinet decision had been reached. So far as the leader of the Tory opposition was concerned, Lord Derby on being approached declared he opposed mediation and recognition, though he was constantly urged to favor these policies. Derby believed the belligerents would reject mediation because "it was clear that the war had not yet marked out the stipulations of a treaty of peace."[36]

News of the Emancipation Proclamation arrived during the British government's deliberation upon a policy, but it wielded no immediate influence in making a decision. What was needed to precipitate England to act was a decisive Southern victory; only this could have cut through the uncertainty, the misgivings, and the opposition to mediation. But the unfolding of the news from America made it plain to Palmerston, as he was to declare, that "to talk to the belligerents about peace at present would be as useless as asking the winds during the last week to let the waters remain calm."

The day before the cabinet was to meet on the American question, Russell postponed the meeting, and Palmerston remarked: "We must continue merely to be lookers-on till the war shall have taken a more decided turn."[37] When, shortly after, France suggested that Britain and France join in proposing a six month's armistice, Britain declined to change her policy of neutrality.

The American question would raise its head again, but for the moment a crisis had been reached and passed. Echoes of gunfire at Antietam had been heard in Downing Street. And repercussions of the Emancipation Proclamation would soon be felt in Exeter Street, Manchester, and elsewhere as religious nonconformists and working classes swung to the support of a war to end slavery.

[36] Adams, *Great Britain and the American Civil War*, II, 51–52.
[37] *Ibid.*, 55–56.

The Emancipation Proclamation

The policy of emancipation, and of employing
black soldiers, gave to the future a new
aspect, about which hope, and fear, and
doubt contended in uncertain conflict.

Abraham Lincoln, December 8, 1863

"I have no purpose, directly or indirectly, to interfere with the institution of slavery in the states where it exists. I believe I have no lawful right to do so, and I have no inclination to do so." This plain statement, first spoken by Abraham Lincoln in a campaign speech, was repeated in his first inaugural address. At this same time, the future author of the Emancipation Proclamation publicly disavowed anti-slavery purposes by announcing his support of a proposed thirteenth amendment that would irrevocably prohibit the Federal government from interfering with slavery in the states. The contradiction between Lincoln's forbearance of 1861 and his fiat of 1862, and the ironic contrast between the proposed thirteenth amendment and the actual one prohibiting slavery in the states, could not be sharper.

Before 1861, abolitionism had been an abominable political failure in national politics. Americans dreaded radical surgery on the body politic. No major party had ever espoused freeing the slaves; no minor party holding this aim had ever been able to endure. The Republican party that had elected Lincoln had met the widest favor of all anti-slavery parties with a moderate stand that upheld the right of a state to control slavery within its limits and the right of the Federal government to eliminate slavery in the territories. This severely limited conception of emancipatory power had borne its protagonist to the presidency, but without the electoral vote of any slaveholding state.

Seven slave states had cut loose from the Union before Lincoln assumed office. It was to reassure his dissatisfied fellow-countrymen that the new President reaffirmed in his inaugural his party's and his own position on slavery in the states. With regard to the territories, he conceded that the Constitution does not expressly say whether Congress may prohibit slavery in them, and he made a plea for majority rule in place of secession when there were controversies over Constitutional interpretation. With regard to the return of fugitive slaves, which the Constitution provided for, Lincoln said he favored enforcement, provided there would be safeguards for the liberty of free Negroes.

If Lincoln's acceptance of Constitutional security for slavery suggests a certain rigor, his outlook on the Negro himself exhibits a greater humanity, though well this side of the image of the legendary Great Emancipator. He stood between the anti-Negro prejudice one might expect of the bias of his slave-state birth and the altruism of the abolitionists. He affirmed as a first premise that the Negro was a man, not property like a dog or horse, as the Supreme Court had ruled in the case of Dred Scott. To deny the humanity of the Negro was a retrograde step, he maintained. The existence of free Negroes, the law that made the foreign slave trade piracy, and the Southern contempt for slave dealers proved, he argued, that the Negro was a man.

Lincoln insisted, secondly—in contrast to Stephen A. Douglas— that the Declaration of Independence originally applied to the Negro as well as to the white. It was a statement for all men and for all time, not just the Revolutionary era. Though his rights were to be unfolded slowly, the Negro was created equal in certain inalienable rights, including the right to be free, to eat the bread he earns, and to be protected by law. Lincoln believed, furthermore, in the education of Negroes; as a congressman he had introduced a bill for Negro education in the District of Columbia; as President he suggested Negro education as a part of the process of reconstructing the seceded states.

"I am naturally anti-slavery," he once affirmed; but to be anti-slavery was not the same as to be in favor of racial equality. Lincoln opposed full equality, flatly declaring:

> I will say, then, that I am not, nor ever have been in favor of bringing about in any way the social and political equality of the white and black races: that I am not, nor ever have been, in favor of making voters or jurors of negroes, nor of qualifying them to hold office, nor to intermarry with white people.

The best solution for race problems was, he felt, separation through colonization; but this does not make him "a flawed hero," as one critic has asserted, for he also believed that the two races could live together peacefully. He did not consider it true that whites were made insecure by freeing blacks or that freedom caused race amalgamation. It was slavery that had bred mulattoes, he observed. Taking up a contention that survives to this day, he argued it was not true that favoring Negro emancipation meant favoring interracial marriages. Historians have criticized Lincoln for failing to live up to the legend, but what may truly be discerned is the mixture of legalism, idealism, and pragmatism with which he regarded the Negro.[1]

The Congress of the United States during the first half or more of the year 1861 held a tempered view toward slavery. The outgoing Thirty-sixth Congress had approved the proposed thirteenth amendment to which the incoming President referred. The Thirty-seventh Congress approved, following Bull Run, the Crittenden resolution, which, "banishing all feeling of mere passion or resentment," declared the war's objects were restricted to maintaining the supremacy of the Constitution and to preserving the Union with the rights of the states unimpaired.

The tribulations of war soon sparked emancipatory measures. As we have related earlier, Senator Lyman Trumbull, on learning of Confederate use of slaves at Bull Run, had successfully amended the First Confiscation Act to embrace slaves used for insurrectionary purposes. General John C. Frémont, confronted by guerrilla war in Missouri, had declared the slaves of all persons resisting the United States free. Lincoln overruled Frémont, as he later overruled General David Hunter in May, 1862, when that commander ordered freedom for all slaves in Georgia, Florida, and South Carolina.

In overruling Frémont, Lincoln acted on grounds both of principle and policy: the principle that the general's proclamation was a political measure not in conformity with the First Confiscation Act, and the policy that Kentucky and the border states should not be alienated. In overruling Hunter, he issued a proclamation announcing he reserved to himself questions concerning military emancipation, and he asked for consideration of the emancipatory policy he had by then presented to Congress.

[1] I have drawn Lincoln's ideas about slavery and Negroes from Basler *et al.* (eds.), *Collected Works of Lincoln, passim*. For the criticism as "a flawed hero," see the *Times Literary Supplement*, July 19, 1963, p. 522.

The anti-slavery impulse quickened with remarkable rapidity during the months spanning the first regular session of the Thirty-seventh Congress. The war was serving as an express train of history. In his message on the state of the Union, Lincoln declared he did not want to see the conflict "degenerate into a violent and remorseless revolutionary struggle." The integrity of the Union was the primary object of the war; and to secure this object he urged Congress to provide compensation for freeing slaves in the border states and to take steps for colonizing Negroes in a climate congenial to them. Apprehensions held earlier in the war of strong support of insurgency north of Mason and Dixon's line had now been allayed, he said, in reviewing events in the states extending from Delaware to Missouri. Congressional approval of his proposal he placed on the pragmatic ground that "the expediency amount[s] to absolute necessity."[2]

Lincoln's proposal seemed lost in a lengthy message that treated many topics. The President, however, continued to meditate upon the subject within the context of his purpose to perpetuate the Republic. Early in March he sent Congress a special message recommending adoption of a joint resolution to implement his program. His message incorporated a draft of the resolution, which read:

> *Resolved*, That the United States ought to co-operate with any state which may adopt gradual abolishment of slavery, giving to such state pecuniary aid, to be used by such state in its discretion, to compensate for the inconveniences public and private, produced by such change of system.

The measure would be "one of the most efficient means of self-preservation," he argued, because it would force the leaders of the insurrection to abandon hope of winning the border slave states. "To deprive them of this hope substantially ends the rebellion."[3]

With this message the lineaments of Lincoln's plan of emancipation were fully rounded out. The President made it pointedly clear his program did not trespass upon state rights, for the decision to

[2] Basler, *Collected Works*, V, 35–53, especially 49.
[3] *Idem*, 144–146.

emancipate was left to the states. Secondly, he favored compensation of slaveowners and not an expropriation of property. A third feature of his plan was gradualism; the decision to emancipate should be taken now, but "in my judgment," he told the Congress, "gradual, and not sudden emancipation, is better for all." Voluntary colonization of free colored persons as the best answer to race relations formed a fourth element of his program. Lastly, he would have the Federal government participate in compensating slaveowners and colonizing Negroes.

This five-point program is strikingly different from the future Emancipation Proclamation. Yet the program, and not the more famous proclamation, best represents Lincoln's thinking about emancipation and race relations. The proclamation differed from the President's program in every point: it excluded the loyal slave states; it emancipated by Federal not by State action; it made no provision for compensation; it declared freedom suddenly and not gradually; it made no provision for colonization; and it did not make the Federal government a partner to the states in aiding them by compensation or colonization. Lincoln embraced emancipation by proclamation with reluctance, and with only one arm.

Believing the border-state congressmen thought his program inimical to their states, Lincoln invited the delegations of the five loyal slave states, including (West) Virginia, to the White House on the morning of March 10. He opened the conference by assuring the congressmen he meant no injury to the loyal slave states.

In response to a question of John W. Menzies of Kentucky, he said only the states had the power to carry out his scheme of emancipation; in response to one raised by Charles A. Wickliffe of the same state, he answered his scheme did not encounter any Constitutional difficulty. He pointed out that the advance of Union armies inevitably attracted slaves to the camps, posing problems to the owners and to the Federal government, and strengthening the hopes of Confederates. Acceptance of his resolution would do more toward shortening the war than the greatest victory on the battlefield.

Later, to a California senator who opposed his scheme, Lincoln argued (March 14, 1862) that "less than eighty-seven days' cost of this war ... would pay for all [slaves] in Delaware, Maryland, District of Columbia, Kentucky, and Missouri." Dividing largely on party lines, with strong opposition from Kentucky, Congress approved the resolution—providing for "the deportation of the institution over a bridge of gold."[4]

Months passed without action by the loyal slave states when Lincoln again invited their representatives to the White House. Appealing to them to accept his plan, he warned that slavery might be extinguished without compensation by mere incidents of the war. Union dissension over emancipation threatened to divide the North, and pressures upon him—such as General Hunter's proclamation, which he had repudiated—were increasing, he said. An immediate decision to emancipate gradually, with Federal assistance in founding a colony in South America, would achieve the two grand results of shortening the war and saving the American form of government.[5]

The border slave states could not bring themselves to accept the Federal government's proposal. One difficulty was its indefiniteness, because the resolution had not been accompanied by an appropriation of funds, and another was the immense cost. Overshadowing all considerations, however, was the dark prospect of reconstructing society in states that might essay emancipation. A majority of the border-state representatives gave first place to the "radical change in our social system" in reciting reasons for opposing the plan.

In Kentucky, a legislative committee recommended the offer be declined; it rejected Lincoln's contention that gradual emancipation in the border states would bring speedy termination of the war, and it charged that the dominant party in Congress was bent on destruction of the Constitution. In Delaware, the legislature turned down—by only one vote—a bill drafted by Lincoln himself that would have freed the slaves (enumerated at 1,798 in 1860, three-fourths of whom were in Sussex County) and would have paid the owners at the rate of $400 per slave. The two houses of Congress failed to agree on terms of a bill that offered compensation to Missouri, and the

[4] Nicolay and Hay, *Abraham Lincoln*, V, 211–214; *Annual Cyclopedia . . . 1862*, p. 788; Basler, *Collected Works*, V, 160–161.

[5] Nicolay and Hay, *Abraham Lincoln*, VI, 108–112.

opportunity passed. Maryland gave the offer no heed. To Lincoln's bitter disappointment not one border state emancipated its slaves under the combined plan of compensation and colonization—his *vade mecum* for winning the war, maintaining state rights, and assuring the future of American democracy.[6]

The executive arm of the government had all the while been lifted against the African slave trade—a nefarious traffic, largely flying the America flag. Although branded as pirates by a law of 1820, slavers had enjoyed relative immunity thanks to the South's sensitivity on the subject of slavery and the nation's sensitivity about Britain's zealous wish to search American vessels. The British fleet was almost indispensable for halting the traffic, but Americans—mindful of a past war with Britain involving the right of search—resisted allowing their ships to be searched.

A startling act by the administration in suppressing the trade was to mete out the death sentence to an American captain, Nathaniel P. Gordon, "taken with a cargo of Africans on board his ship." Lincoln withstood efforts to secure mitigation of the severe sentence, and on February 21, 1862, in the Tombs prison in New York City, the government for the first time in its history hanged an American citizen as a pirate.[7]

This dramatic crackdown on the slave trade was followed by negotiations with Britain for a treaty that accorded British vessels the privilege of searching and arresting ships flying the American flag off West Africa and Cuba. Civil war made an Anglo-American agreement feasible. The United States had been compelled to withdraw its squadron from West African waters; the South had withdrawn from Congress; and the North was ready to end an admitted evil if in the process she might enlist English sympathy. The treaty, accepted by the Senate on April 25, 1862, was a turning point in the history of the Atlantic slave trade. The Cuban traffic during the war years fell off: from 30,473 in the year ending September 30, 1861, to 143 five years later—and all 143 were rescued. Spain joined in

[6] *Annual Cyclopaedia . . . 1862*, pp. 541–542; Nevins, *War for the Union*, II, 115; Blaine, *Twenty Years*, II, 447.

[7] Basler, *Collected Works*, V, 46–47, and n. 22; 128–129, and n. 1.

suppressing the traffic, and by 1870 the slave trade had virtually disappeared from the Atlantic world.[8]

The Republican party had not secured control of the Thirty-seventh Congress by the election of 1860, but it had managed a comfortable majority by expulsion and secession. Congress met in December, 1861, irritated by the misconduct of the war, eager to initiate an aggressive policy, and intent on asserting the authority of the legislative arm of the national government. Two actions of the opening days suggest a change in temper. By a vote of 71 to 65, the House declined to reaffirm the Crittenden Resolution on the objects of the war. With near-unanimity, the two houses created a joint Committee on the Conduct of the War—as an outgrowth of dis-satisfaction with the military reverses at Bull Run and Ball's Bluff, and with McClellan's deliberation, and in the belief that in a democratic government the public ought to keep an eye on the military.

Conceived as an agency to investigate and to advise the President, the committee became the vehicle of that spirit called Radicalism. The Radicals' aims were succinctly defined by Edward Channing:

> They wished to have all the slaves freed at once, to hang Jeff. Davis and as many other rebels as could be caught, to seize all the property of traitors and keep it forever, and to bring the war to a short and successful conclusion.

The "Radical" senator from Ohio, Benjamin F. Wade, became the committee's first chairman, and though he and Senator Zachariah Chandler of Michigan felt an animus toward the President, most of its members at first sought to cooperate with Lincoln. In recent years historians have exaggerated the conflict between Lincoln and the radicals; members of his party, they cooperated with him and helped enact an impressive body of law.[9]

[8] A. Taylor Milne, "The Lyons-Seward Treaty of 1862," *American Historical Review*, XXXVIII (April, 1933), 511–525.

[9] William W. Pierson, Jr., "The Committee on the Conduct of the Civil War," *American Historical Review*, XXIII (April, 1918), 550–576; Channing, *History*, VI, 587; T. Harry Williams, *Lincoln and the Radicals* (Madison: University of Wisconsin Press, 1960).

The Congress, with a substantial Republican majority, and with radicalism in embryo, enacted a series of anti-slavery measures so comprehensive (on their face) as to make the Emancipation Proclamation seem anticlimactic. This legislative attack went on throughout the war; when the Thirty-eighth Congress had ended, Senator Henry Wilson of Massachusetts could list twenty-six legislative enactments against slavery.[10]

Congress cooperated with Lincoln, as we have seen, in approving aid to the states to emancipate their slaves and in ratifying the Lyons-Seward Treaty to suppress the African slave trade. Congress then took up a third measure, diplomatic recognition of the Negro nations of Haiti and Liberia, which the President had recommended in his first annual message. It encountered stout resistance in the House, where John J. Crittenden flaunted his pride in white superiority and shuddered at the thought of black diplomats in Washington. But the bill to open diplomatic relations with the black republics became law June 5, 1863. This victory over prejudice in international affairs had long been frustrated by sectional deadlock. Sumner observed: "A full generation has passed since the acknowledgment of Haiti was urged upon Congress."[11]

Early in the war, fugitive slaves had begun to find their way into army lines in the hope of protection and freedom, and their masters often followed them to demand their rendition. Army officers dealt with the problem of fugitives in various ways. General B. F. Butler, while commanding at Fort Monroe in May, 1861, had refused to release fugitive slaves on the ground they were "contraband." Other officers refused to permit owners to search their camps, while still others allowed masters or their agents to carry Negroes back to servitude.

Lincoln himself had ordered General McClellan to enforce the fugitive slave law in Maryland. Military advantage and moral indignation later combined to make rendition of fugitives by the army impolitic. On the initiative of Senator Henry Wilson, Congress—

[10] Henry Wilson, *History of the Antislavery Measures of the Thirty-seventh and Thirty-eighth United States Congresses, 1861–65* (Boston: Walker, Fuller & Co., 1865).

[11] *Idem*, p. 176.

bypassing objections based on the Fugitive Slave Act—solved the vexatious question by adding an article of war to army regulations to prohibit military personnel from returning fugitive slaves. The President signed it into law March 13.

For a generation or more, slavery in the District of Columbia had offended many Northerners. Opponents of slavery had succeeded in abolishing the slave trade in the district (as part of the Compromise of 1850), but slavery itself endured—bolstered by doubts about the Constitutional authority of Congress to end it and by the argument that consent of Maryland and Virginia, which had made the Federal district a national domain, was needed.

With Senator Wilson again taking the lead, and with the border states standing athwart the proposal, Congress decreed the abolition of slavery in the District of Columbia, with up to $300 compensation to the owners for each slave. The lawmakers appropriated $1 million for compensation, and $100,000 to assist in colonization (in accordance with Lincoln's policy), but this is the single instance of compensated emancipation during the four years of war. The Senate divided 29 to 14 in approving the bill, the House 92 to 39, and the President gave it his approval April 16.

The question of prohibiting slavery in the territories had been the most profoundly divisive issue in the history of the American republic. The power to bar slavery from territorial possessions had been asserted in the Northwest Ordinance of 1787. Thereafter, two developments caused Southerners to reconsider congressional restriction of slavery in the territories. One of these was the further spreading of slavery because of the invention of the cotton gin; and the second was the spreading of the nation across the continent. Step by step—in the Louisiana Territory, in Oregon, in the Mexican Cession—the South had resisted exclusion, and had achieved compromises in two of the three contests. The repeal of the Missouri Compromise in 1854, in connection with the organization of Nebraska and Kansas territories, outraged Northerners, gave birth to the Republican party, disrupted the Democratic party, and presented the nation with the issue that rent it asunder in 1861.

When in early May of 1862 the House began debate on a bill that would prohibit slavery in the territories, with no provision for compensation, Representative John W. Crisfield of Maryland sought the floor to cry: "I denounce this bill as a palpable violation of the rights of States, and an unwarrantable interference with the rights of private property." Thaddeus Stevens, a Pennsylvania radical, pointed out the Northern states had abolished slavery without compensation, and he claimed that both John Quincy Adams and Henry Clay had declared "within my hearing, the entire competency of Congress to abolish slavery, without compensation." The House approved the bill 85 to 50, the Senate readily ratified it 28 to 10, and the President made it law on June 19—"thus closing forever," Henry Wilson wrote, "the long contest between freedom and slavery for the vast Territories ... of the United States."[12] The Republican party had realized the purpose of its founding fathers.

On December 5, 1861, Senator Lyman Trumbull of Illinois, by whose amendment the First Confiscation Act had been extended to slaves used for military purposes, introduced a bill that took the high ground of freeing the slaves of all persons taking up arms against the United States or in any manner aiding or abetting the rebellion. Repeatedly amended by radicals, staunchly resisted by moderates, and worked over by special committees, a sweeping measure— known as the Second Confiscation Act—became "one of the most drastic laws ever enacted by the American Congress."[13]

Senator Garret Davis of Kentucky arraigned the bill in a long, exhaustive speech. He declared that "neither the Declaration of Independence nor the Constitution was ever intended to embrace slaves, nor any of the negro race.... The only partners to our political partnership were the white men. The negro was no party, and he cannot now constitutionally be any party, to it."[14] Senator Orville H. Browning of Illinois objected on grounds both of expediency and Constitutionality, arguing the bill would make peace and reunion impossible, and that it violated the attainder clause of the Constitution.[15]

[12] *Idem, passim,* and especially pp. 98, 103, 109.
[13] Randall and Donald, *Civil War,* p. 284.
[14] Wilson, *Antislavery Measures,* p. 122.
[15] J. G. Randall, *Constitutional Problems under Lincoln* (New York: D. Appleton & Co., 1926), pp. 277–278.

Extreme and punitive, the Second Confiscation Act covered three subjects: treason, confiscation, and emancipation. The emancipatory provisions, which are our concern, were several. The slaves of persons found guilty of treason were declared and made free. Freedom was accorded slaves of persons convicted of setting on foot, assisting, or engaging in rebellion, or giving aid and comfort thereto. Escaped and captured slaves, including those in places occupied by Union armies, were declared free; and the military was prohibited from judging the claims of alleged owners, as well as from surrendering slaves. Lastly, the bill authorized the President "to employ as many persons of African descent as he may deem necessary and proper for the suppression of this rebellion," and to provide for colonization of freed slaves willing to emigrate. Under the bill's terms, the President was directed to bring about the seizure of estates and property.

Here was a formidable legislative assault against property and slavery—nothing less than congressional conduct of war by confiscation. The House approved 82 to 42, and the Senate 28 to 13. After certain Presidential scruples about the bill's Constitutionality had been partially met by an explanatory joint resolution of Congress, Lincoln on July 17 signed the measure and the resolution "as ... substantially one." That his scruples persisted is suggested by his extraordinary procedure of attaching his *proposed* veto message to his message that notified Congress he had signed the act.[16]

On the same day, July 17, Lincoln signed the Militia Act, which, though essentially concerned with white soldiers, authorized the President to employ colored soldiers at his discretion; it also provided freedom for colored soldiers—and their mothers, wives, and children—unless they belonged to loyal owners. The emancipatory amendment had been added at a late hour by Senator Henry Wilson. There had been bitter protests—such as Senator Willard Saulsbury of Delaware uttered when he denounced the attempt "made on every occasion to change the character of the war, and to elevate the miserable nigger, not only to political rights, but to put him in your army." The amendment was accepted by a narrow margin in the Senate, and agreed to by the House.[17]

[16] Basler, *Collected Works*, V, 328–331.
[17] Wilson, *Antislavery Measures*, p. 204.

The Thirty-seventh Congress made its second session one of the most fruitful in our history. It granted homesteads to settlers; it subsidized the building of the first transcontinental railroads; it endowed agricultural and mechanical colleges—while it was providing for an army, a navy, and a financial program to wage a vast war. Its emancipatory achievements were substantial, "and amounted to a complete reversal of the policy of the General Government."[18] In the international field, Congress had ratified the treaty for the suppression of the African slave trade, and had extended diplomatic recognition to Haiti and Liberia, both Negro republics. In the field of national authority, it had freed the slaves in the District of Columbia (with compensation) and in the Federal territories (without compensation), had forbidden return of fugitive slaves by military personnel, and had offered to help state emancipation. Moving beyond these areas, Congress had entered the state field, and had freed slaves coming within Union lines and slaves of rebel ownership, together with their families.

So very much had been done, indeed, that it is sometimes said that emancipation was accomplished by acts of Congress instead of by Presidential proclamation; and all this had been done by July 17. The Emancipation Proclamation was issued September 22—two months after Congress had completed laying its hands on the peculiar institution.

Why should Lincoln issue an emancipation proclamation when Congress had seemed to do all? Close study shows Congress had in actuality attacked slavery piecemeal and indirectly. Its exemption of the military from enforcement of the fugitive slave laws left the laws on the statute books until they were repealed on June 28, 1864. Emancipation in the District of Columbia and in the territories freed only a fraction of those in bondage. In 1860, census-takers counted 3,185 slaves in the district, 29 in Utah, 15 in Nebraska, 2 in "bleeding Kansas," and none in the other territories: 46 slaves in the territories in all.[19] Liberation under the confiscation acts rested upon a cumbersome judicial process and slow military progress. Trumbull said in 1864 of the First Confiscation Act: "So far as I am advised not a

[18] Nicolay and Hay, *Abraham Lincoln*, VI, 97.
[19] *Annual Cyclopaedia . . . 1862*, pp. 777–778.

single slave has been set at liberty under it"; and Lincoln said on September 13, 1862, of the Second Confiscation Act: "I cannot learn that that law has caused a single slave to come over to us."[20]

Congress had not, in point of fact, fundamentally touched slavery. Its most drastic emancipatory measures had been confiscation laws—primarily to take property of rebels and punish treason, and only secondarily to give freedom. Probably a general law of emancipation, even if it made exception of the border states, could not have been passed by a Congress numbering many members who believed the states kept jurisdiction over this subject.

Sumner's resolutions of February, declaring state slavery abolished because state authority under which it existed had been extinguished by secession, failed of passage. What was needed, in the abolitionist view, was a clean sweep at slavery. Executive action could meet this demand, but the executive was not disposed to act. How was his reluctance overcome? How did "the slavehound of Illinois," as Wendell Phillips once termed Lincoln, become "the Great Emancipator"?

If we glance back at what we already know about Lincoln, we can understand why he was averse to proclaiming freedom for the slaves. He was not a revolutionary or even a radical reformer. His essential aim was to perpetuate the nation and the principles it lived by. He had long believed that slavery, which he hated, could not be abolished without a series of extended preliminary preparations. Recognizing the complexities of emancipation, he had observed in 1854: "If all earthly power were given me, I should not know what to do, as to the existing institution."[21] So far as political and social equality were concerned, he knew that the great mass of white people would not consent. Race prejudice and a conservative sentiment to keep "the Union as it was" blew briskly in the winds of Northern opinion.

The chronicler of the life of the Union soldier, Bell Wiley, was struck by the "enormous amount of antipathy toward Negroes"

[20] Randall, *Constitutional Problems*, p. 357, n. 35; p. 363, n. 44.
[21] Basler, *Collected Works*, II, 255.

he found in letters and diaries.[22] When Lincoln visited McClellan at Harrison's Landing on the Peninsula in early July, he was handed a letter, addressed to Lincoln by the general, which later was made public; it stated, in part: "A declaration of radical views, especially upon slavery, will rapidly disintegrate our present armies."[23]

If aversion to allowing the war to turn into a social revolution deterred the President from freeing the slaves, a second consideration was the border states. From early on, he had reckoned their loyalty indispensable to winning the war. To drive the border states out of the Union now, by a precipitate proclamation, was a risk not lightly to be assumed. So long as he cherished a chance they would accept his plan of emancipation, he would refrain from more radical action. Crucial Kentucky, in particular, evinced hostility to seeing the mold of its society broken.

The preferability of voluntary state emancipation—combined with gradualism, compensation, and colonization—was a third reason why the President should not act. Such a program would erase most persons' Constitutional scruples and would ease the social, economic, and racial stresses inherent in an immense unsettling of society.

Yet each of these reasons not to act had its counterweight—with something thrown into the balance—of reasons to act. Whether or not he wished it, a revolutionary movement was occurring. "You cannot, if you would, be blind to the signs of the times,"[24] he exhorted the people of the border states, when in countermanding General Hunter's decree he asked them to act. The anti-slavery measures of Congress were evidence of these signs; and the moderating influence of men like Crittenden had waned during the second session.

Borderland leaders appeared defensive and despondent. The border states, which had essayed the delicate tasks of compromise and adjustment in the years before Sumter, now in the midst of carnage evaded the bold course by which the war might be shortened and the Union saved. The scepter of power was passing to men like

[22] Bell Wiley, *The Life of Billy Yank* (Indianapolis: Bobbs-Merill, 1951), p. 109.
[23] McPherson, *Political History . . . during the Rebellion*, pp. 385–386.
[24] Basler, *Collected Works*, V, 223.

Sumner and Wilson in the Senate and Stevens and Lovejoy in the House. Outside Washington, radicalism was vehemently voiced by a minister, Henry Ward Beecher, in a series of articles in *The Independent*, intended to spur the President to pronounced action. James Russell Lowell wrote in June, 1862:

> 'Hosee,' sez he, 'I think you're goin' to fail:
> The rettlesnake ain't dangerous in the tail;
> This 'ere rebellion's noth' but the rettle,—
> You'll stomp on thet an' think you've won the bettle:
> It's Slavery thet's the fangs an' thinkin' head,
> An' ef you want selvation, cresh it dead.'

The refusal of the border states to initiate emancipation under the joint resolution of Congress drove Lincoln to the alternative, as he later phrased it, "of laying strong hand upon the colored element." The border states, he anticipated, "would acquiesce, if not immediately, soon; for they must be satisfied that slavery had received its death-blow from slaveowners—it could not survive the rebellion."[25]

Neither the running of a revolutionary current nor the refusal of loyal slave states to emancipate exerted as much force upon the President as military necessity. The war effort was flagging, perhaps failing. The brilliant prospects of early 1862 had clouded over with Shiloh and with the Seven Days. On the Peninsula, General McClellan, after several months' prelude of massive preparations, at last launched what was meant to be the great offensive to end the war. But he had met his match in Lee, had failed to take Richmond, and now posed for Lincoln the problems of evacuating his forces and replacing him.

The President repaired to the Peninsula for a firsthand interrogation of McClellan and his generals; in particular, he inquired about the numerical strength of the Union armies and pondered upon the problems of command. He concluded that Richmond could be taken with additional Union troops, that McClellan must be replaced by General Pope, and that overall command ought to be entrusted to General Halleck in the restored post of General-in-chief.

During the Seven Days, Lincoln had anticipated the need for new troops, and had devised an astute plan to avoid the general panic an

[25] *Ibid.*, VII, 281–283; Nicolay and Hay, *Abraham Lincoln*, VI, 163.

administration appeal might start. At his bidding, Seward arranged a "voluntary" request of the Northern governors to the President to call for as many men as might be required. On July 2, Lincoln called upon the states for 300,000 volunteers, but the result was disappointing; fewer than 90,000 volunteered. When a call for 300,000 militia (the "Draft of 1862") a month later brought meager results, abolitionists blamed slow enlistment on the administration's timid policy of emancipation. They pointed out that slavery "was contributing nearly all the subsistence by which the enemy in arms was supported; it built the greater part of their fortifications; it dug the greater number of trenches; it alone enabled nearly all the able-bodied whites to join the Confederate army, &c."[26]

Lincoln himself was to justify his Emancipation Proclamation by the need for manpower. "Take from us, and give to the enemy, the hundred and thirty, forty, or fifty thousand colored persons now serving us as soldiers, seamen, and laborers," he told a Wisconsin War Democrat in August, 1864—who objected to abolition—"and we cannot longer maintain the contest."[27]

Lincoln could not have been unmindful, in deliberating upon a policy of liberation, of the attitude of Europe. Shortly after the *Trent* affair had underscored the peril of war with Europe, the American minister to Spain returned home and urged emancipation to prevent foreign intervention. "You may be right," Lincoln replied. "I cannot imagine that any European power would dare to recognize and aid the Southern Confederacy if it became clear that the Confederacy stands for slavery and the Union for freedom."[28]

For months the subject of emancipation was on Lincoln's mind, "by day and by night, more than any other," he acknowledged in mid-September. Of all the influences at work—military, political, diplomatic—it was probably the collapse of the Peninsula campaign that served as the catalytic agent. On Sunday, July 13, during a carriage ride to attend the funeral of an infant child of Secretary

[26] William B. Hesseltine, *Lincoln and the War Governors* (New York: Alfred A. Knopf, Inc., 1948), pp. 181 ff.; *Annual Cyclopaedia . . . 1862*, p. 792.

[27] Basler, *Collected Works*, VII, 500.

[28] E. D. Adams, *Great Britain and the American Civil War*, II, 91–92.

Stanton, Lincoln confided to two cabinet officers, Seward and Welles, his determination to proclaim freedom for the slaves should the war persist. He had given much thought to it, he said, "and had about come to the conclusion that it was a military necessity absolutely essential for the salvation of the Union."[29]

Two events of the preceding day may well have firmed his resolve. He had met with the border state congressmen to make a third appeal on behalf of voluntary state emancipation; and they were plainly disinclined to institute his plan. On the same day, Congress had completed approving the drastic Second Confiscation Act, imposing upon the executive certain responsibilities for liberating rebels' slaves. The failure of moderation and the progress of extremism mark the course of revolutions; and application of these attributes to the problems of slavery and race in America—problems intricated with national survival—narrowed the President's ground for choice. Though colonization was a chimera, the rest of Lincoln's scheme was sound, and the border states were behaving with the same blind stubbornness about slavery and the race question that had characterized the states of the Confederacy. Though sudden, uncompensated emancipation by Federal fiat was unwise as a means, the radical insistence on abolition of human bondage during a war originating over slavery was wise as an end.

The progress of emancipationist sentiment may be less accurately measured by the contrast between Lincoln's opposition to abolition in March, 1861, and his espousal of it in July, 1862, than by congressional approval of the Crittenden Resolution in July, 1861, and passage of the Second Confiscation Act in July, 1862.

Lincoln met with his cabinet on July 21 and 22. On the first day he announced an order to military commanders that authorized them to employ Negroes as laborers; and there was discussion of arming Negroes, to which Lincoln said he was averse. On the second day discussion was resumed, without reaching a final conclusion. Apparently to the surprise of most of the cabinet, Lincoln then read the draft of a policy of emancipation. All his advisers appeared struck by the sweep and magnitude of the step; only two, the secretary

[29] Basler, *Collected Works*, V, 425; Gideon Welles, *Diary of Gideon Welles* (3 vols.; Boston: Houghton Mifflin Co., 1911), I, pp. 70–71.

of war and the attorney general, gave unqualified endorsement.

Chase, the nearest to being an abolitionist, said the proposal went beyond anything he had recommended, and he would prefer to see emancipation accomplished by military commanders. Blair, the postmaster general, opposed the proclamation on the ground it would cost the administration the fall elections. Lincoln had already considered all these objections, and was struck by only one: Seward's sage advice that the proclamation be postponed until the Union enjoyed military success. "His idea," the President later said, "was that it would be considered our last shriek on the retreat.... The result was that I put the draft of the proclamation aside ... waiting for victory."[30]

Antietam, the battle on which the grand policy of emancipation would pivot, lay two months ahead; Second Bull Run—another Union defeat and retreat, entirely relieving Richmond from Union threat and leaving Washington endangered—intervened. The Confederacy readied its triple offensive. Europe wondered at the moral and intellectual obliquity of free men fighting to perpetuate a slave-keeping republic.

During the two months preceding Antietam, Lincoln labored to disarm his critics, conservative and radical, who complained and counseled plentifully. Conservatives, for example, complained that military operations and administration weakened the loyal element in Louisiana and injured the interests of slaveholders. In reply Lincoln pointed out that the necessity to send armies into Louisiana had been forced upon him. The people of Louisiana "very well know the way to avert all this is simply to take their place in the Union upon the old terms. If they will not do this, should they not receive harder blows rather than lighter ones?"[31]

The Radical editor of the *New York Tribune*, Horace Greeley, long a gadfly to the moderate Lincoln, published a two-column open letter to the President, entitled "The Prayer of Twenty Millions." Greeley charged Lincoln was unduly influenced by "certain fossil politicians" from the border states, was remiss in executing the

[30] F. B. Carpenter, *Six Months at the White House with Abraham Lincoln* (New York: Hurd & Houghton, 1866), pp. 2–22.

[31] Nicolay and Hay, *Abraham Lincoln*, VI, 149.

Confiscation Act, and was deferring to slavery. In a public statement
of policy, Lincoln gave a masterly answer, placing the issue of slavery
in the context of his nationalist purpose and distinguishing between
official duty and personal wishes.

> My paramount object [he wrote Greeley] *is* to save the Union,
> and is *not* either to save or destroy slavery. If I could save the
> Union without freeing any slave, I would do it; and if I could save
> it by freeing some and leaving others alone, I would also do that.
> What I do about slavery and the colored race, I do because I
> believe it helps to save the Union; and what I forebear, I forebear
> because I do not believe it would help save the Union.... I
> intend no modification of my oft-expressed personal wish that all
> men, everywhere, could be free.

Later, when Greeley renewed his urging on a visit to the White
House, Lincoln objected he could not antagonize Kentuckians and
drive them into rebellion.[32]

Would he issue a proclamation of freedom? A group of free
Negroes summoned to the White House in mid-August listened to
his opinion that freedom would not solve race problems. "You and
we are different races.... Even when you cease to be slaves, you are
yet far removed from being placed on an equality with the white
race." Colonization was the remedy. "It is better for us both to be
separated."[33] And when a deputation from the religious denomina-
tions of Chicago urged him to issue a proclamation, he asked the
delegates: "What good would a proclamation of emancipation from
me do.... I do not want to issue a document that the whole world
will see must necessarily be inoperative, like the Pope's bull against
the comet."[34]

Then the Antietam campaign began. Maryland was invaded.
Lincoln a few weeks later told a friend how Antietam was decisive in
announcing the great commitment.

> When Lee came over the river, I made a resolution that if McClellan
> drove him back I would send the proclamation after him. The battle

---

[32] Basler, *Collected Works*, V, 388–389, and n. 1; see also 357;
Richard N. Current, *The Lincoln Nobody Knows* (New York: Hill & Wang,
1958), p. 225.

[33] McPherson, *Political History ... during the Rebellion*, pp. 374–375.

[34] *Ibid.*, pp. 231–232.

of Antietam was fought Wednesday, and until Saturday I could not find out whether we had gained a victory or lost a battle. It was then too late to issue the proclamation that day; and the fact is I fixed it up a little Sunday, and Monday I let them have it.[35]

That Monday, September 22, a state department messenger had summoned the cabinet members to meet at twelve. The president opened the historic cabinet session not with a note of solemnity but with a chapter from a book by the dialect humorist, Artemus Ward. Then, turning solemn, he declared he had determined to issue the proclamation. On this decision, the main matter, he wished no advice, but he would read his draft and receive suggestions about any minor matters.

The cabinet discussed the draft long and earnestly. Seward spoke first, suggesting some changes of phrasing. Chase said that while the course was not what he would prefer, he would support it as the President's right and duty. Stanton made a very emphatic speech in support of the proclamation, remarking upon the vast consequences involved. Montgomery Blair, of the border state of Missouri, doubted the expediency of Presidential action at this time, raising the possibilities of sending the border states into secession and of handing party opponents a club that would be used against the administration. The President reminded Blair that he had labored to get the border states to move, and that his opponents would use as a club against any course he might take.[36] So it was that the cabinet concurred that the President of the United States would proclaim the emancipation of slaves.

What precisely did Lincoln decree? First of all, the proclamation was monitory, or preliminary to a formal one, which would be issued January 1, 1863. Second, it proclaimed freedom for the slaves only of persons in rebellion, thus exempting the border states and any state or portion of a state that abandoned rebellion before January 1. Next, it was not primarily an abolitionist or humanitarian document, for the President announced, in the opening

[35] Nicolay and Hay, *Abraham Lincoln*, VI, 164–165.

[36] *Ibid.*, VI, 158–164; David Donald (ed.), *Inside Lincoln's Cabinet: The Civil War Diaries of Salmon P. Chase* (New York: Longmans, Green & Co., 1954), pp. 149–152; Welles, *Diary*, I, 142–145.

paragraph, that the war would continue to be prosecuted for the object of preserving the Constitutional framework of the United States. The second paragraph announced that the Chief Executive would again recommend that Congress offer all slave states voluntary, compensated emancipation, combined with colonization. Lincoln also called attention to the new article of war and the Second Confiscation Act, and enjoined enforcement upon the military, promising he would recommend compensation for any slaves lost by loyal persons. The nub of it all, however, was that on January 1 he would recognize the slaves of all persons then in rebellion to be "forever free."

The prosaic, legalistic tone of the preliminary proclamation, without eloquence or apparent idealism, carried over to the definitive pronouncement one hundred days later. The formal proclamation withheld freedom from the slaves in the border states, Tennessee, and portions of Louisiana and Virginia. It emanated from the power vested in the Commander-in-chief of the army and navy, and was justified as "a fit and necessary war measure for suppressing the rebellion." It urged freedmen to abstain from violence and assured them that qualified Negroes would be received in the armed service. Only the final paragraph aspired to a lofty note. "And upon this act, sincerely believed to be an act of justice, warranted by the Constitution upon military necessity, I invoke the considerate judgment of mankind and the gracious favor of Almighty God."

The proclamation differed markedly from Lincoln's plan of emancipation, for it contained none of the five essential points: state action, compensation, Federal aid, gradualism, or voluntary colonization. The President, to be sure, declared in the September document that he would renew his recommendation of compensated emancipation, which he renewed in December, but after the definitive proclamation, which omitted mention of colonization, he appears to have abandoned all but a wistful hope of removing Negroes from the United States.

Myth-makers have often construed Lincoln's act as a virtual Promethean liberation of the black bondsman, as a striking of shackles from millions of slaves, as a "deliverance from Egypt." The legend of the Great Emancipator has been erected on the shaky foundation of misconception, which the foregoing analysis of the proclamation destroys. Cynics, on the other hand, have asserted the proclamation freed no slaves, was callously indifferent to slavery in loyal portions of the Union, and spoke no high principle. It has been interpreted as an incitement to a slave uprising, as a surrender to the Radicals, as a bid for foreign sympathy, as a strategem to delay freeing the slaves, as political warfare. Censorious persons have condemned Lincoln for violating his inaugural promise, the platform pledge of the Republican party, and the Constitution as well.

A truer judgment lies somewhere between the sweet and the sour. To be sure, the proclamation had many shortcomings, and there was a wide chasm yet to be bridged by victory and by Constitutional amendment between a mere executive statement and a binding, lawful guarantee of freedom. Even Lincoln's own support of the course suggested by his proclamation lay open to doubt, especially since, as his friend David Davis put it: "Lincoln's whole soul is absorbed in his plan of remunerative emancipation."[37]

Within his own party the new policy of the President stirred opposition. Thurlow Weed, veteran political boss of New York, judged "it has strengthened the South and weakened the North"; and Frank Blair, Sr., thought Lincoln "had ruined himself by his proclamation." In the President's own state of Illinois, a Democratic legislature resolved that the proclamation was "a gigantic usurpation" that invited "servile insurrection" and that would be "an uneffaceable disgrace to the American people." In Kentucky, Governor Robinson expressed certainty emancipation was an act of usurpation that would fire the South with "inextinguishable hatred."[38]

General McClellan was still commanding the Army of the Potomac when the preliminary proclamation was promulgated to the army

[37] Current, *Lincoln Nobody Knows*, ch. 9; *New York Times*, September 28, 1862; Nicolay and Hay, *Abraham Lincoln*, VI, 167, 171; Welles, *Diary*, I, 142–145; Nevins, *War for the Union*, II, 235.

[38] Randall and Donald, *Civil War*, p. 389; John Hope Franklin, *The Emancipation Proclamation* (New York: Alfred A. Knopf, Inc., 1963), p. 66.

in general orders. In his Harrison's Landing letter he had warned the President against a declaration of radical views. Now he impulsively wrote out a defiant protest against the proclamation, which on the advice of friends he withheld. Next, he considered resigning his commission; and finally, after a fortnight, he issued an extraordinary order to his army, deprecating intemperate discussion of "public measures determined upon and declared by the Government.... The remedy for political errors, if any are committed, is to be found only in the action of the people at the polls."[39]

In England, the preliminary proclamation failed to win immediate favor. Lord Palmerston called it a "singular manifesto that could scarcely be treated seriously. It is not easy to estimate how utterly powerless and contemptible a government must have become which could sanction with its approval such...trash."[40] The London *Spectator* scornfully remarked: "The government liberates the enemy's slaves as it would the enemy's cattle, simply to weaken them in the ... conflict ... The principle is not that a human being cannot justly own another, but that he cannot own him unless he is loyal to the United States."[41]

Montgomery Blair's warning about the ill effects of a proclamation on the fall elections was vindicated by the voters. The election, of course, turned on more than the issue of emancipation: military failure, arbitrary arrests, and the normal veering away from an administration in congressional elections. But the proclamation contributed to the decline in administrative fortunes. As a distinguished authority has put it: "What it amounted to was that the harassed President, without winning the hearty support of abolitionists, had alienated moderate Republicans and war Democrats. As for the opposition Democrats, he had put excellent ammunition into their hands."[42]

In the House of Representatives, on whose support the President must depend for the duration of the war, the Republican margin narrowed to eighteen votes. The Democrats swept five leading

[39] Nicolay and Hay, *Abraham Lincoln*, VI, 179–181.
[40] Quoted in Franklin, *Emancipation Proclamation*, p. 71.
[41] Quoted in Randall and Donald, *Civil War*, p. 381.
[42] *Ibid.*, p. 457.

Northern states that Lincoln had carried in 1860: New York, Pennsylvania, Ohio, Indiana, and his home state of Illinois. In this reversal of Republican fortunes, the border states, which Lincoln had dealt with so tenderly in the preliminary proclamation, sustained the administration.[43]

All the same, the proclamation seized on the popular imagination in its own day, even as it does now. Although there was a broad spectrum of feeling, the proclamation won endorsement from important sources. "There has been no more important and far-reaching document ever issued since the foundation of this Government," pronounced the *New York Times*.[44] The day after the proclamation was published, a group of Northern governors, alarmed about Lee's invasion and the course of the war, met at Altoona, Pennsylvania. The repulse at Antietam abated their concern, and they joined in sending a written address to the President endorsing his proclamation.[45] Radical politicians in general supported the measure, including Senator Charles Sumner, who gave his approval in a sententious speech at Faneuil Hall, Boston. In the House of Representatives, George H. Yeaman of Kentucky offered resolutions denouncing the proclamation as unwarranted by the Constitution and not well chosen as a war measure, which were tabled by a vote of 94 to 45. By a vote of 78 to 51, the House soon after, on the initiative of S. C. Fessenden of Maine, endorsed the proclamation. Northern free Negroes held jubilant meetings to celebrate the "day of days"—in the District of Columbia, in New York's Cooper Union, in Boston's Tremont Temple, and elsewhere across the North. At the largest meeting held to celebrate the formal proclamation—in Boston's Music Hall—Emerson read his "Boston Hymn."[46]

Strongest support came from the race that had inspired the proclamation. It was not that the Negroes revolted—far from rising, many were unmoved by the proclamation, and remained loyal to their owners—nor was there a wholesale exodus from slavery to

[43] Nevins, *War for the Union*, II, 318–322.

[44] *New York Times*, September 23, 1862.

[45] Hesseltine, *Lincoln and the War Governors*, pp. 258 ff.

[46] Franklin, *Emancipation Proclamation, passim*.

freedom. But news of the proclamation encouraged slaves to become restive, to refuse to work, and to steal within Union lines when armies advanced into their sections. The organization of Negro military units went forward rapidly after January 1, 1863. As early as August, Lincoln could write a critic: "Some of the commanders of our armies in the field, who have given us our most important successes, believe the emancipation policy, and the use of colored troops, constitute the heaviest blow yet dealt to the rebellion."[47] The numbers grew, and in the end 186,000 Negroes bore arms for the Union, of whom 104,000 were recruited in Confederate territory—24,000 from Louisiana alone.

In England, as we have seen, liberal opinion did not immediately thrill to the preliminary proclamation. Even John Bright, steadfast friend of the North, failed at first to give hearty approval; and the change in public favor did not begin to show until the turn of the year. President Davis contributed to this alteration by a proclamation, issued two days before Christmas, ordering delivery of slaves captured in arms to their states, where local law decreed death. On the eve of the formal proclamation, the workingmen of Manchester, England, a center of Union sympathy, sent an address to Lincoln: "You have attracted our warm and earnest sympathy."[48]

Lincoln's redemption of his September pledge to issue a formal proclamation, combined with the absence of slave insurrections, served to win English popular support of his policy. The widely read radical paper, *Reynolds's*, ceased to call Lincoln a tyrant, and by late January had accepted the proclamation as the beginning of abolition. "This marked the turning point in radical opinion on the war," writes G. D. Lillibridge.[49] Public meetings in great number endorsed emancipation.

Late in January, English anti-slavery elements held an enthusiastic mass meeting in London's Exeter Hall, the celebrated center of reform assemblies. Textile workers in Lancashire, though idled by the "cotton famine," warmly upheld the proclamation—and conducted

[47] Basler, *Collected Works*, VI, 408.
[48] *Ibid.*, VI, 65 n. 1.
[49] G. D. Lillibridge, *Beacon of Freedom* (Philadelphia: University of Pennsylvania Press, 1955), p. 117; also see p. 120.

themselves with a dignity that commended them to Gladstone's future consideration when suffrage expansion was discussed. Governmental circles—the Establishment—did not respond with zeal, or even friendliness, to the new American policy. On January 1, 1863, Gladstone told Russell: "I think it cannot be very long before the American question crops up again." Nonetheless, the Union cause wore a new face, which British and European statesmen could not stare out of countenance in confronting the question of mediation.[50] In France, from the first pronouncement it appears the Northern cause did "daily grow in grace"—to use the phrase of John Bigelow, American consul in Paris.[51]

By his formal proclamation Lincoln had committed the United States to ending property in human beings. Its popular reception made the pronouncement irrevocable. Without meaning to do so, he had inspired a belief that the war had broadened in purpose, to embrace not only saving the nation's life but also redeeming the enslaved. That he renewed his plea for compensated emancipation in his second annual message made little impression either upon politicians or posterity.

The Emancipation Proclamation was looked upon in Lincoln's time, and in the generations since, as the turning point in the history of abolition in America. The anti-slavery measures of Congress, the futility of the proclamation in a practical sense, the necessity to amend the Constitution to legalize executive fiat—these finicky caveats of the sober historian bow before the authority of the myth. The myth became the master. The great proclamation trumpeted a powerful blast of freedom that filled the Union cause with the purpose of the Divinity:

> He has sounded forth the trumpet that shall never call
> retreat;
> He is sifting out the hearts of men before his judgment-seat:
> Oh! be swift, my soul, to answer Him! be jubilant, my feet!
> Our God is marching on.

[50] E. D. Adams, *Great Britain and the American Civil War*, II, 101–110.
[51] Randall and Donald, *Civil War*, p. 391.

The July Days: Gettysburg and Vicksburg

Surely and swiftly the coil was tightening around us.

Mrs. Roger A. Pryor of Virginia

After Antietam and the preliminary proclamation, much remained to be done to restore the Union, free the slaves, and forestall foreign intervention. The tempestuous storms of Fredericksburg, Chancellorsville, Gettysburg, Vicksburg, Chickamauga, Atlanta, the Wilderness, and Nashville lay ahead. While the shore was still only dimly to be seen, the question of continuing Lincoln in command would inexorably arise. With the Emancipation Proclamation, the course followed by the American republic had decisively shifted; yet the chart did not reveal whether the ship of state could be kept on its perilous course through heavy, unknown seas. It had survived the shoals of Kentucky's neutrality, First Bull Run, and the *Trent* affair. Would it founder and wreck at Gettysburg?

The battle of Gettysburg has conventionally been regarded as the turning point of the Civil War, the victory that won the war for the Union, the great divide. Historians have recently reevaluated Gettysburg in relation to the claims of Antietam as a greater turning of the tide, for the victory at Antietam, as we have noted, produced two major results. England was constrained to postpone mediation in the war at a time when she was nearer recognition of the Confederacy as a separate nation than ever before—or after. The other great consequence of Antietam was the Emancipation Proclamation, projecting a potent moral ideal into the Union cause and amplifying the meaning of the war for the nation's history. Union defeat at Antietam would almost surely have eventuated in Southern independence.

This appraisal of Antietam is correct, and it of course serves to subtract from the former pleas for Gettysburg's pretensions to first place in importance. Admittedly, then, Antietam was more consequential, but this does not signify that Gettysburg was not also a turning point. Let us examine what the battle of Gettysburg meant in effecting ultimate Northern victory.

We should note, first of all, that Lee made a deeper penetration of the North at Gettysburg than at Antietam. It was the northernmost

Confederate offensive, the "high tide" of the Confederacy; after July, 1863, the Confederacy never again mustered the strength to carry the war to the enemy. Looked at as a military engagement, the three-day battle of Gettysburg was the greatest battle of the Civil War; indeed, the greatest battle ever fought on the North American continent. In both battles the Union placed the larger armies in the field, but the Confederacy posed a more formidable threat at Gettysburg than at Antietam. If Antietam provided the bloodiest day of the war, Gettysburg provided the bloodiest battle.

For sheer, massive military weight bearing down upon the Confederacy, Gettysburg takes precedence over Antietam. Though numbers and losses in the Civil War represent educated guesswork, the careful compiler, Thomas Livermore, furnishes these statistics.

CASUALTIES[1]

	Union	Confederate
Antietam		
Effectives	75,316	51,844
Killed	2,108	2,700
Wounded	9,549	9,024
Total Casualties	11,657	11,724
Missing	753	2,000
Gettysburg		
Effectives	90,626	75,000
Killed	3,155	3,903
Wounded	14,529	18,735
Total Casualties	17,684	22,638
Missing	5,365	5,425

As a military operation, therefore, Gettysburg enjoys greater stature than Antietam. Perhaps more than any other battle, it was the decisive engagement of the war. Its diplomatic and political consequences were far-reaching. If Antietam meant British postponement of intervention, Gettysburg, as we shall see, meant British abandonment of it. If Antietam, after an initial sense of relief, was followed by gloom in the North and hope in the South, Gettysburg was succeeded by gloom in the South and hope in the North. Lee escaped censure for being repulsed at Antietam. "It is all my fault,"

[1] Livermore, *Numbers and Losses*, pp. 102–103.

he said of his failure at Gettysburg, anticipating the crosswinds of controversy that have blown to this day.

After McClellan's dismissal in November, 1863, command of the Army of the Potomac had been given Ambrose E. Burnside, a West Pointer with a promising record. He advanced upon Richmond at the head of a mighty army that vastly outnumbered Lee's. But the Confederate commander took advantage of Burnside's procrastination, and fortified Marye's Heights above Fredericksburg. Successive frontal attacks yielded a senseless slaughter. After these heavy losses, Lincoln was compelled to replace Burnside.

In January, 1863, "Fighting Joe" Hooker, who had earned a good name as a soldier, took command of immense Union forces, 130,000 strong. He advanced upon Richmond, leading "the finest army on the planet," but Lee divided his army, and in a surprise move sent Jackson around the Union right at Chancellorsville. Stunned by the move, Hooker fell back across the Rappahannock (May 5), leaving Lee to rejoice over a victory and to mourn the loss of Stonewall Jackson—"his right arm." It is a part of Confederate folklore that, had Jackson lived, the South would have won its independence.

The struggle had worn on for two years; the North had won only one meaningful victory in the East, at Antietam; and within six months Lee had whipped the enemy twice without scoring a decisive victory. What to do next? Three courses of action lay open to Lee. He could assail the Army of the Potomac on Virginia soil, where it now sat. He could send a portion of his troops to the Western front to reinforce the hard-pressed forces of Pemberton, besieged at Vicksburg by Grant, and those of Bragg, who had been pushed back to Chattanooga. Third, he could invade the North, and carry the war to the enemy. In Richmond the consensus of Confederate military opinion opposed a northern offensive, but Lee, backed by Secretary of War James Seddon, favored it, and in the end the fateful campaign that closed at Gettysburg was determined upon.[2]

Why did Lee invade the North? What did his offensive portend? To begin with, the military opportunity was open. He had been

[2] Archer Jones, "The Gettysburg Decision," *Virginia Magazine of History and Biography*, 68 (July, 1960), 331–343.

successful up to now; and, as he wrote Seddon, there was nothing to be gained by "remaining quietly on the defensive." He had frustrated a series of Federal commanders—McClellan, Pope, Burnside, Hooker—and there was no one in sight whom he feared. Invasion of the North would relieve Virginia of Union forces. The political harvest also was tempting. Military failure and arbitrary arrests nursed Northern pacifism. The legislature of New Jersey passed a series of peace resolutions, protesting a war for "unconstitutional or partisan purposes." Secret organizations, notably the "Knights of the Golden Circle," gave aid and comfort to the Southern enemy. Congressman Clement Vallandigham of Ohio placed himself at the head of the Peace Democrats, cried "Stop this war!" and ran for governor of Ohio in a Copperhead campaign following his arrest and banishment from the North. Vallandigham, whose story inspired "The Man without a Country," had struck a chord Lee hoped to play on by encouraging, through his invasion, the emerging peace faction of the North. With the help of appeasers and dissidents he might dictate a peace on Northern soil.[3]

The possibility of foreign help was also present. France in particular appeared prone to intervene. The French army was conquering Mexico, and in June it entered Mexico City, placing Napoleon III in an admirable position to wield the balance of power in North America. Shortly after the Union defeat at Fredericksburg, the French emperor offered his good offices to shorten the period of hostilities in the United States. Secretary of State Seward squarely refused the offer of mediation, and both houses of Congress resolved —by substantial majorities—that attempted mediation would be looked upon as "an unfriendly act."[4]

Though the formal Emancipation Proclamation worked as a powerful leaven on English sentiment, Confederate hopes for aid and recognition kept an awesome form. In the Laird shipyards at Liverpool, formidable ironclad steam warships were under construction. Fitted with 9-inch rifled guns and wrought-iron rams, they

[3] Wood Gray, *The Hidden Civil War* (New York: Viking Press, 1964), pp. 118–147; Rhodes, *History*, IV, 223 ff.

[4] Perkins, *A History of the Monroe Doctrine*, p. 127; *Congressional Globe*, 38th Cong., 1st sess., p. 1408.

could easily have bombarded Northern seaports and sunk Union wooden-hulled ships. All the world seemed to know the mighty rams were being built for the Confederacy, but the Lairds could show papers stating they were under private contract, and the British government was reluctant to seize property and expose itself to a damage suit.

News of Chancellorsville cheered the Confederacy's supporters in Parliament, and their leader, John A. Roebuck, M.P. from Sheffield, knowing in advance Lee's plan of Northern invasion, pressed a resolution in Parliament requesting the Queen to enter into negotiations with foreign powers for cooperation in recognition of the Confederacy. If Lee should prove victorious, and if European powers should extend a friendly hand to the Confederacy, a new nation might emerge in North America.[5]

Lee reorganized his army—a necessity after the death of Jackson—dividing it into three corps, under Generals James Longstreet, Richard S. Ewell, and A. P. Hill. A known risk for Lee was undertaking a major action without his "right arm," Stonewall, and with a new army organization. Beyond this, Lee bore an unknown risk: Jeb Stuart's failure to be his "eyes," which, combined with the loss of Stonewall, vitiated his chances of victory.

Though Longstreet urgently advised against a campaign on Northern soil while Vicksburg lay in danger, Lee ordered an advance early in June, his armies rested and eager.[6] Hooker, after contemplating an attack on Richmond, turned toward Lee's marching forces. He followed the tactical counsel of Lincoln, who wrote: "If the head of Lee's army is at Martinsburg [near the Potomac], and the tail of it on the plank-road between Fredericksburg and Chancellorsville, the animal must be very slim somewhere. Could you not break him?... Fret him and fret him," the President enjoined.[7]

Hooker screened the capital and Eastern seaports, keeping his army parallel to Lee, neither fretting nor halting the stout-hearted

[5] E. D. Adams, *Great Britain and the American Civil War*, II, 106–164.

[6] Clifford Dowdey, *Death of a Nation* (New York: Alfred A. Knopf, Inc., 1958), *passim*.

[7] Basler *et al.* (eds.), *Collected Works of Lincoln*, VI, 273, 257.

Army of Northern Virginia. By mid-June the Northeast was in panic. Ewell had swept through the Shenandoah Valley, "gobbled up" (as Lincoln phrased it) the Union forces there, and had pushed on into Pennsylvania. He seized Chambersburg, proceeded to Carlisle, and terrified Harrisburg with a cannonading only four miles from the state capital. By June 27, Lee had been joined at Chambersburg by A. P. Hill and Longstreet, and Hooker had made his headquarters at Frederick, Maryland.

Lincoln on June 15 called for 100,000 militia, and Governor Andrew Curtin of Pennsylvania on June 26 called for 60,000 men to defend their firesides. Philadelphia was rife with rumors of Confederate movements, and the Pennsylvania Railroad suspended shipments. From Pittsburgh to Baltimore, alarm gripped the Northern public. "Give us McClellan," went up a cry, to which Lincoln replied, speaking to Governor Joel Parker of New Jersey: "I beg you to be assured that no one out of my position can know so well as if he were in it, the difficulties and involvements of replacing General McClellan in command, and this aside from any imputations upon him."[8]

Hooker, quarreling with General-in-chief Halleck, asked to be relieved. The President quickly acceded to this request. "We cannot help beating them if we have the man," he exclaimed in his quest for a winning general. "How much depends in military matters on one master mind! Hooker may commit the same fault as McClellan." At 3:00 A.M. June 28—three days before Gettysburg—Major General George Meade learned from a solemn-faced messenger that he had been named commander of the Army of the Potomac.[9]

Along with the order giving him command, Meade found a letter from Halleck. "Considering the circumstances, no one ever received a more important command.... You will not be hampered by any minute instructions from these headquarters. Your army is free to act as you may deem proper under circumstances as they arise."[10]

[8] Rhodes, *History*, IV, 278; *OR*, Ser. I, Vol. XXXVII, part 3, 136–137.
[9] *Idem*, p. 369; *ibid*., part 1, p. 61; Freeman Cleaves, *Meade of Gettysburg* (Norman: University of Oklahoma Press, 1960), p. 124.
[10] *OR*, Ser. I, Vol. XXVII, part 1, 61.

West Point, class of 1835, veteran of the Peninsula, Second Bull Run, Fredericksburg, and Chancellorsville, steadfast and eagle-faced—tall, manly, and spare—Meade swiftly assumed command, resolved to give his best to his country. He had three duties: to shield the Northern cities of Washington and Baltimore, to prevent Lee from crossing the Susquehanna River, and to defeat Lee in battle.[11]

He took up the northwestward march Hooker had been making, cautiously looking for the enemy and selecting a battle site in northern Maryland. Neither commander knew the other's whereabouts; Lee was without his "eyes," for on June 25 the dashing Stuart had set out on an audacious but useless cavalry raid around the Union army and had not returned. Like two blindfolded titans, Meade and Lee groped for one another.

Quite by chance, the clash at arms, which might sunder or unite the nation, began on July 1. Part of A. P. Hill's corps had gone to the quiet college town of Gettysburg, Pennsylvania—looking for new boots, not Federals. But John Buford's Union cavalry was there, and a stand had to be made at an unintended battlefield. Confederate and Federal troops hastened to the scene of action.

The accident of having to fight at Gettysburg placed Lee under an additional disadvantage, for he labored under a numerical inferiority of about 15,000 fewer men than Meade, he had irretrievably lost Stonewall, and had momentarily lost Stuart. He commanded a newly reorganized army, in which Hill and Ewell were poor replacements for the dead Jackson. He suffered from President Davis's strategy of defense by dispersal instead of being able to pursue a policy of concentration. There were 190,000 graycoated soldiers scattered between the Rappahannock and the Mississippi rivers—beyond his call, for a campaign that might win the war. Now, besides all this, he—with the smaller army—was drawn into taking the offensive. It had been his plan to assume a strong defensive position near Cash-town and there await attack. Chance had operated against Lee.[12]

[11] "George Gordon Meade," *Dictionary of American Biography*, XII, 476; Isaac R. Pennypacker, *General Meade* (New York: D. Appleton & Co., 1901), p. 139.

[12] Cleaves, *Meade*, pp. 132–135; Dowdey, *Death of a Nation*, pp. 119 ff.; Douglas S. Freeman, *R. E. Lee* (4 Vols.; New York: Charles Scribner's Sons, 1940), III, 53 ff.

Gettysburg lasted three days. On the first day the Federals appeared to have the better of the fighting—until mid-afternoon, when Ewell, pressing down from the north, outflanked them and sent them scurrying to Cemetery Ridge, south of town. General John F. Reynolds, Meade's "right arm," and second in command, fell dead at the battle's beginning.[13] On Cemetery Ridge the Union forces found a strong defensive position. Ewell now developed a paralysis of will and failed to storm Cemetery Hill (contrary to what Jackson possibly would have done) before Federal reinforcements arrived under General Winfield Scott Hancock. Even so, the first day of Gettysburg must be counted a Confederate success, the men in gray having driven the bluecoats south of the town to the ridge that became the Union stronghold.

At one in the morning, Meade—gaunt and hollow-eyed—arrived at the battlesite. Through the night the Federal troops kept coming in, so that the next morning they occupied the fishhook-shaped Cemetery Ridge, from Culp's Hill at the north to the Round Tops at the south. Not quite a mile to the west stood a height, Seminary Ridge (the location of a Lutheran college). The Confederates made their stand on the western ridge, and on the second day Lee ordered Ewell to attack head-on the Union right, while Longstreet was to assail the Union left; Hill, along Seminary Ridge, was to strike at the center. Longstreet, as we have seen, disfavored the invasion of the North, and now he urged Lee to turn the enemy's flank rather than attack directly. Lee was adamant, leaving "Old Pete"—as Longstreet was called—no choice.[14]

Clearly, there was a want of harmony between Lee and Longstreet; but that Longstreet delayed carrying out Lee's "sunrise attack" order on July 2—as has so often been charged—is probably untrue. The order has never been substantiated, and Longstreet later adduced testimony from Lee's staff members that refuted the charge.[15] Be that as it may, Longstreet attacked in mid-afternoon,

[13] *OR*, Ser. I, Vol. XXXVII, part 2, 317–318, for Lee's report.

[14] Dowdey, *Death of a Nation, passim*; *Battles and Leaders*, III, 339 ff.; Glenn Tucker, *High Tide at Gettysburg* (Indianapolis: Bobbs-Merrill, 1958), *passim*.

[15] Freeman, *Lee*, III, 84, n. 53; Glenn Tucker, "Longstreet: Culprit or Scapegoat?" *Civil War Times Illustrated*, I (April, 1962), 5 ff.

having only one division on hand in the morning, gaining a second at noon, and proceeding without Pickett's division. For a good part of the day Little Round Top had been undefended, but just before Longstreet's attackers could seize it it was manned. The key to the Federal position, Little Round Top, if in hostile hands would have enabled the enemy to enfilade the Union line. The Confederates held the Peach Orchard in the valley, but failed to take Little Round Top.[16] On the Union right, Ewell—moving tardily—occupied part of Culp's Hill, then failed to take Cemetery Hill.

Meade met with his generals at a midnight council. The Federals had been hit hard and had yielded a little on both flanks. The unanimous decision was against retreat—to fight again the next day. Meade spoke to General John Gibbon of the Second Corps: "If Lee attacks tomorrow, it will be in *your front*. He has made attacks on both our flanks and failed, and if he concludes to try again it will be on our center."[17]

On the third day, at first light, a struggle began for possession of Culp's Hill, and after seven hours of battle the Federals drove Ewell off the hill. But throughout the morning the center was silent. Lee had determined on a frontal assault against the enemy's center, and had designated Pickett's division of Longstreet's corps to lead the charge of 15,000 men. "Old Pete" expostulated: "It is my opinion that no fifteen thousand men ever arrayed for battle can take that position." Lee, unmoved, replied: "The enemy is there, and I am going to strike him." At one in the afternoon the Confederate cannonading started up, and the Federals answered for an hour and a half. Then the Union guns ceased firing, not because the Confederates had silenced them, as the men in gray believed, but because Meade wished to cool the guns and save ammunition.[18]

Pickett, about three o'clock—unable to get a verbal order to attack from the disapproving Longstreet, led his division into the "valley of death." An immense gray wedge that lost its contours and

[16] *OR*, Ser. I, Vol. XXXVII, part 2, 317–320.

[17] Quoted in Cleaves, *Meade*, p. 157. There are variant wordings of Meade's statement, but the sense is always the same.

[18] Quoted in Rhodes, *History of the American Civil War*, p. 237; *OR*, Ser. I, Vol. XXXVII, part 2, 32–321.

size as it moved forward, the Confederate host paused before the renewal of deadly Federal fire. A valiant vanguard of over one hundred under General Lewis Armistead, his cap held high on his sword, pierced the "bloody angle" on top of the ridge, held their ground for a moment of triumph—and then fell back. Slowly the Confederates rolled rearward, leaving the flower of Southern manhood on the battlefield. Lee, alone, rode out to meet the fractured throng. "It was all my fault: now help me to do what I can to save what is left."[19]

The chance for Confederate success was gone. It had been a near thing, but after three days Lee was unable to strike again. His brilliant offensive, so shining with promise, had been frustrated in a quiet college town in southern Pennsylvania. Lee's total losses had been 28,063, Meade's 23,049.[20] Lee now awaited the seemingly inevitable counterattack, but Meade allowed July 4 to pass without a stroke. For this he has been criticized, but in his defense it may be argued he had assumed command only five days before, that he and his troops were exhausted, that the trusted Reynolds lay dead, and that he did not know Lee's condition atop Seminary Ridge.

In heavy rain on the night of the fourth Lee started his retreat, and Meade followed. Vicksburg surrendered that July 4, and, on confirming this news, Lincoln told Halleck: "Now, if General Meade can complete his work, so gloriously prosecuted thus far, by the literal or substantial destruction of Lee's army, the rebellion will be over."

"Push forward and fight Lee before he can cross the Potomac," Halleck telegraphed Meade. But soon after, on further thought, he advised: "I think it will be best for you to postpone a general battle" —until Meade was ready; and he left the decision to Meade.[21] Lee learned that rains had raised the Potomac beyond fording stage, and on July 8 he wrote President Davis he thought it would be a week before the river would have receded enough to permit passage. He

[19] Quoted in Rhodes, *History of the American Civil War*, p. 243; F. H. Haskell, *The Battle of Gettysburg* (Boston: Houghton Mifflin Co., 1958).

[20] Livermore, *Numbers and Losses*, pp. 102–103.

[21] *OR*, Ser. I, Vol. XXVII, part 1, 83, 88, 89.

gained the banks of the Potomac on the 11th, Meade only a short distance away.

The Union general purposed to attack on July 13, but, not sure of himself, he referred the decision to a council of war. Five of his seven corps commanders advised against attack, and instead of fighting on the 13th he spent the day examining Lee's position. The next day he brought his army up—for reconnaissance, or for attack if the situation was suitable. It was too late, for during the night Lee had slipped across the river.

Informed by Halleck that Lee's escape "has created great dissatisfaction in the mind of the President," Meade, good soldier that he was, offered his resignation, which was not accepted. In anguish, Lincoln penned a letter to Meade that he never posted: "He [Lee] was within your easy grasp, and to have closed upon him, would, in connection with our late successes, have ended the war. As it is, the war will be prolonged indefinitely." Later he said: "Still, I am grateful to Meade for the great service he did at Gettysburg." And the Congress of the United States voted Meade its thanks for his "skill and heroic valor ... at Gettysburg."[22]

Simultaneously with that at Gettysburg, the Union scored a meaningful victory in the West. In the Gettysburg campaign the Confederacy was on the offensive, at Vicksburg on the defensive. What Meade did was to repel a sword thrust at the heart of the North; what Grant did at Vicksburg was to rip the armor from the enemy's flank, exposing him to a spear thrust.

We have seen how Kentucky and western Tennessee passed under Union control. Mastery of the Mississippi, the lifeline of the West, was a challenge to the Federals until mid-summer of 1863. Following the loss of forts Henry and Donelson, the Confederates fortified Island No. 10 in the Mississippi, at the southern boundary of Missouri, and New Madrid. Here, at a great bend in the river, they built low-lying batteries to sweep the stream of commerce. At the

[22] *Ibid.*, 92; Rhodes, *History*, IV, 295–296; Garnet Wolseley and James A. Rawley (ed.), *The American Civil War: An English View* (Charlottesville: University Press of Virginia, 1964), p. 174; "Meade," *Dictionary of American Biography*, XII, 476.

direction of General Halleck, John Pope, working hand in hand with the navy, effected the abandonment of New Madrid and went on to subdue the island and its garrison (April 7, 1862), securing control of the upper Mississippi.

The Union gunboats moved south on the river, and on June 7—after a naval engagement watched by crowds on the bluffs—Memphis surrendered. Meantime to the south, control of the lower Mississippi had been gained by Flag Officer David Farragut, who memorably ran the forts below New Orleans and fired but one broadside on the city, which surrendered April 26. By the end of the summer of 1862 the Union controlled the upper and lower reaches of the great river—all but 250 miles, guarded by Vicksburg and Port Hudson.

After the campaigns of early 1862, Halleck had been named General-in-chief of all the land forces of the United States, with headquarters in Washington. Grant now became commander of the Department of the Tennessee, embracing the forces in western Tennessee and northern Mississippi, with headquarters in Memphis. His target was Vicksburg.

High on a bluff, strongly fortified, Vicksburg was a natural stronghold. It reposed two hundred feet above the river, on a hairpin bend. Unassailable from the river side, to the north it enjoyed the protection of the Yazoo River delta—an impassable network of waterways and malarial marshland. The only possible approaches were from the east and south.

Yet Vicksburg was the key to the West. It dominated the Mississippi River, the free navigation of which was in actual fact and popular fancy of vast significance. It also commanded the rail connections between the cis-Mississippi Confederate states and those in the trans-Mississippi West, especially Texas. The Lone Star State, bordering on the Gulf and on Mexico, was thinly blockaded, and was a channel for supplies to the East. Munitions through Mexico, beef and grain from Texas, and sugar from Louisiana went on to Confederate troops. The Vicksburg campaign looms as the most important event in the West in 1863.

Twice in 1862, unsuccessful attempts were made to take the city. In May and June an effort by means of a naval expedition failed. In

November and December efforts by means of a land expedition, in cooperation with a column that moved down the river, likewise failed. Sherman, who was in charge of the approach through the Yazoo waterland, concluded the plan was "hopeless." Grant next tried to divert the channel of the Mississippi River, setting his men to digging a canal; he also sought to make a channel to the Yazoo River by smashing a levee. Neither engineering expedient succeeded. On January 20, Grant took personal command of the Vicksburg expedition.

He then made an audacious move. "It is generally regarded as an axiom in war that all great armies moving in an enemy's country should start from a base of supplies, which should be fortified and guarded, and to which the army is to fall back in case of disaster," he later wrote.[23] Grant now slammed shut the textbooks and tossed orthodox military theory to one side. He was no longer the sluggish Grant of Shiloh, but the emergent genius, cool and lucid, who would win the war. "Rebellion," he observed, "has assumed that shape now that it can only terminate by the complete subjugation of the South or the overthrow of the government." Heterodox in method, clear in intent, resolute in execution, he refused to fall back on Memphis as Sherman advised, and instead determined "*to go forward to a decisive victory.*"[24] The result was his greatest achievement—Grant's finest hour—victory at Vicksburg.

Late in March, when the rains had abated sufficiently to leave the roads only "intolerably bad," he began concentration of his forces on the western bank of the river at Milliken's Bend, above Vicksburg. His campaign required the cooperation of the navy, under Admiral D. D. Porter, for transports and gunboats were needed to convey troops back across the Mississippi below Vicksburg, at Bruinsburg, from which a good road ran to the city of Port Gibson. As an experiment in amphibious warfare, the Vicksburg campaign was a huge success. "The navy, under Porter," Grant wrote, "was all it could be during the entire campaign. Without its assistance the

[23] U. S. Grant, *Personal Memoirs of U. S. Grant* (2 vols.; New York: Charles L. Webster & Co., 1885), I, 422 ff.; *Battles and Leaders*, III, 493.

[24] Rhodes, *History of the American Civil War*, p. 251; Grant, *Memoirs*, I, 443.

campaign could not have been successfully made with twice the number of men engaged.... The most perfect harmony reigned between the two arms of the service."[25]

On the night of April 16, Porter, leading the way on board the flagship *Benton*, ran past the batteries of Vicksburg. It was a deed of valor and skill. The elevated fortress on the river's bend kept the flotilla under fairly close fire for nearly nine miles. The flotilla consisted of seven ironclads, one ram, and three transports, together with some coal barges. Ably commanded, returning gunfire vigorously, the ironclads raced downriver, bringing the flotilla safely through (except for one transport and some barges).

Grant meantime had marched his army across the peninsula opposite Vicksburg to the point at Bruinsburg where Porter could ferry the force to the east bank. On the last day of April, Grant landed his army sixty miles below Vicksburg—in enemy country. "I feel that the battle is now more than half won," he wired Halleck.[26] His achievement was vast. He had cut loose from a safe base above Vicksburg, and had moved his army through difficult terrain to lodge it—with magnificent assistance from the navy—in enemy country. The problems he had solved in moving and massing his army through the river bottoms seem insuperable. There is no parallel in the annals of the Civil War for what Grant had done: not Lee in the Gettysburg campaign, nor Jackson in the Valley campaign, nor McClellan in the Peninsula campaign.

Still, the battle was scarcely more than half won. The theater of operations in which Grant had placed himself so adroitly was a triangle, extending from one apex, at Bruinsburg, northeast to Jackson, Mississippi, and thence westward fifty miles to Vicksburg. Grant's forces, within a week after crossing the river, grew to 33,000 when Sherman joined him; by the end of the campaign he commanded 75,000 men. For their part, the Confederates mustered a total strength of no more than 60,000; about two-thirds of this number were under Pemberton in Vicksburg and along the railroad,

[25] Quoted in William W. Wood, *Captains of the Civil War* (New Haven: Yale University Press, 1921), p. 262.

[26] *OR*, Ser. I, Vol. XXIV, part 1, 32; Rhodes, *History of the American Civil War*, p. 252.

and the other third was under Joseph E. Johnston, guarding the state capital at Jackson.

At Bruinsburg, Grant had made a foothold in hostile territory, had cut himself off from supplies, and now faced operations in a terrain thick with woods and laced with waterways. His army had to thread its way through unfamiliar country, live off the land, and carry war to the enemy. The next eighteen days witnessed a masterly operation. In a series of swift strokes he scored five distinct victories, including the capture of the capital city. By May 19 he had traversed two sides of the triangle, and stood behind Vicksburg on high, dry ground. He completely invested the fortress. Twice—on May 19 and 22—he essayed to carry the Confederate works by assault. Both ventures were failures; and then began the siege of Vicksburg.

It lasted six weeks, during which time men in blue and gray fraternized with one another, exchanging Yankee bread for Rebel tobacco. Confederates deserted, and Union forces planted mines. All the while, Grant's lines, extending in an arc from Hayne's Bluff on the Yazoo to Warrenton on the Mississippi below Vicksburg, separated the Confederate forces and kept a watch on the element under Johnston to the east. Pemberton sought to escape across the river, but, hearing of this, the Union flotilla increased its vigil, and before Pemberton could attempt to carry out his plan, the Union side fired a large mine that blew off the top of the hill.

Grant was readying for assault. Another mine was exploded July 1. Soldiers and citizens in beleaguered Vicksburg were suffering acutely from short rations, and were driven to eating mules and rats. Pemberton's generals advised him against trying to join Johnston, and on July 3 he met Grant under the "Vicksburg Oak"; the following day he surrendered his entire force of 33,000 men, whom Grant permitted to go home on parole. Once home, many of them refused to return to military service when the exchange of prisoners made it possible for them to do so.[27]

The Confederate loss before capitulation had been nearly 10,000.

[27] Grant, *Memoirs*, I, 522 ff.; John C. Pemberton, *Pemberton, Defender of Vicksburg* (Chapel Hill: University of North Carolina Press, 1942), pp. 178–240.

To this must be added Pemberton's troops, and 170 cannon and 50,000 small arms. The Union loss totaled 9,362.[28] To make the river war complete, Port Hudson on July 8 yielded to a siege begun in mid-May. Symbolic of the free navigation of the Father of Waters, the steamboat *Imperial*, sailing from St. Louis, deposited its cargo on the levee at New Orleans on July 16.

These operations split the Confederacy in two and gave the Union mastery of the Mississippi. Grant's achievement was perhaps the most constructive, the most positive in conquering an enemy, wrought thus far in the war. Gettysburg was a famous victory, but the war could not be won by defense and repulse. The North had to take the offensive and wage a war of aggression.

Grant was to spend a few more months in the West, tackling the problems of subjugating eastern Tennessee, but he had already earned the reputation that lifted him to the supreme field command.

On February 29, 1864, Congress revived the rank of lieutenant general expressly for U. S. Grant, and the long Federal search for a winning general had ended. With Grant's appointment to the rank (by Lincoln, on March 2), the Union achieved a modern command system. The President, as Commander-in-chief, stated policy and broad strategy; Grant, as General-in-chief, executed policy and strategy in detail; and General Halleck, as a chief of staff, coordinated military and civil relationships.

In its military organization and policy the United States had moved a vast distance from the disarray of Bull Run, the diffidence of McClellan, and the dictatorial threat of Hooker. The historian T. Harry Williams holds that the 1864 command system of the Union was a major factor in the North's final victory. It provided, he has pointed out, a sound basis for participation by civil and military branches in formulating strategy; it gave the Union a modern command system for a modern war; and it expressed what he has described as the national genius to improvise to meet the requirement of the moment.[29] The aggressive and brilliant Grant, together

[28] Rhodes, *History of the American Civil War*, pp. 257–258.
[29] T. H. Williams, *Americans at War* (New York: Collier Books, 1962), pp. 87–91.

with the sound and dependable Meade and the implacable Sherman, would in the spring of 1864 begin slowly unfolding the strategy and power that effected the downfall of the Confederacy.

At Vicksburg the South had suffered the loss of a mighty bastion, but at Gettysburg she had suffered the loss of her proud belief that Lee was invincible (Lee's request to be relieved was refused).[30] The long siege had helped prepare minds for surrender at Vicksburg, but the blow at Gettysburg had been sudden. Together, the defeats sank deeply into the South's spirit. "The news from Gettysburg," wrote Mrs. Roger A. Pryor of Virginia, "plunged our state into mourning and lamentation," and the sequel at Vicksburg made many realize that "surely and swiftly the coil was tightening around us."[31]

Gettysburg and Vicksburg had a salutary effect abroad for the Union. Roebuck's motion, which never had much chance of adoption, had been exposed to ridicule by its sponsor's indiscretion, and was withdrawn July 13. Learning of Parliament's unfriendliness, the Confederacy on August 4 ordered Mason to end his mission and withdraw from London. The Southern diplomat and his colleague, Slidell, over whose capture, Britain had risked war with the Union, had never been officially received.

The question of the Laird rams remained. The American minister maintained firm pressure on the British foreign office. On September 3 Lord John Russell ordered the rams detained, and soon after avoided the problem of confiscating private property by buying the formidable fortresses. Diplomatic relations between the Confederacy and Britain, such as they had been, were fully severed in October, when the Confederacy expelled the British consuls from her cities. It was "the end of the King Cotton philosophy," the historian Frank Owsley observed.[32]

[30] Rhodes, *History*, IV, 319.

[31] Quoted in F. B. Simkins and J. W. Patton, *The Women of the Confederacy* (Richmond: Garret & Massie, 1936), p. 215; Earl S. Miers, *The Web of Victory: Grant at Vicksburg* (New York: Alfred A. Knopf, Inc., 1955), pp. 294–296.

[32] E. D. Adams, *Great Britain and the American Civil War*, II, 170–179, 134–148; Frank L. Owsley, *King Cotton Diplomacy* (Chicago: University of Chicago Press, 1931), p. 527.

As for France, Napoleon III gave up his efforts to intervene in the American war. Seward, emboldened by victory, sent France a warning in late September against foreign interference in the republics of the New World; and thereafter he continued to warn and protest—until, after the war, the United States could flourish military force against France in Mexico.[33]

In domestic politics North and South, Gettysburg and Vicksburg colored the elections. Lincoln capitalized upon the victories in a notably felicitous letter that was read at a mass meeting of Republicans in his home town of Springfield, Illinois. He wrote, in part:

> The signs look better. The Father of Waters again goes unvexed to the sea.... The Sunny South ... in more colors than one... lent a hand.... And while those who have cleared the great river may well be proud, even that is not all. It is hard to say that anything has been more bravely, and well done, than at Antietam, Murfreesboro, Gettysburg, and on many fields of lesser note. Nor must Uncle Sam's webfeet be forgotten.... Thanks to all. For the great republic—for the principle it lives by, and keeps alive—for man's vast future—thanks to all.[34]

In the same letter he skillfully parried criticisms of his so-called dictatorship—an issue especially important in the gubernatorial contest in Kentucky. In the Bluegrass State the voters' choice was between two factions of the Democratic party. Thomas E. Bramlette, a former Federal army officer, was nominated for governor by the Union faction—more nearly friendly to the Lincoln administration than its rival. Anti-administration Democrats exploited the issue of military interference in the state's civil government, and favored compromise and peace: "the Union as it was." The Peace Democrats nominated Charles A. Wickliffe, who had served as a delegate to the Washington Peace Conference in 1861.

In an election policed by Federal soldiers, Union Democrats swept the state. Bramlette polled 68,000 votes to Wickliffe's 18,000. Both chambers of the state legislature fell to the Union Democratic

---

[33] Perkins, *A History of the Monroe Doctrine*, pp. 121 ff.

[34] Basler, *Collected Works*, VI, 409–410.

faction. Gettysburg and Vicksburg (and Union bayonets at the polls) had done their work in sustaining the national administration and discrediting peace and compromise in Kentucky. The issue of whether Kentucky would continue to support the war was resolved. However, her support would remain qualified; in his inaugural address Governor Bramlette strongly objected to arming Negroes.[35]

In Ohio, where Vallandigham was running against Unionist John Brough, the outcome also strengthened the administration, as Brough received a majority of more than 100,000 votes. On the same day, Pennsylvania voters reelected Andrew J. Curtin governor by a good majority—after a campaign in which McClellan had publicly endorsed the Democratic nominee, Judge Woodward. The general, who had spent the winter and spring preparing a report on his military operations, issued a letter reciting his personal views of politics, which won him favor among Democratic politicians.[36]

Throughout the North, except in New Jersey, voters sustained the Union party in the state elections, and even in the border states of Delaware and Maryland, as well as in Kentucky. The historian-diplomat John L. Motley wrote from the American ministry in Vienna:

> The elections I consider of far more consequence than the battles; or, rather, the success of the anti-slavery party and its steady increasing strength made it a mathematical certainty that, however the tide of battle may ebb and flow with varying results, the progress of the war is in one direction. The peculiar institution will be washed away, and with it the only possible dissolvent of the Union.[37]

In the Confederacy, elections were held for a new Congress. Party lines had been erased, and though on the surface there appeared to be a one-party system, a factional split existed between administration and anti-administration men. Military success during the first half of the war had held anti-administration forces in fairly effective check, but the fall elections of 1863 brought a change. The new

[35] Frank Klement, *The Copperheads in the Middle West* (Chicago: University of Chicago Press, 1960), p. 128; Coulter, *Kentucky*, pp. 170–178; Moore, ed., *Rebellion Record*, VII, 47.

[36] McPherson, *Political History of the Rebellion*, p. 386.

[37] Rhodes, *History*, IV, 416.

Congress was made up largely of new legislators, and the number of anti-Davis men had risen from twenty-four to forty-one in the 106 congressional districts.[38] The President of the Confederacy, like the President of the Union, had incurred hostility by his nationalizing measures, affronting state rights and individualistic sentiments of Southerners. Attacks in the press had been common, and attacks in the Congress soon broke out.

Davis's message to the Confederate Congress in December sounded repeated notes of despondency. Referring to Gettysburg, Vicksburg, and other campaigns, he declared: "Grave reverses befell our arms soon after your [Congress's] departure from Richmond." In the field of foreign affairs, he lamented that the conduct of some European nations "has assumed a character positively unfriendly." And "the state of the public finances is such as to demand your earliest and most earnest attention," he informed the lawmakers. "We have lost many of the best of our soldiers and most patriotic of our citizens," he noted sadly. And, most mournful of all: "The hope last year entertained of an early termination of the war has not been realized."[39]

Lincoln's message to the Union Congress the next day affords striking contrast. The President recalled the dissatisfaction and uneasiness that had dominated public feeling the year before, and that had been expressed in the congressional election of 1862—and in the pitying words of Europe. Since then, the Emancipation Proclamation had been issued, and had grown in favor. Over 100,000 former slaves were now serving in the Union army; two of the border states, Maryland and Missouri, had dropped their hostility to self-emancipation and were debating how best to accomplish it. Rebel boundaries had been pushed back, the Mississippi opened, and the Confederacy divided into two parts. The state elections were highly encouraging to the administrators of the Union.

The future cast by the proclamation had wrought a new reckoning. "The crisis which threatened to divide the friends of the Union is past." Indeed, the time had come to consider reconstruction of the

[38] W. B. Yearns, *The Confederate Congress* (Athens: University of Georgia Press, 1960), p. 58.

[39] Rowland (ed.), *Jefferson Davis*, VI, 94–127.

Union, and in this third annual message Lincoln took up the problem of reviving loyal state governments in the South.[40]

A further outcome of Gettysburg was the noble expression by Lincoln of the war's meaning in world history. So many soldiers had fallen at Gettysburg a special burying ground was set aside to inter them. At Gettysburg National Cemetery, November 19, 1863, Lincoln compressed into a few words his vision of liberty and equality, conceived and dedicated in the American nation. He said the American system was in a trial by battle, and expressed his hope it would survive: "that this nation, under God, shall have a new birth of freedom—and that government of the people, by the people, for the people, shall not perish from the earth."

But a year and a half of war, and another crisis of the nation, lay ahead.

[40] Basler, *Collected Works*, VII, 48–53.

The Election of 1864

This morning, as for some days past, it seems exceedingly probable that this Administration will not be reelected. Then it will be my duty to so cooperate with the President-elect as to save the Union between the election and the inauguration; as he will have secured his election on such ground that he cannot possibly save it afterwards.

Abraham Lincoln, August 23, 1864

It was a perilous experiment, to hold a general election in wartime, and doubly perilous to hold one during the crisis of domestic strife. Only once before 1864 had the United States conducted a presidential election in time of war—in 1812—and then during a foreign war that had barely begun. "Alone of democratic governments before World War II," the historian Henry Commager has observed in connection with the election of 1864, "the United States faced a general election in wartime."[1]

Yet no one seems to have proposed postponement of the election. As President Lincoln remarked: "We cannot have free government without elections; and if the rebellion could force us to forego or postpone a national election, it might fairly claim to have already conquered and ruined us."[2]

Still the hazard was great, like the gambler staking his purse on a throw of the dice or the windswept victim walking toward the eye of the storm. The dangers were several: of diverting attention from a war for the nation's life, of subjecting the conduct of the war to partisan conflict, of inviting violence at the polls, of risking demoralization of troops fighting on distant battlefields, of changing governments in the midst of war, and—not the least—of expecting a rational choice among issues and candidates in the fury and agony of fratricidal strife.

If such were the dangers involved, the possible benefits were equally great: to clarify issues in debate, to be a safety valve, to unite dissident groups, to reaffirm the national purpose, to hear the voice of the people, and possibly to secure a mandate to continue the work the nation was in. What was more, the Constitution of the United States plainly required an election, and at a time when the Constitution was being strained and tested in many particulars it was of first importance to ascertain that a people's war had the people's approval.

[1] Morison and Commager, *Growth of the American Republic*, I, 776.
[2] Basler, *Collected Works*, VIII, 101.

171

From early in the war, Northerners had been divided in their opinions about how the war should be waged: improvising or planning, volunteering or drafting, maintaining Constitutional safeguards or placing military restraint upon liberty, and conventional financing or printing money. Even more divisive, early in 1864, was the peace movement. To advocate peace while a war for national survival was being fought smacked of disloyalty, if not treason, neither of which governments lightly risk in peace or war, and most especially not in a civil war. Persons of doubtful patriotism abounded in the border slave states, in New York, and in the states of Ohio, Indiana, and Illinois in the Old Northwest.

In the exigency of domestic conflict, the Federal government limited traditional liberties. The most questionable action was Lincoln's suspension, without legislative sanction, of the privilege of the writ of *habeas corpus*. The number of military arrests had risen high before Congress tardily authorized Presidential suspension, but the passage of the Habeas Corpus Act in March, 1863, did not end the larger issues of arbitrary arrests and martial law. In all, well over 13,000 persons were arbitrarily arrested in the North during the Civil War. A number of hostile newspapers were suppressed or suspended. The leader of the Copperheads, Clement Vallandigham, Democratic congressman from Ohio, found much support for his insistence on the maintenance of free speech and on the restoration of peace on any terms. He was tried by a military tribunal for expressing treasonable ideas, and was banished to the Confederacy, from where he escaped to Canada.[3]

The peace movement fed on this storehouse of civil liberties abridged. "Without peace," cried Vallandigham, "you will not have one remnant of civil liberty left among yourselves."[4] On Washington's birthday, 1864, at a so-called national meeting in New York, leaders of secret anti-war societies organized on a national basis, assumed the name Sons of Liberty, and prescribed strict obedience by members to projects determined on by the officers. Clement Vallandigham, still in exile in Canada, accepted the post of Supreme Commander.

[3] Wood Gray, *The Hidden Civil War: The Story of the Copperheads* (New York: Viking Press, 1942).

[4] *Idem*, p. 120.

This peace movement, centering among Democrats in the North-west, soon leagued itself with Confederate agents in Canada. On June 11, 1864, Vallandigham initiated into the Sons of Liberty Jacob Thompson, one of a three-man commission sent by President Davis to Canada to further Confederate schemes. Talks were begun, looking to the creation of a "Western Confederacy" through an uprising, which the Confederate agents thought, even if it failed, would divert Federal troops from the Southern front. In mid-June, Vallandigham returned to Ohio, anticipating arrest, which would be a signal for a revolt that might force abandonment of the war. Lincoln, who had been embarrassed by the congressman's arrest, made no move against him. Vallandigham's success would hinge upon the failure of Union arms.[5]

The spring of 1864, which brought the dogwood to bloom in Virginia and the small cotton plants to blossom in Georgia, bore with it the fresh promise for the North of an end to the fratricidal carnage that had now for three years despoiled the American republic. Victories the year before had contracted the theater of war to the Southeastern states below the Potomac and east of the Appalachians. Along the Atlantic and the Gulf, most of the coastal fortresses had fallen under Federal control. The new Union command system, which apportioned military functions among Commander-in-chief Abraham Lincoln, Chief of Staff Henry Halleck, and the general commander of the Union armies, U. S. Grant, had been perfected.

In early March the Army of the Potomac, under the personal supervision of Grant, stood on Virginia soil, poised to do battle against Lee. In the Lower South, William T. Sherman had succeeded to Grant's command, and at the head of a blue host nearly 100,000 strong he confronted Confederate forces of about 53,000 under Joseph E. Johnston. Together, Grant and Sherman, poring over maps in the Burnet House in Cincinnati, had determined upon the strategy of victory. With a stark simplicity that his admirers call genius, Grant understood that his objective was not the enemy's capital at Richmond but the enemy's army, that politics were the

5 Frank L. Klement, *The Copperheads in the Middle West*, *passim*.

civil preserve of the President, not to be poached on by a general, and that by the resolute application of manpower against waning Confederate strength an indecisive struggle could be concluded in triumph.

But the sands of the Confederacy had not run out. What survived of the South was its heartland—from Virginia through Georgia—the center of its food supply, its manpower, its rail system, and its iron industry. Two redoubtable commanders, seasoned in battle and adroit in defensive generalship, guarded the region: at the Virginia front, Lee—the perfect, gentle knight—and at the gateway to Georgia, Johnston—the stormy petrel of the Confederacy. The lush Shenandoah Valley that ran down to the Potomac, at once a Confederate cornucopia and a high road leading North, remained under Southern arms. On its coasts, the Confederacy had kept open the ports of Wilmington, N.C., Charleston, and Mobile. The strategy of dogged defense, with the advantage of interior lines, could well eventuate in independence from a North rent by internal dissension and weary of war.

Early in the morning of May 4 the Army of the Potomac began to cross the Rapidan River and enter the Wilderness, a thickly wooded area near Fredericksburg, Virginia. Outmaneuvering the invader, Lee inflicted severe losses—some 18,000 casualties—on his enemy. Undeterred, Grant ordered another forward movement—and in five bloody days at Spotsylvania suffered another 18,000 casualties. In the battle of Cold Harbor, near the Chickahominy, Lee exacted a further toll. In the month ending June 12, Grant had lost nearly 60,000 men—equal to Lee's whole army. The Army of Northern Virginia, for its part, had lost from 25,000 to 30,000 men—about half its strength. When would the national hemorrhage stop?

Grant's telegram to Halleck—"I propose to fight it out along this line if it takes all summer"—bespoke determination, but it did not bode a swift end to the war. Lee resisted inexorably, realizing what was at stake for the North, for, as he wrote Jefferson Davis in mid-May: "The importance of this campaign to the administration of Mr. Lincoln and to General Grant leaves no doubt that every effort and every sacrifice will be made to secure its success."[6]

[6] Grant, *Memoirs*, II, 177 ff.; Freeman, *Lee*, p. 337; Livermore, *Numbers and Losses*, pp. 110–114.

When Grant's army started its slow and costly campaign, Sherman began his famous invasion of Georgia. His opponent, Johnston, fell back slowly, offering a skillful delaying action throughout May and June. In his Fabian retreat, Johnston burned bridges, destroyed railroads, and avoided open battles by fighting at positions of his own choosing, behind prepared entrenchments. By retarding Sherman's progress he sought to promote disaffection in the North and effect the downfall of the Lincoln administration. Prevention of the capture of Atlanta, whose military value had been exaggerated by the Northern press, "would have strengthened the peace party greatly," Johnston later declared, "so much, perhaps, as to have enabled it to carry the presidential election, which would have brought the war to an immediate close."[7]

Beyond the Rio Grande rose still another danger to the Union. In April, 1864, Maximilian of Austria, a puppet of the French Emperor Napoleon III, accepted the crown of Mexico. The United States was temporarily helpless in the face of the French challenge to the Monroe Doctrine. "Why should we gasconade about Mexico when we are in a struggle for our own life?" asked Secretary of State Seward.[8] The impotence of the United States had offered a golden opportunity for the overthrow of the Mexican republic, establishment of a New World monarchy, and extension of unfriendly European influence to the western hemisphere.

It is against the background of military development that one must view the presidential election of 1864. The political fortunes of the Lincoln administration rose and fell with the fortunes of war. The wartime elections of 1862, 1863, and 1864 are fairly accurate barometers of popular responses to leading events. The election of 1862 had narrowed the base of the administration's support in Congress; the state elections of 1863 then broadened the base throughout the North; and the election campaign of 1864 would

[7] W. T. Sherman, *Memoirs of Gen. W. T. Sherman* (2 vols. in one, 4th ed.; New York: Charles L. Webster & Co., 1891), II, 5 ff.; Johnston, *Narrative*, p. 363.

[8] Quoted in Bailey, *A Diplomatic History of the American People*, p. 352; Perkins, *A History of the Monroe Doctrine*, p. 118.

mark the success of Northern arms in the subjugation of the South and the termination of the war. The outcome of the election would in turn influence the outcome of the war. The election of 1864, broadly viewed, was the final turning point of the American Civil War.

For one living in the twentieth century, reared in the knowledge of Lincoln's place in history and legend, it is difficult to reach back to the contemporary Lincoln. It comes with a start to realize that the Great Emancipator and Savior of the Union might not have had a second term—that the route to reelection was not as smooth as the path to a village church. Many members of his party opposed his renomination; some supported third-party candidates; some wanted to postpone the convention in order to gain time to seek another candidate; some moved to set aside his nomination once it had been made; and throughout the whole, strange proceeding ran a wide streak of detraction and vilification—a disfiguration not found in the grand portrait that historians and sculptors have executed for posterity.

Great numbers of Northerners—weary of war, grieving for loved ones, burdensomely taxed, fearful of arbitrary government and conscription—had abundant reason to project their resentments upon the Union President. In his own party, a considerable array of political leaders believed that he was not adequate to his great office in a time of unparalleled crisis. He did not cut the figure of a statesman in appearance, with his ill-fitting clothes and swarthy face, or in his manner, with his homely levity and frontier pronunciation. Indifferent to administrative detail, he was thought by some persons to be too easy-going, and to spend his time with trifles. His assumption of vast executive power offended many Radical and moderate congressmen, particularly after the issue of reconstruction emerged; and his retention of the moderates Seward and Blair in his cabinet, together with a prudent policy on emancipation, offended Radicals. Senator Lyman Trumbull wrote from Washington to a friend (in February, 1864):

> You would be surprised, in talking with public men we meet here, to find how few, when you come to get at their real sentiments, are for Mr. Lincoln's re-election. There is a distrust and fear that he is too undecided and inefficient to put down the rebellion.[9]

[9] Pierce, *Sumner*, IV, 194–196; White, *Trumbull*, pp. 217 ff.

The Republican party of 1864—the party of Lincoln—was not a monolith. The Republican party changed its name, if not its identity, during the war. It had enacted its platform and fulfilled its founders' purposes; but war thrust new issues upon it, threatening to divide the Republican house against itself. It took as its new title the Union party—stressing the nationalistic aim that engrossed the moderate men at the helm of the party's affairs.[10]

From early in the war, an extremist faction known as the Radicals had differed with the President over various issues, which by 1864 included abolition of slavery, Negro rights, extent of reconstruction, and control of reconstruction. Early in the year 1864, there was a movement to nominate Secretary of the Treasury Salmon P. Chase, but the Chase pudding failed to rise—as a contemporary remarked—and the secretary announced he was not a candidate.

The outer edge of Radicalism now turned to General John C. Frémont, promulgator of premature emancipation in Missouri. A little more than a week before the national convention of the Union party, a convention attended by some 350 delegates assembled in Cleveland, Ohio. The creed it adopted had been adumbrated in a pre-convention letter of the Boston abolitionist, Wendell Phillips:

> Subdue the South as rapidly as possible. The moment territory comes under our flag reconstruct States thus: Confiscate and divide the lands of the rebels; extend the right of suffrage broadly as possible to whites and blacks; let the Federal Constitution prohibit slavery throughout the Union, and forbid the States to make any distinction among their citizens on account of color or race.

Frémont accepted the nomination promptly, "to prevent the misfortune," as he put it, of Lincoln's reelection.[11]

The party split at Cleveland, even though it had nominated a prominent and colorful personality for president—"the West's

[10] William A. Dunning, "The Second Birth of the Republican Party, *American Historical Review*, XVI (October, 1910), 56–63.

[11] McPherson, *A Political History of the United States during the Rebellion*, pp. 411–414 for Phillips's and McClellan's letters and other documents.

greatest adventurer"—had not materially fractured Lincoln's following.

What the convention had done was underscore Radical ideals, foremost of which was completion of the work of emancipation. The emancipatory measures of Congress and President had not provided a comprehensive solution for the problem of slavery. The vast bulk of Negroes from Virginia to Texas remained in slavery. Even Lincoln questioned whether his proclamation was legally valid. In the border slave states and occupied Tennessee, the institution of slavery, untouched by the proclamation, remained secure under state law. Only in newly formed West Virginia, where emancipation was decreed as a condition of admission into the Union in 1863, had a border state abolished slavery. Conceivably, the war could end with slavery protected by state rights in the Borderland, and confused in legal status in the Confederate states. A mere act of Congress abolishing slavery would not suffice, for it was widely conceded that the national legislature could not prohibit slavery in the states. Only a Constitutional amendment could silence doubts about legality and effectually complete the emancipation of slaves. An amendment would be, as Lincoln was to remark, "a king's cure-all for all evils."

In January, 1864, a resolution was introduced in the Senate to amend the Constitution by abolishing slavery in the United States. Senator Garret Davis of Kentucky led the opposition. After ten days of debate, however, on April 8, 1864, the Senate approved the resolution by a vote of 38 to 6. In the House of Representatives, border-state men and Democrats powerfully opposed the resolution. George H. Pendleton of Ohio, a leader of the Peace Democrats, contended slavery lay beyond the reach of the Federal government, even by constitutional amendment. The House vote of 93 to 65, on June 15, failed to muster the necessary two-thirds majority. The issue of the ultimate extinction of slavery was carried over to the presidential campaign.[12]

From early in the year, Lincoln's friends had actively labored for his renomination; and though numerous party leaders held misgivings, and there was much silent disapprobation, and there were

[12] Randall, *Constitutional Problems under Lincoln*, pp. 385 ff.

those who favored Grant, a second nomination appeared probable. Shortly before the national convention was to begin, Lincoln called the chairman of the national executive committee to him at the White House. "Senator Morgan," he is said to have remarked, "I want you to mention in your speech when you call the convention to order, as its keynote, and to put into the platform as the keystone, the amendment of the Constitution abolishing and prohibiting slavery forever."[13]

At noon of June 7, in Baltimore, Senator Edwin D. Morgan, the Republican party's only chairman since its founding in 1856, his lantern-jawed face worn and coarse hair gray from his arduous service as New York's first Civil War governor, called to order the Union national convention. An esteemed moderate, he evoked prolonged applause, followed by three cheers, when he urged the delegates to root out the cause of "terrible civil war" by endorsing an amendment to "prohibit African slavery in the United States."[14]

Morgan's sponsorship of the Thirteenth Amendment was one mark of the progress of Northern anti-slavery sentiment during wartime. Four years before in Chicago, the Republican platform had expressly recognized "the right of each State to order and control its own domestic institutions exclusively." Now, in the dread ordeal of a brothers' war, assertedly caused by slavery, the party of Lincoln demanded the complete extirpation of this "gigantic evil." On another issue, in a clear riposte against Peace Democrats, the Baltimore platform disowned compromise with the rebels and upheld a determination to maintain the integrity of the Union. A resolution declaring that "harmony should prevail in the National Councils" seemed a covert attack on the moderate Montgomery Blair, postmaster general.

On the roll call of states to renominate Lincoln, only Missouri withheld its vote, giving it at first to Grant, but, before the result was announced, it climbed on the bandwagon and made the renomination unanimous. In selecting a vice-presidential candidate, the convention was permitted by Lincoln—outwardly at least, for

[13] Current, *Lincoln Nobody Knows*, p. 229.
[14] Rawley, *Edwin D. Morgan*, p. 199.

the point is controversial—to make its own choice.[15] The designation of Johnson, a Tennessee War Democrat, for whatever motives—whether political balance or partisan rivalry—was more crucial than had been anticipated. It did, doubtless, contribute to the success of the Union ticket, but beyond that it gave the Republic its next President, who, untried—and in many ways unfitted for his task—was to be charged with binding up the nation's wounds.

The making of the platform and the ticket represented an effort to unite the North on the common ground of supporting an experienced President and pursuing the ideal of universal freedom. But the Frémont faction had not been appeased, and the general, who had resigned his commission, continued to be a candidate. Chase resigned from the cabinet in late June, after a losing struggle with Senator Morgan over New York patronage. Within a short time he was conniving with Republican malcontents, and contemplating support of the Democratic nominee—if not angling for that post for himself.[16]

The menace to Lincoln's reelection, however, came less from Republican factionalism, or as yet unorganized Democratic opposition, than from the fortunes of war. In mid-June, Grant's campaign halted before Petersburg, whose defenders resisted a four-day assault and took a toll of 8,000 Union soldiers. Grant now dug in for a nine-month siege—the longest of the war. Confederate forces, under Jubal A. Early, cleared the Shenandoah Valley of Federals in June, crossed the Potomac, and gave Washington its worst scare of the war—before returning to Virginia in mid-July. In his march through Georgia, Sherman had bogged down, at first frustrated by Johnston's masterly delaying action, and then, after President Davis impatiently replaced Johnston with John B. Hood, stalled by Hood's offensives. "Sherman is checked before Atlanta," the Northern press reported to a discouraged public. This wilting under the summer sun of the bright military promise of the springtime left its mark on the North. The value of greenbacks—Federal printing press money—

[15] McPherson, *Political History*, pp. 403–407; James F. Glonek, "Lincoln, Johnson, and the Baltimore Ticket," *The Abraham Lincoln Quarterly*, VI (March, 1951), 255–271.

[16] Rawley, *Edwin D. Morgan*, pp. 195–197.

fell to 39 cents on the gold dollar. Between the Rapidan and the Potomac, Union dead lay thick as autumnal leaves. Volunteering for military service failed. On July 18, President Lincoln called for half a million men for one year's duty—to be drafted if not furnished before September 5.[17]

In the early summer of 1864 much hung in the balance: the outcome of the general election, the course of the peace movement, the extinction of slavery, and—outweighing all else—the question of whether American nationality was to be unbroken or Confederate independence achieved. The Democrats, hoping the distress of their partisan foes might persist, if not deepen, postponed their convention from July 4 to late August. The summer stalemate intensified peace sentiment among Democrats, and impelled it to crop up, amazingly, in the President's party.

The notion of a negotiated peace found a strange champion in Horace Greeley, the editor of the *New York Tribune*, who in the summer of 1861 had shrilly sounded the battle cry "On To Richmond!" An incorrigible idealist and erratic reformer, Greeley was drawn by his pacifism into reluctantly undertaking (in July, 1864) a peace mission, after he had been informed two Confederate agents were in Canada "with full and complete powers for a peace." Jogged by a letter from Greeley charging that many persons thought the administration was not anxious for peace, Lincoln insisted that Greeley himself make the trip to Canada. There the editor learned that the agents had no credentials; it appeared they were endeavoring to stir up peace sentiment in the North.

Lincoln exploited the episode by publishing an announcement that sought to give assurance of his wish for peace, at the same time stating a basis for peace. "To Whom It May Concern. Any proposition which embraces the restoration of peace, the integrity of the whole Union, and the abandonment of slavery, and which comes by and with the authority that can control the armies now at war against the United States will be received and considered..." Thus

[17] Harold M. Dudley, "The Election of 1864," *Mississippi Valley Historical Review*, XVIII (March, 1932), 510; E. C. Kirkland, *The Peacemakers of 1864* (New York: The Macmillan Co., 1927), pp. 66–67.

the "To Whom It May Concern" letter of July 18 laid down two conditions of a peace: reunion and abolition.

A second peace mission now followed, testing at the summit the Confederacy's attitude toward peace. Lincoln welcomed the request of Colonel James Jaquess and James R. Gilmore, self-constituted envoys, who wished to discuss peace with President Davis in Richmond. The whole episode, Lincoln calculated, would expose the illusion of Northern peace advocates; namely, that the Confederacy was willing to abandon its struggle for independence if only the North would abandon its demand for abolition.

Jaquess and Gilmore, bearing a statement of Lincoln's peace terms, met with Davis and his secretary of state, Judah P. Benjamin, that "short, plump, oily little man in black," in Richmond. "If Jefferson Davis had been adroit he could have completed the distraction of Union councils by proposing an armistice or a peace conference on any terms, for once the fighting had stopped, it would have been impossible to get it started again," Henry S. Commager has observed. Instead, Davis delivered an ultimatum. "We will go on unless you acknowledge our right to self-government. We are not fighting for slavery. We are fighting for independence, and that, or extermination, we will have."[18]

Davis threw the North's failure to subdue the South into the faces of the envoys.

> If your papers tell the truth, it is your capital that is in danger, not ours.... Grant has lost seventy-five or eighty-thousand men— *more than Lee had at the outset*—and is no nearer taking Richmond than at first; and Lee, whose front has never been broken, holds him completely in check, and has men enough to spare to invade Maryland and threaten Washington! Sherman, to be sure, *is* before Atlanta; but suppose he takes it? You know that the farther he goes from his base of supplies the weaker he grows, and the more disastrous defeat will be to him. And defeat *may* come. So, in a military view, I should certainly say our position was better than yours.[19]

[18] Kirkland, *op. cit.*, pp. 94–95; Morison and Commager, *Growth of the American Republic*, I, 778.

[19] Rhodes, *History of the United States*, IV, 515–516.

One more unofficial peace effort, in Toronto between two former colleagues in Buchanan's cabinet, underscored the hard truth that the Confederacy would entertain no proposals of peace that did not embrace disunion. Southern independence was the *sine qua non* of a negotiated peace.[20]

August was the "cruelest month" of the year 1864 for the Union and its President. Reflecting on the probability that the Democratic convention would espouse a negotiated peace, Lincoln wrote: "Thus, the present Presidential contest will almost certainly be no other than a contest between a union and a disunion candidate." The military outlook had turned even darker just before the month opened, when an elaborate effort to take Petersburg by exploding a mine dug under Confederate works resulted in what Grant himself admitted as a "stupendous failure" and in the loss of almost 4,000 Union soldiers.[21]

The multiplication of Union difficulties provoked a vindictive attack on Lincoln by extremists in his own party, long restive about his nomination. The issue was the reconstruction of the South, which the President had taken into his own hands in December, 1863. Under his lenient plan, he had installed loyal governments in Arkansas and Louisiana. Congressional hostility to executive reconstruction mounted until the Radicals, by a narrow vote at the end of a session, passed the Wade-Davis Bill, providing for a stringent plan of reconstruction under Congress. Lincoln gave the bill a pocket veto and issued a temperate proclamation, with characteristic pragmatism stating he was not "inflexibly committed" to any single plan of reconstruction but that he was unwilling to have the new governments of Arkansas and Louisiana "held for naught" or to recognize "a Constitutional competency in Congress to abolish slavery in States," as the bill contemplated.

A savage assault on Lincoln—the Wade-Davis manifesto—appeared in Horace Greeley's *New York Tribune* on August 5.

[20] Randall and Donald, *Civil War and Reconstruction*, p. 472; *New York Times*, July 24, 1864.

[21] Nicolay and Hay, *Abraham Lincoln*, IX, 246; *Battles and Leaders*, IV, 544–562; Grant, *Memoirs*, II, 315.

Without let or dignity, its two congressional authors accused the President of vetoing the bill to hold "the electoral votes of the rebel States at the dictation of his personal ambition." After reviewing the President's proclamation, they charged that "a more studied outrage on the legislative authority of the people has never been perpetrated. ...He must understand that our support is of a cause and not of a man... and if he wishes our support, he must confine himself to his executive duties ... and leave political reorganization to Congress." Finally, in an appeal to the supporters of the government, they exhorted: "Let them consider the remedy for these usurpations, and having found it, fearlessly execute it."[22]

The *New York Times* branded the manifesto "the most effective Copperhead campaign document thus far," and the Richmond *Examiner* called it a "blow at Lincoln under the fifth rib."[23] Discontent with Lincoln's candidacy quickly spread among politicians fearful of defeat in the fall. On August 14 a group of political leaders met in New York City and decided to issue a call for a new convention to rally the Union party supporters to Lincoln or some other candidate. From both extremes of the party, despairing judgments agreed: "I told Mr. Lincoln that his re-election was an impossibility," conservative Thurlow Weed reported to Seward: "Mr. Lincoln is already beaten," pronounced Greeley.[24]

At no time in the war had Northern disaffection seemed so marked. Peace meetings were being held widely; the Democrats were about to convene in Chicago; election day was near at hand in certain states. Gloom descended like a pall over the Republican National Executive Committee. Its new chairman, the conservative Henry J. Raymond, editor of the *New York Times* and an antagonist of Greeley, summoned his committee to meet in New York City on August 22. That day he wrote the President: "The tide is setting strongly against us.... Two special causes are assigned for this great reaction in public sentiment—the want of military successes, and the impression in some minds, the fear and suspicion in others, that we

[22] Nicolay and Hay, *Abraham Lincoln*, IX, 124–127.

[23] *New York Times*, August 13, 1864; the *Examiner* is quoted August 16.

[24] Quoted in David Donald, *Lincoln Reconsidered* (New York: Alfred A. Knopf, Inc., 1961), p. 114; also see pp. 117–118.

are not to have peace in any event under this Adminstration until slavery is abandoned." Raymond proposed that Lincoln send a commission to proffer peace to Jefferson Davis, which would doubt-less be rejected, thereby dispelling all illusions about peace and uniting the North "as nothing since the firing on Fort Sumter has hitherto done."

The day he received this counsel of despair from the chairman of the party to which he owed his nomination, Lincoln wrote out a private memorandum and put it away in his desk. "This morning, as for some days past, it seems exceedingly probable that this Administration will not be reelected. Then it will be my duty to so cooperate with the President-elect as to save the Union between the election and the inauguration; as he will have secured his election on such ground that he cannot possibly save it afterwards." When the committee, depressed in spirit and stricken with panic, came to the White House two days later to urge its views on Lincoln, he succeeded in persuading it to abandon the idea of a peace offer.[25]

It may be as Carl Sandburg and W. F. Zornow have contended, that popular support of Lincoln was at this time greater than the politicians'; there is some evidence that small-town editors remained loyal to Lincoln.[26] But Lincoln himself, a sensitive barometer of the climate of opinion, was deeply pessimistic; and his pessimism, as we have seen, was shared by Radical supporters of Fremont, veteran political boss Weed, Republican National Chairman Raymond, and the North's most influential editor, Greeley.

It was in August that the astounding probability arose that Lincoln was willing to accept slavery as the price of peace. To this time one might think of emancipation as a *sine qua non* for accepting Confederate surrender. The Emancipation Proclamation had appeared unequivocal in freeing all slaves in regions in rebellion against the United States. Was it Lincoln's policy there would be no peace without the ending of slavery? Had the war become an abolitionist war? Had emancipation become an obstacle to the

[25] Nicolay and Hay, *Abraham Lincoln*, IX, 217–220.
[26] William F. Zornow, *Lincoln and the Party Divided* (Norman: University of Oklahoma Press, 1954), pp. 117–118.

cessation of bloodshed? A worried Wisconsin editor of a War Democratic newspaper anxiously wrote the President: "As we understand it ... no steps can be taken towards peace from any quarter, unless accompanied with an abandonment of slavery. This puts the whole war question on a new basis, and takes us war Democrats clear off our feet."

In a reply that was apparently never sent or completed, Lincoln outlined views at variance with the traditional interpretation that he insisted upon emancipation as one of his terms of peace. "To me it seems plain," he wrote, "that saying reunion and abandonment of slavery would be considered, if offered, is not saying that nothing *else* or *less* would be considered, if offered." Lincoln affirmed that he was still true to the purpose stated in his Greeley letter; that is, to save the Union with or without slavery, and to do more or less about slavery if doing more or less would help the Union cause. The Emancipation Proclamation, he said, had been the doing of more about slavery to help save the Union. The way in which the proclamation was to help the cause, he explained, was "by inducing the colored people to come bodily over from the rebel side to ours." Lincoln pointed to the already large number of colored soldiers in the North's service. They could not be reenslaved, he emphasized. What he appears to be saying is that he would entertain proposals of peace without abandonment of slavery, except in the case of Negro soldiers. As if to clinch the matter, he remarked: "If Jefferson Davis wishes for himself, or for the benefit of his friends at the North, to know what I would do if he were to offer peace and reunion, saying nothing about slavery, let him try me."[27]

Most historians have ignored this acceptance of peace with slavery extant. The view that Lincoln was in earnest in saying he would consider peace without emancipation, and that he was subsequently consistent to the policy of the unsent letter, has recently been cogently argued by Richard N. Current. In a draft of instructions Lincoln prepared for Henry Raymond to carry to rebel authorities, he wrote: "You will propose, on behalf of this Government, that upon the restoration of the Union and the national authority, the war shall cease at once, all remaining questions to be left for

[27] Nicolay and Hay, *Abraham Lincoln*, IX, 215–217.

adjustment by peaceful modes." As we have seen, Raymond and his committee relinquished the idea of a peace offer. To visitors in the White House on August 19 and September 12, Lincoln iterated and reiterated that the sole object of the war was to preserve the Union. His remarks on the Negro mentioned only colored soldiers, who he insisted could not be sent back to slavery.

In his last Annual Message, in December, Lincoln stated "a single condition" of peace: "The war will cease on the part of the Government, whenever it shall have ceased on the part of those who began it." As for slavery, he said he would not retract the Emancipation Proclamation or return to slavery any person freed by it or by acts of Congress. Again, he seems to be saying he would not insist upon total emancipation as a condition of peace. His willingness to separate emancipation from peace carries over to the instructions he wrote in January, 1865, for Seward's conference with Confederate authorities: "No receding, by the Executive of the United States, on the Slavery question, from the position assumed thereon, in the late Annual Message to Congress, and in preceding documents."

Early in February, Lincoln joined Seward for the peace discussions at Hampton Roads. Vice-President Stephens asked what effect the Emancipation Proclamation would have on the slaves. Lincoln said that this was a judicial question. "His own opinion was, that as the Proclamation was a *war measure*, and would have effect only from its being an exercise of the war power, as soon as the war ceased, it would be inoperative for the future. It would be held to apply only to such slaves as had come under its operation while it was in active exercise."[28]

How are we to evaluate Lincoln's willingness to clasp slavery to the bosom of peace? One point to be discerned is that though he would have entertained a proposal of peace with slavery, and possibly have accepted it, he would not make the proposal. Initiative lay with the Confederacy, and, as Lincoln told the Wisconsin editor, no offer had been made; it was "an abstract question." A second point to be noted is that he differed with the War Democrats, who insisted upon reunion but who disfavored Federal interference with slavery. Running for reelection on the party plank that called

[28] Current, *Lincoln Nobody Knows*, ch. 10.

for the Thirteenth Amendment, he would use his victory, as we shall
see, as a lever to pry approval of the amendment from a reluctant
House of Representatives. Lincoln, in short, favored peace *and*
emancipation; the one inseparable, the other separable, from
reunion. But, though peace might come without emancipation, he
would exert his influence to secure emancipation through means
other than peace terms.

It was the eve of the Democratic national convention, postponed
in this "summer of discontent." On August 29, at the Wigwam in
Chicago—where Lincoln had been nominated in 1860—the convention opened. Its two great concerns were the drafting of a platform
and the selection of a candidate. Clement Vallandigham, leader of
the peace faction, secured a place on the platform committee, where
he exerted a pernicious influence. The platform was given priority
over nominations, and Vallandigham said he wrote the most
important plank—the notorious "war failure" resolution.

It declared that, "after four years of failure to restore the Union
by the experiment of war, ... immediate efforts be made for a
cessation of hostilities ... to the end that at the earliest practicable
moment peace may be restored on the basis of the Federal Union
of the States." What is proposed, astoundingly, was a proffer of
peace to the Confederacy without exacting any *quid pro quo*. First,
there would be an armistice, and *then*, after fighting had stopped,
there would be "an ultimate convention of the States, or other
peaceable means to restore peace." Nothing was said about stipula-
ting the Union as the basis for stopping the fighting. There could be,
in hard truth, only one outcome of this maneuver—the division of
the nation—for, as Lincoln later observed, "An armistice—a
cessation of hostilities—is the end of the struggle, and the insurgents
would be in peaceable possession of all that has been struggled for."

The issue of civil liberties formed a long plank that, in denunciatory
language, decried "usurpation," "subversion," "arbitrary" denial
of civil law, "suppression" of freedom, and disregard of state
rights. These abridgments, it said, erected a barrier to reunion, and
the aim of the Democratic party was "to preserve the Federal Union
and the rights of the States unimpaired." The phrase about the rights

of the states asserted, as closely as any words in the platform, the party's position on slavery, for the Democrats made no express reference to this issue, second in significance only to reunion. The contrast between the abolitionist plank of the Baltimore platform and the state rights stand of the Chicago platform looms as one of the most meaningful differences in their political creeds, though it is curiously often disregarded by historians. The election was bidding to become a referendum on peace and emancipation. Would the nation live? Would slavery die? These were the two grand questions being asked of the electorate.

Once it had adopted the platform, the convention took up nominating a candidate. The peace faction, which had prevailed in writing the platform, hoped to name Governor Horatio Seymour of New York, a prominent foe of the Lincoln administration. But Seymour withdrew his candidacy the day before the convention opened, clearing the way for George B. McClellan.[29] Beloved by the soldiers, whose vote in 1864 might swing the election, the Little Napoleon, former general-in-chief of the United States Army— young, vital, full of dash and charm—McClellan was a figure calculated to attract many voters.

> O General McClellan, he is the man:
> He licked the Rebels at Antietam.[30]

...so ran a popular song of the hour. His failures, on the Peninsula and after Antietam, could be attributed to Lincoln's interference; and his great services to the country in organizing a national army after First Bull Run and in repelling Lee in Maryland were worthy of grateful remembrance. His inexperience in political life could be brushed aside—as the voters had done in 1848 in making General Zachary Taylor president.

From 1861 on, General McClellan's career had had a political character. His conduct of the war had consistently been in opposition to the stand of the Radicals. McClellan's interest in the presidency probably dates from his endorsement of the Democratic candidate

[29] Zornow, *Party Divided*, ch. 10; McPherson, *Political History during the Rebellion*, pp. 417–421.

[30] Quoted in A. Nevins and M. H. Thomas (eds.), *The Diary of George Templeton Strong* (4 vols.; New York: The Macmillan Co., 1952), p. 475.

for governor of Pennsylvania, in October, 1863. In his letter of endorsement, McClellan gave his support to the candidate of the Peace Democrats, Judge Woodward, who had ruled that the draft act was unconstitutional. McClellan had also outlined the principles of conservative Democrats. He insisted that "the military power of the rebellion" must be destroyed, but he held there must be no interference with private rights, property, or slavery, nor should there be any punitive action against the vanquished. By his endorsement of a Peace Democrat, he had perhaps unwittingly encouraged the Copperheads to write the "war failure" plank into the platform of 1864; and, by stating a creed that promptly won the backing of conservative Democrats, he had entered the political arena.

The Peace Democrats at first appeared lukewarm about a warrior nominee, but Seymour's withdrawal and the peace plank made them less resistive to McClellan's nomination. At the close of the first ballot, none other than Vallandigham moved that McClellan's nomination be unanimous. In the choice of a vice-presidential nominee, the peace faction was conciliated by the naming of a representative of the defeatist movement in Ohio, George H. Pendleton, who had joined with Vallandigham during the secession crisis in contending the national government had no right to coerce a state.[31]

The "Chicago surrender" was the culmination of the desperation of August—the midsummer madness that had seized the North; in the last week of August, the prospect for the American Union could hardly have worn a darker visage. Lee held Grant immobilized before Petersburg. Hood seemed to have stalled Sherman before Atlanta. Lincoln and his party were bitterly divided over war and reconstruction aims. Peace sentiment surged across party lines, and wrote the most significant article in the creed of the "loyal" opposition. An interminable stalemate, a negotiated peace, division of the nation, a change of administration—all lurked as possible paths of the future. "Lincoln manifestly loses ground every day," George Templeton Strong noted. "The most zealous Republican partisans talk doubtfully of his chances."[32]

[31] Michie, *McClellan*, pp. 444–445; Zornow, *Party Divided*, pp. 123–140; Myers, *McClellan*, passim.
[32] Nevins and Thomas (eds.), *Strong Diary*, III, 478.

The Chicago compromise, which was perhaps the price of preventing a schism in the Democratic party, at first outraged and frightened loyal citizens in the North. Before McClellan had indicated whether he would accept nomination on a Copperhead platform, and before men could ponder the implications of the party compromise, the war took a decisive turn. The four-month campaign against Atlanta ended in the evacuation of the beleaguered city, on the night of September 1. The next day Union army soldiers, showing signs of strain and fatigue, took possession.

The capture of Atlanta was the turning point of the presidential election of 1864.[33] It followed closely upon Admiral David Farragut's victory at Mobile Bay, which closed the great Gulf port and tightened the blockade of the Confederacy. In a pithy phrase, Seward rejoiced that "Sherman and Farragut have knocked the bottom out of the Chicago nominations."[34] The fall of Atlanta influenced British and Confederate opinion. The London *Times* performed a *volte-face*, turning from a prediction that the Democrats were sure to win to a concession that Lincoln would be reelected.[35] The Richmond *Examiner* condemned President Davis for replacing Johnston with Hood. "The result is disaster at Atlanta in the very nick of time when a victory alone could save the party of Lincoln from irretrievable ruin.... It will obscure the prospect of peace, late so bright."[36]

"There is fatuity in nominating a general and a warrior in time of war on a peace platform," Gideon Welles had noted in his diary.[37] The extremists of the peace faction hoped McClellan—who six weeks before the Chicago convention, in a speech at West Point, had called for "vigor to complete the work thus begun"—was impaled on the horns of a dilemma. McClellan labored a week over his acceptance letter. The platform had put peace first, union second. "If these fools will ruin the country I won't help them," he had said

[33] *New York Times*, July 26, 1864; Zornow, *Party Divided*, p. 142.

[34] Quoted in Dudley, "Election of 1864," *MVHR*, XVIII, 515.

[35] E. D. Adams, *Great Britain and the American Civil War*, II, 234.

[36] Quoted in Lloyd Lewis, *Sherman, Fighting Prophet* (New York: Harcourt, Brace & World, 1932), p. 409.

[37] Welles, *Diary*, II, 136.

before his nomination. Now, however, in the first two drafts of his letter he accepted the peace faction's stand of an unconditional armistice, without assurance of reunion and with the risk that the war once halted could never be resumed. His first draft had also asserted that the Democrats "do not wage war for the abolition of slavery."

McClellan, having swung from one extreme to another, in his final draft accepted the nomination and declined the peace plank. More accurately, perhaps, he reversed the party stand and assigned reunion priority over peace. "The Union is the one condition of peace—we ask no more," he declared. Of the charge that the war was a failure, he avoided self-stultification by stating: "I could not look in the face of my gallant comrades of the army and navy . . . and tell them that their labor and the sacrifice of so many of our slain and wounded brethren had been in vain." He dropped the direct disavowal of abolitionism, but declared the sole object of the war ought to be preservation of the Union. "When any one State is willing to return to the Union, it should be received at once, with a full guarantee of all its constitutional rights." In sum, there would be no Federal effort at emancipation, no reconstruction of the Union, but mere restoration.[38]

McClellan's letter repudiated the naive assumption of the peace faction that an unconditional armistice might be followed by reunion through negotiation. He had attached the essential condition of reunion to the cessation of hostilities. W. F. Zornow, the historian of the election of 1864, has interpreted McClellan's move as one that placed him "on the same platform with Lincoln." A similar interpretation was advanced by James G. Randall, who, writing of the "false emphasis" upon the peace plank, asserted that McClellan as president would have prosecuted the war with the object of restoring the Union, and that "on the main issues of the day— secession, war, and reconstruction—Lincoln and McClellan were not opposites." Both political parties were Union parties, he observed,

[38] Charles R. Wilson, "McClellan's Changing Views on the Peace Plank of 1864," *AHR*, XXXVIII (April, 1933), 498–505; McPherson, *Political History during the Rebellion*, p. 421 for McClellan's letter of acceptance.

and if the Democrats had a peace faction, the Republicans had a radical faction.[39]

This blurring of issues and reducing of distinctions to mere partisan rivalry fails to satisfy us. It minimizes the seriousness of the Democratic split, the depth of the Northern peace sentiment, and the impact of a Lincoln victory on the Confederacy. The Democratic party, encumbered by a peace platform repudiated by its standard-bearer, presented two faces to voters; it was obviously more seriously split than the so-called "party divided" of Abraham Lincoln, which offered no contradiction in principle between its platform and its nominee. It has been a fault of some historians to make the friction between Lincoln and the Radicals more weighty than the division between the two major parties. The Union party, to be sure, had been beset by factionalism, but (as we shall see) there was a healing of party rifts before the election, while the schism of the Democrats could not be bridged, even with Vallandigham campaigning for McClellan.

One must also ponder the effect on morale, Northern and Southern, of a victory by a candidate backed by a faction substantial enough to write his party's peace platform. Thurlow Weed sapiently observed:

> The objections to the election of General McClellan are found less in himself than in his political surroundings. These are largely disloyal, and it requires a higher degree of moral courage than he possesses to shake them off. The influences which surround a President usually shape his action.[40]

We have noted already that Lincoln thought a victorious rival would have secured election on such ground that he could not save the Union after his inauguration. Henry Commager has remarked that though McClellan repudiated the peace plank, he "was willing to ride into the White House on a wave of pacifism."[41] A Lincoln victory in November would dishearten the South and would feed the

[39] Zornow, *Party Divided*, p. 140; Randall and Donald, *Civil War and Reconstruction*, p. 478.

[40] Thurlow Weed, *Life of Thurlow Weed* (2 vols.; Boston: Houghton Mifflin Co., 1884), II, 446.

[41] Morison and Commager, *Growth of the American Republic*, I, 778.

growing peace movement in the Confederacy. General Sherman waited until the South was dismayed by news of Lincoln's reelection before he started his march from Atlanta to the sea, writing Grant on November 6:

> Now Mr. Lincoln's election, which is assured, coupled with the conclusion just reached [that a march would demonstrate a military power Davis could not resist], makes a complete, logical whole.[42]

The assertion that after his letter of acceptance McClellan stood on the same platform with Lincoln evades the issue of slavery—a "main issue" not listed by Randall. McClellan and his party were opposed to abolition by the Federal government, and Lincoln and his party were committed to it. The victory of McClellan would have probably produced a backlash against emancipation. It would have meant a national apostasy, not only against the Emancipation Proclamation but also against state acquiescence in Federal emancipation measures as a condition of reconstruction—and against the proposed thirteenth amendment. Lincoln's plan of reconstruction required state acceptance of the acts of Congress and of executive proclamations having reference to slaves. McClellan would restore the states with a "full guarantee of all constitutional rights."

The Union party had incorporated an abolitionist plank in its platform, with Lincoln's urging; the Democratic party had re-affirmed its aim to keep the rights of the states unimpaired, with McClellan's endorsement in his letter of acceptance. As for the status of slavery before November, 1864, it may be recalled, the border states either opposed or wavered on emancipation, and the House of Representatives had failed to approve the proposed thirteenth amendment. The future of slavery in the United States was uncertain before the election, and would have been complicated by the defeat of Father Abraham. The interregnum between the election of McClellan and his inauguration could have seriously deflected the course of the war. Thus the election contest revolved around the issues of peace, the capacity of parties to attain their programs, sectional morale, and the future of slavery.

[42] Lewis, *Sherman*, p. 431.

In the aftermath of Atlanta there was a quickening of Republican fortunes. Early elections in the bellwether states, Vermont and Maine, gave victories to the Republicans. The Chicago platform sparked a reaction that drew Republicans closer together. Chase, Greeley, Sumner, Henry Winter Davis, and others who had wanted Lincoln to withdraw now swung their support to him. The projected convention to displace him was abandoned. In the third week of September, General Philip Sheridan defeated General Jubal A. Early in the Shenandoah Valley; a month later he began to devastate the valley as thoroughly as Sherman was doing in Georgia. The Radical candidate, Frémont, withdrew from the presidential race on September 22, and at the same time the *bête noire* of the radicals, Montgomery Blair, retired from the cabinet. Whether or not there was a bargain between Lincoln's managers and Frémont's friends, as has been charged, is less significant than the fact of emerging party harmony.[43]

Further elections took place in October, in pivotal Pennsylvania and Indiana, as well as in Ohio and Maryland. All four states gave their support to the Union party, with the important help of soldiers' votes in the first two states. Maryland voters, in addition, approved a new constitution that provided for the extinction of slavery.[44]

Most of the Northern states held their elections November 8. The day passed without violence or disorder—to the surprise of many observers, who had expected a different outcome of an atmosphere charged with excitement, bitterness, and suspicion of treason. With the South shorn off from the Union, the Democratic candidate carried only three states: New Jersey, Delaware, and Kentucky. Lincoln won 212 votes in the electoral college, against 21 for McClellan. His majority was in excess of 400,000 votes.

Looking at these figures, one might assume Lincoln had won a tidy victory; moreover, with 55 per cent of the popular vote he would no longer be a minority president. Closer analysis, however, reveals the

[43] Zornow, *Party Divided*, ch. 15; Charles R. Wilson, "New Light on the Lincoln-Blair-Frémont 'Bargain' of 1864," *AHR*, XLII (October, 1936), 71–78.

[44] McPherson, *Political History during the Rebellion*, p. 424.

Democrats did surprisingly well, despite the handicaps of being termed Copperheads, of military successes, of administrative use of martial law, and of soldier votes. In New York, with 33 electoral votes, Lincoln won a majority of only 6,749 out of 730,723 votes; in Pennsylvania, with 26 electoral votes, he won a majority of 18,849 out of 573,375 votes. In Connecticut and New Hampshire his margins were also narrow; but he enjoyed the support of states he had helped create: West Virginia and Nevada (the latter was admitted to the Union eight days before the election). Lincoln polled fewer votes than in 1860 in four states, and a smaller percentage than in 1860 in nine states (including the four). A change of a few thousand votes in key states would have given the victory to McClellan;[45] a different pattern of voting could have turned the presidency over in the midst of war to a man innocent of political experience.

It is worth trying to imagine what kind of a president McClellan would have made. His admirers point to his attractive personal manner, his capacity to capture the popular imagination, and his patriotism and energy. Given the office of commander-in-chief, they hold, he would have prosecuted the war until Union had been restored. As president during reconstruction, it could be supposed he would have pursued a clement policy toward the South, respectful of state rights and Southern sensibilities about Negroes. He would have opposed civil rights for Negroes, if they had been freed, and abridgment of civil rights of white men.

On the debit side, one can point to his inexperience (he had never held civil office), his naivete (revealed in his letters to his wife), his indecision if not vacillation (shown in the Peninsula campaign and in drafting his letter accepting the presidential nomination), his tendency to blame his enemies for his shortcomings and to excuse himself (found in his correspondence with the war department). In view of his military record, it is open to question whether he would have pushed the war effort more ardently as president than he had as general—and in this connection it is to be noted he disfavored the draft.

A clement policy of reconstruction would have encountered radical opposition perhaps even more bitter than President Andrew

[45] Zornow, *Party Divided*, ch. 16; McPherson, *op. cit.*, p. 623.

Johnson, elected on the Union ticket, met. And to have delayed emancipation, as well as the rapidly emerging issue of civil rights for Negroes, might have embroiled the nation in another civil war—that knew no North or South, and as sanguinary and destructive as the conflict of 1861–65. Certainly the nation would not have had the impulse we know Lincoln's reelection gave to Union arms and emancipation.

Moreover, the election was meaningful for the future of democracy and for reconstruction. "I think our last election fairly legitimizes democracy for the first time," James Russell Lowell wrote the American minister in Vienna, John L. Motley. "It was really a nobler thing than you can readily conceive so far away, for the opposition had appealed to every base element in human nature, and cunningly appealed too."[46]

"The election having passed off quietly, no bloodshed or riot throughout the land, is a victory worth more to the country than a battle won. Rebeldom and Europe will so construe it," declared Grant.[47] The general election gave the Union party a gain of thirty-seven seats in the House of Representatives—fateful for the Thirty-ninth Congress, which was to shape reconstruction of the nation. United States senators were then elected by state legislatures, and the Union party won control in most of the states.

The canvass in Kentucky—the state that had walked the tightrope of neutrality in the summer of 1861—holds special interest. During most of the war Kentuckians formed but one party: Democrats, divided into Union and peace factions. The name Republican was a stigma until 1864. In the spring of that year the party split over appointing delegates to the national convention in Chicago, which, when it finally met, admitted all the delegates, assigning a half vote to each. Supporters of the Lincoln administration had meanwhile cried that the peace faction had stolen the party machinery and had sent delegates, under the leadership of Robert J. Breckinridge, to the Union convention in Baltimore. "This marked the real beginning of the Republican party in Kentucky." Breckinridge had served as

[46] Quoted in Hosmer, *Outcome of the Civil War*, p. 268.
[47] *OR*, Ser. I, XLII, part 3, 581.

temporary chairman of the Republican convention in 1860; he occupied the same position for the Union convention in 1864.

Guerrilla bands, largely made up of disorganized soldiers and deserters from Confederate service, roamed about Kentucky in the summer of 1864. On July 5 Lincoln suspended the privilege of the writ of *habeas corpus*. His action, matched by suspensions in other border slave states, incurred the ire of the Democratic party, which devoted a plank of its Chicago platform to denunciation of military interference in elections. The suspension deepened other vexations nursed by Kentuckians against the administration, including restrictions of their trade with the Confederacy. Early in September, Governor T. E. Bramlette, leader of the Peace Democrats, wrote Lincoln to decry extreme military measures and to assert flatly that he was opposed "to your election, and [I] regard a change of policy as essential to the salvation of our country." In 1864, as in 1860, Kentucky cast its ballot against its native son; the vote was 64,301 for McClellan and 27,786 for Lincoln. Arbitrary government and abolition alienated men in the Bluegrass State; to the end of the war the spirit of Crittenden—"the Union as it was"—prevailed.[48]

The election had discredited the peace movement and peace sentiment. On the whole, this was a positive benefit in time of war; but the denigration of the Democrats went to extremes—branding the whole party with opprobrium: the name Copperhead, and the taint of disloyalty. Such extremism was of course unjust to the great number of loyal Democrats; and the injustice, founded on charges of war responsibility and pacifism, persisted long after the war.

The election vastly enhanced the historical reputation of Abraham Lincoln. It seems most doubtful that American historians, who twice have rated him in a poll as the nation's greatest president, would have accorded him that honor had he been defeated for a second term. Much of the glamor would have been rubbed off by an unfavorable vote in 1864. Influenced by the voters' verdict, historians would have probed for the reasons why Lincoln failed to be elected. Nothing

[48] W. E. Connelley and E. M. Coulter (eds.), *History of Kentucky*, II, 896–898.

succeeds like success; and Lincoln's reelection helped him on his climb up Mount Olympus.

To Lincoln, the election demonstrated the vitality of free government. "It has long been a grave question whether any government, not *too* strong for the liberties of its people, can be strong *enough* to maintain its own existence, in great emergencies," he told a crowd on the White House lawn just after the election. The American republic had passed a severe test. "Until now it has not been known to the world ... that a people's government can sustain a national election, in the midst of a great civil war."[49]

In his annual message to Congress—his last State of the Union message—Lincoln dwelt upon the significance of the election. He reminded Congress that the present House of Representatives had failed to pass the proposed amendment abolishing slavery. The intervening election, he said, "is the voice of the people now, for the first time, heard upon the question." He recommended that this Congress reconsider and pass the amendment, for it if did not, the new one would. As he had done in issuing the Emancipation Proclamation, he continued to maintain that the abolition of slavery would serve the end of perpetuating the Union. He noted the progress of freedom in reconstructed Arkansas and Louisiana, and in the border states—movements having the effect "of moulding society for durability in the Union."

Besides expressing the will of the majority on the abolition of slavery, the election expressed a second grand purpose—"to maintain the integrity of the Union." No candidate for office, high or low, Lincoln said, sought votes on the basis of disunion, and the election showed the people and the world a firmness and unanimity of purpose.

The Chief Executive discerned a third heartening fact in the election, the increase in the number of voters: 145,551 more than in 1860. Notwithstanding wartime losses, the growing Union had more men after three years of war than when the war began. With an abundance of human and material resources, the government must continue in its unchanged public purpose of reestablishing the national authority. No negotiation with the Confederate leader would be fruitful, for he insisted upon independence, Lincoln

[49] Basler (ed.), *Collected Works*, VIII, 149–152.

declared; but Lincoln used his message to make an indirect appeal to the Southern people to lay down their arms and submit to national authority.[50]

The House of Representatives was loath to heed Lincoln's urging to approve the thirteenth amendment. Though slavery may appear to us as an anachronism, doomed by the march of events, it was protected against immediate destruction by several barricades. Partisan politics was one obstacle to passage of the amendment. What was involved was not merely the Democratic party's past attitude toward slavery and the South but also its fear that in the future the Republican party might indefinitely control the government through the Negro. A second obstacle was the fact that emancipation seemed a stumbling block to peace. Why prolong the war by this bitterly divisive measure?

Beyond questions of politics and peace lay human prejudice. The question of race is ever one that excites passions, making rational decisions difficult. Slavery had served historically as a means of race adjustment. What would happen to the white race if the Negro were freed? Apart from fears of miscegenation, there were real questions of civil rights, employment, education, and of safeguarding white and Negro interests that mere emancipation did not resolve. Finally, there were the Constitutional scruples of those, such as George H. Pendleton, who argued that the power to amend did not give the "power to revolutionize."

On January 6, 1865, Representative James M. Ashley called up his resolution to amend the Constitution. The opposition pounced upon it, Pendleton leading the attack. It was plain the resolution lacked the necessary votes, and its proponents decided to postpone balloting. Ashley, Lincoln, and Seward exerted extraordinary pressures upon the House in order to induce Democrats either to vote for the resolution or be absent when the vote was taken. Ashley appears to have made promises: to one Democratic member, an office for his brother; to another, favorable consideration for his contested seat in the next Congress; and to a third—in exchange for his absence—a bill the member opposed either would not be reported or not

[50] *Idem*, 149–152.

reported soon. Lincoln met with border-state representatives, let it be known he would call a special session if the resolution failed, and kept an experienced hand on the patronage.[51]

Seward supervised a lobby (whose existence has only recently been discovered), which focused its attention upon New York Democrats. It held out the prospect of swift and generous reconstruction of the nation on the basis of emancipation completed. It played "a critically important role" in securing passage of the resolution, declare La Wanda and John Cox, discoverers of the lobby.

On January 31, friends of the resolution brought it to a vote. To the last, no one knew whether enough Democrats would come over to the Republicans, would hold firm, or would absent themselves to make possible the necessary two-thirds majority. In the afternoon, the time the balloting was scheduled, persons favoring the amendment thronged the House galleries, their faces anxious and suspenseful. Every Republican member was present on the floor as Ashley called for the main question. A quiet solemnity overhung the roll-call vote, until at last it was clear the measure had passed. Members jumped to their feet, cheered, clapped, and embraced one another. The galleries seethed with excitement, and, after several minutes of enthusiastic demonstration, the House adjourned "in honor of this immortal and sublime event."[52]

If we analyze the balloting we can see how critical the decision was. By a thin margin of only three votes was the requisite majority secured: 119 to 56. Sixteen Democrats had voted for the resolution, eight had absented themselves; the two-thirds majority in fact represented less than two-thirds of the whole membership. Only two of the sixteen Democratic votes had come from members who had been reelected to the next Congress; the others were lame ducks, with little to lose. Six of the Democratic votes had been cast by New Yorkers, the target of the Seward lobby.[53]

[51] Randall and Donald, *Civil War and Reconstruction*, p. 396; McPherson, *Political History during the Rebellion*, p. 590.

[52] La Wanda Cox and John H. Cox, *Politics, Principle, and Prejudice, 1865–66* (New York: Free Press of Glencoe, 1963), p. 24; White, *Trumbull*, p. 228.

[53] Cox and Cox, *op. cit.*, p. 25.

The amendment now went before the states for ratification. All of the loyal states, except Kentucky and Delaware, approved it; all of the seceded states approved it—in a paradoxical exercise of state authority—as a requirement for the restoration of state authority. In December, 1865, the secretary of state proclaimed the end of slavery in the United States of America.

What difference did it make that the outgoing Thirty-eighth Congress approved the amendment? Would not its successor, the Thirty-ninth, have approved it? Granted that it would, nonetheless the future of political reconstruction would have been altered. The fact that the amendment had been given congressional sanction loomed prominently in the working out of events. If Lincoln had called the Congress into special session, and it had acted and adjourned before his death, the outcome would have been the same. But if the legislature had been in session at the time of the assassination, or after, President Johnson would have had to reckon with it in his reconstruction measures. As it was, he made ratification a part of his policy and went forward with executive reconstruction, without Congress, until December. If there had been no special session of Congress, the seceded states could not have been committed to ratification as a stipulation of presidential restoration. Finally, the Seward lobby had done its work in an atmosphere that suggested clemency toward the South and the formation of a conservative party made up of moderate Democrats and Republicans, excluding the radicals. House approval of the amendment—before the South surrendered and before Johnson took office—conditioned the future of reconstruction politics. It is the Coxes' judgment that "postponement would have critically altered the course of American post-Civil War history."[54]

The reelection of Lincoln, renewing the vitality of the American political system, discrediting defeatism, and giving impetus to emancipation, was the last turning point of the American Civil War. This view, we have noted, runs contrary to respected historical interpretation. James G. Randall has argued that Lincoln and McClellan were not opposites, the differences being more "a matter

[54] *Idem*, p. 30.

of shading than of glaring contrast." His account of "Peace Movements and the Election of 1864" curiously stresses the peace movement in the Union party and minimizes it in the Democratic party, although the latter incorporated a peace plank in its platform and nominated a Copperhead for the vice-presidency. The peace plank, Randall rightly contends, was distorted in significance by partisan propagandists, but he judged emphasis upon it is "false" after McClellan repudiated it.[55] Randall did not consider the psychological effects of a McClellan victory on Northern peace-lovers and Southern resisters. Nor did he examine the issue of emancipation, which was at stake in the election.

Substantially similar views appear in the history of the election written by W. F. Zornow. His book, *Lincoln and the Party Divided*, stressed the divisions in the Union party and not among Democrats, which was at least as badly riven as the party of Lincoln. He, too, scanted the emancipation issue, and ignored the impact of a defeat for Lincoln upon public and soldier support of the war. He separated the presidential and congressional results—as if the voters might have broken time-honored habit and split their tickets— and stressed the election of a Congress that he mistakenly assigned to radical control immediately after 1864—about two years prematurely.[56]

Frank Klement, in his *The Copperheads in the Middle West*, endeavored to defend the Democrats of the Upper Mississippi Valley against the charges of irrationality, disloyalty, and treason; yet he emphasized the retrogressive nature of their Jeffersonian outlook, their propensity in wartime to exalt partisanship over the nation's needs, and their failure to produce a statesman of the stature of Stephen A. Douglas. Moreover, he showed that, when in control of the Indiana and Illinois legislatures, the Copperheads—not without provocation from Republican governors—obstructed war measures and usurped powers that Constitutionally belonged to the state executives. We can agree that the Democrats, as a party, were not disloyal or treasonable, but we are not persuaded they had the vision, the philosophy, or the statesmanship that would have

---

[55] Randall and Donald, *Civil War and Reconstruction*, ch. 27.
[56] Zornow, *Party Divided*, especially pp. 218–221.

completed the war in a national victory, which would at the same time have assured the end of human bondage.

Though not an overt campaign issue, the economic program of the Union party was at stake. During the war, a new blueprint for the American economy had been translated into fact. Protective tariffs, paper money, national banks, subsidies for railroads and colleges, and homesteads for farmers characterized a Northern system that Southern agrarians historically had opposed. The Copperheads in the Middle West, in particular, were a nostalgic, backward-looking group, faithful to a Jeffersonian order of state rights and agrarianism. Throughout the war they opposed strong central government and the ascendancy of industry over agriculture, taking the railroads as the special target of their protest. A Democratic victory in 1864 would probably have led to dismantling the new political edifice that had been built for industrial capitalism.[57]

The war did not endure many months after the election. Sherman's army, imbued with its commander's conviction that war is cruelty unrefined, had disemboweled Georgia before Christmas Day, and Thomas had smashed Hood's forces at Nashville. Lee's attenuated line below Richmond was broken at Five Forks on April 1; and the Confederate retreat began that ended eight days later at Appomattox. Before the end of the month, General Joseph Johnston surrendered to Sherman near Durham Station, North Carolina. The fate of the Confederacy was sealed. Disunion and slavery were doomed. The American nation, after four years of travail, was given a new birth of freedom.

American nationality had withstood the atomizing doctrines of state sovereignty and secession. Unimpaired, the power of the Republic abided, ready to be exerted in the affairs of the western hemisphere, and in the fullness of time in the world at large.

[57] Klement, *Copperheads*, especially pp. 266–267.

Afterword

The Civil War was a major turning point in United States history. From the beginning of the Republic to the end of isolation, with the Second World War, there is no higher watershed than the decision of Appomattox. The vindication of American nationality was meaningful, primarily for political democracy and human equality, but its effects stretched out in many other directions.

The price of victory, human and material, was vast. The war's imprint on the American economy deeply stamped its future. The American Constitution was substantially revised by amendment and interpretation. The structure of American political parties today, particularly in the South, is a legacy of the war; and the South retains a separate identity largely because of the war. American literature is richer, the study of military history profounder, the pantheon of heroes larger, the American presidency stronger as a result of the conflict.

What the success of the American experiment denoted for democracy, at home and abroad, was best voiced by Lincoln at Gettysburg when he dedicated his generation to the resolution "that this nation, under God, shall have a new birth of freedom— and that government of the people, by the people, for the people, shall not perish from the earth." The vindication of majority rule gave a new dimension to the meaning of the word democracy.

European liberals hailed the triumph of democratic principles in the United States. English workingmen, struggling for the franchise, turned the victory to their advantage. "Our opponents told us that Republicanism was on its trial," declared an English liberal newspaper in April, 1865. "They may rely upon it that a vast impetus has been given to Republican sentiments in England, and that they will have to reckon with it before long." The Reform Bill of 1867 was the fruition of a British movement that had been quickened by American developments.

The playwright Ibsen saw in the war's outcome a challenge to conservative Europe:

> Thou Europe old, with order and law,
>   With maxims that never fail,
> With an unstained name, without blemish or flaw,
> With a virtue that keeps all meanness in awe,
>   Why grew'st thou so strangely pale?

And the Italian patriot and republican, Mazzini, paid homage to America: "You have done more for us in four years than fifty years of teaching, preaching, and writing from all your European brothers have been able to do."

In international affairs, the American democracy—reunited—was able at once to confront the French threat in Mexico to the Monroe Doctrine by sending about 50,000 troops to the Texas border. Under a variety of pressures, among them American military might, Napoleon III ultimately withdrew, removing the threefold threat to our national security and prestige of French influence in Mexico, of a Mexican monarchy, and of possible expansion in the New World. A century of Anglo-American hostility passed into eclipse with the settlement of the *Alabama* claims in 1872, and a new century of Anglo-American friendship dawned; today the Anglo-American *entente* is the firmest bastion of American foreign policy. The might of the United States in two world wars, in partnership with Britain, has perpetuated freedom in the Western world. A United States divided at the Potomac would doubtless have been less equal to the international challenges of the twentieth century.

Second in impressiveness only to the preserving of the American polity and the principles it lived by was the freeing of four million human beings by the brute force of war. By 1861, slavery was an anachronism in the Western world—its existence in the United States had violated the whole tenor of the American experiment. Not only had liberty and equality been denied the blacks, but slavery had fettered the freedom of whites, North and South. The war inadvertently broke a log jam, and a movement long-delayed gave freedom to the millions. Few events in nineteenth-century American history can rival in importance the abolition of human bondage. However, we must note, the violence of the context of emancipation and the abruptness of the act failed to secure civil liberties and equality to the freedmen. Nonetheless, the doctrine of equality passed beyond old bounds of American democratic thought during the Civil War.

The cost in human lives exceeded that of any other American war. National unity was purchased at a price of 617,000 lives—a figure that overtowers the 112,000 American fatalities of World War I and the 322,000 of World War II. The incidence of 258,000 fatalities among the 5,500,000 people of the South bore heavily upon this regions that lost so great a proportion of young men—the flower of the Confederacy, the seedcorn of its future.

The material cost to the nation was five billion dollars, to the South inestimable. Southern destitution after the war is embedded in Southern tradition. Long swaths of land lay devastated by marching and countermarching armies. Houses, buildings, fences, and railways had been torn down, or stood neglected. Fortunes had been obliterated, social classes dissolved, political leaders proscribed, the gentry disfranchised.

All this is true, or nearly enough true, not to warrant a quibble. But what is arresting is the South's loss of economic eminence. If cotton had been king before the war, steel, oil, wheat, and meat wielded the scepter in the new generation. Though one can demonstrate the recovery and growth of the cotton growing and cotton spinning South in the decades immediately after Appomattox, the general picture is one of regional retardation in a nation being transformed by industrialization. Notwithstanding the presence of abundant resources, Southerners long continued to subsist on an inadequate living standard, as the Federal government's *Report on Economic Conditions of the South* pointed out in 1938. In that year President Franklin D. Roosevelt declared: "It is my conviction that the South presents right now the nation's No. 1 economic problem." And, for a generation or more after the war, the whole nation bore an onerous burden of taxes to redeem war bonds and to rescue veterans from penury and defecting from the Republican party.

The war transformed American economic institutions. The United States maintained its policy of protectionism for two generations;

not until 1913 did the nation scale down its tariff wall to a moderate height. The printing of greenbacks to finance the war nurtured debtors' dreams of easy escape from creditors throughout the panics and depressions of succeeding epochs. The nation reorganized its banking institutions during the war by establishing a system of national banks, creating a new kind of national money, and terminating the chaotic issue of notes by state banks. The Federal government used the public domain to promote homesteading, transcontinental railroads, and agricultural and mechanical colleges. Contrary to what is usually said, the war may well have retarded industrialization instead of accelerated it. Analysis of statistical series indicates economic growth, which had been advancing very rapidly before the war, sank to a low level in the sixties.

As a result of the war the American Constitution was amended, both in body and spirit. Three amendments ended slavery, extended citizenship to Negroes, and banned denial of the right to vote on account of race, color, or previous condition of servitude. Collectively, the amendments disinherited the states of traditional rights. The victory of American nationalism won its classic formulation in 1869 in the decision of *Texas* v. *White*, when the Supreme Court repudiated the secession theory and ruled that "the Constitution... looks to an indestructible Union, composed of indestructible States."

In astounding acts of judicial legerdemain, the Court subsequently withdrew privileges of the Fourteenth Amendment from Negroes, conferred them on corporations, denied them to labor unions, and guaranteed the *Federal* Bill of Rights against *state* encroachment. Only in recent years has the Court sought to restore the amendment to its pristine meaning. Grave as were the abuses made by a false construction of the Fourteenth Amendment, the nation had made a Constitutional commitment to human equality, which is tortuously being realized in the second half of the twentieth century.

In the realm of party politics, the Civil War was a vital issue through the period of Republican ascendancy, into the time of William McKinley—the last Civil War veteran to serve as president. The Democratic party wore the taint of Copperheadism, the Republican party brandished the bloody shirt, and the GAR gave its votes for Republicans and pensions; in the campaign of 1884 a partisan smeared the Democrats as the party of "Rum, Romanism, and Rebellion." The "Confederacy" maintained itself as the "Solid South"; it disenfranchised the Negro, entrenched itself on congressional committees through the seniority system, and continued for a century after the cessation of hostilities, to keep a watch on the Potomac.

Defeated, humiliated, impoverished, and reduced in political influence, the South suffered a psychic scar—perhaps the most intangible but most enduring outcome of the war for white Southerners. If Southern nationalism was defeated at Appomattox, it rose again from the ashes of Reconstruction. Ambivalent between the Old and the New South, the section adjusted its labor system to a new form of peonage in share-cropping and mill towns, pursued Northern industry but eschewed trade unionism, fought in American wars but continued to sing "Dixie," accepted Federal funds but preached state rights, claimed power in the councils of the Democratic party but organized a Dixiecrat revolt. Whatever their vagaries of behavior, Southerners remained keenly conscious of themselves as Southerners, sensitive to external criticism, and unable to laugh at themselves.

Southern agrarians defiantly offered their manifesto in the book, *I'll Take My Stand* in 1930. Margaret Mitchell's *Gone with the Wind* resoundingly resurrected, in 1936, a romantic past for delighted Southerners. The so-called Southern Renaissance of literature, absorbed in Southern themes, was a latter-day witness of the stamp made by the Civil War upon *belles-lettres* and upon historical writing. In earlier generations, Mary Johnston and Ellen Glasgow had drawn inspiration from the war and its aftermath.

The Civil War has been an endless battlefield for students of military history. Its strategy and tactics formed textbook lessons at West Point, Annapolis, and Sandhurst. The generalship of Lee, Jackson, Grant, Sherman, and others influenced later generations of soldiers. The military use of railroads, entrenchments, the conception of total war, the method of conscription—all provided matter for deliberation in Western nations. The United States drew bountifully on its Civil War experience in organizing for the First World War.

A war of sabres and ironclad ships, the Civil War was the last of the romantic and the first of the modern wars.

The Civil War broadened the American presidency. The office had been limited by the Constitution and tradition before Lincoln's accession to it. Only one president, Andrew Jackson, had construed his powers in a nationalistic and popular sense; and he had provoked an anti-executive opposition that took the name Whig party, in remembrance of opponents of Stuart tyranny. Lincoln discovered a new source of national authority: the war power claimed by the executive, and he inaugurated war, proclaimed a blockade, raised an army, suspended the writ of *habeas corpus*, and spent Federal funds—all without authorization by Congress. His issuance of the Emancipation Proclamation flaunted the presidential prerogative in a manner without parallel in American history, invading the rights of the states, and confiscating billions of dollars. True, presidential power subsequently deteriorated under the congressional assault on Andrew Johnson and his successors, but Lincoln's legacy to Theodore Roosevelt, Woodrow Wilson, Franklin Roosevelt, and others was a vigorous executive, identified with the popular interest.

The war lengthened the gallery of national heroes. Lincoln became, in popular esteem, one of the greatest American presidents. The Confederate general, Robert E. Lee, was transfigured into a national hero, second only to George Washington in perfection of character. U. S. Grant was celebrated as the warrior who saved the Union, and was twice rewarded with the presidency. The dour and indomitable Stonewall Jackson perhaps stands unrivaled for the brilliance of his tactics. A host of lesser men in blue and gray—among them Sherman, Thomas, Stuart, Forrest—occupy conspicuous pedestals.

The Civil War was America's tragedy. It was a tragic failure of the democratic process, of national statesmanship, of Constitutional government. Compromise and reason receded in the face of rigidity and passion. Fellow citizens went to war and killed one another by the hundreds of thousands. Property was expropriated by the hundreds of millions. The black race was freed, exalted, and then abandoned.

Yet the Civil War, once thrust upon the Republic, was a mitigated tragedy. It perpetuated the American nation, the democratic experiment, and Constitutional government. It extinguished human slavery in the United States of America. Nationalism, democracy, and constitutionalism preserved—and freedom gained—are no mean heritage of a war.

In 1865 the United States turned away from state sovereignty, minority rule, secessionism, and slavery. It faced the future.

Bibliography

PRIMARY SOURCES

BASLER, ROY P., *et al.* (eds.). *The Collected Works of Abraham Lincoln.* 9 vols.; New Brunswick, N.J.: Rutgers University Press, 1953–55.

BEALE, HOWARD K. (ed.). "The Diary of Edward Bates, 1859–1866," *Annual Report of the American Historical Association, 1930.* Washington: Government Printing Office, 1933, Vol. IV.

BLAINE, JAMES G. *Twenty Years of Congress: From Lincoln to Garfield. With a Review of the Events which Led to the Political Revolution of 1800.* 2 vols.; Norwich, Conn.: Henry Hill Publishing Co., 1884–86.

CARPENTER, F. B. *Six Months at the White House with Abraham Lincoln.* New York: Hurd & Houghton, 1866.

COMMAGER, HENRY S. (ed.). *Documents of American History.* 2 vols., 7th ed.; New York: Appleton-Century-Crofts, 1963.

DAVIS, JEFFERSON. *The Rise and Fall of the Confederate Government.* 2 vols.; London: Longmans, Green & Co., 1881.

DONALD, DAVID (ed.). *Inside Lincoln's Cabinet: the Civil War Diaries of Salmon P. Chase.* New York: Longmans, Green & Co., 1954.

GLADSTONE, WILLIAM E. *Papers.* British Museum.

GRANT, U. S. *Personal Memoirs of U. S. Grant.* 2 vols.; New York: Charles L. Webster & Co., 1885.

GUEDELLA, PHILIP. *Gladstone and Palmerston.* New York: Harper & Brothers, 1928.

HASKELL, FRANK A. *The Battle of Gettysburg.* Boston: Houghton Mifflin Co., 1960.

JOHNSON, ROBERT U., and BUEL, CLARENCE C. (eds.). *Battles and Leaders of the Civil War.* 4 vols.; New York: Thomas Yoseloff, Inc., 1956.

JOHNSTON, JOSEPH E. *Narrative of Military Operations, Directed during the late War between the States.* New York: D. Appleton & Co., 1874.

KIRWAN, ALBERT (ed.). *The Confederacy.* Cleveland: World Publishing Co., 1959.

LINCOLN, ABRAHAM. Robert Todd Lincoln Collection of the "Abraham Lincoln Papers." New York: Columbia University Library (microfilm).

LONGSTREET, JAMES. *From Manassas to Appomattox.* Philadelphia: J. B. Lippincott Co., 1896.

MOORE, FRANK (ed.). *The Rebellion Record: A Diary of American Events.* . . . 11 vols.; New York: G. P. Putnam, 1861–64.

MORGAN, EDWIN D. *Papers*. Albany: New York State Library.

NEVINS, ALLAN, and THOMAS, M. H. (eds.). *The Diary of George Templeton Strong*. 4 vols.; New York: The Macmillan Co., 1952.

New York Times, 1861 to 1865.

ROWLAND, DUNBAR (ed.). *Jefferson Davis, Constitutionalist*. 10 vols.; Jackson, Miss.: Mississippi Department of Archives and History, 1923.

RUSSELL, JOHN. *Papers*. London: Public Record Office.

U.S. Congress. *Congressional Globe*. Washington: F. & J. Rives and George A. Bailey, 1861 to 1865.

War of the Rebellion: . . . Official Records of the Union and Confederate Armies. 128 vols.; Washington: Government Printing Office, 1880–1901.

WELLES, GIDEON. *Diary of Gideon Welles*. 3 vols.; Boston: Houghton Mifflin Co., 1911.

SECONDARY WORKS

BOOKS

ADAMS, EPHRAIM D. *Great Britain and the American Civil War*. 2 vols. in one. New York: Russell & Russell, n.d.

The American Annual Cyclopaedia and Register of Important Events of the Year 1861 [1862, etc.]. New York: D. Appleton, 1866—.

ASHLEY, EVELYN. *The Life and Correspondence of Henry John Temple, Viscount Palmerston*. 2 vols.; London: Richard Bentley & Son, 1879.

BAILEY, THOMAS A. *A Diplomatic History of the American People*. New York: Appleton-Century-Crofts, 1964.

CHANNING, EDWARD. *A History of the United States*. 6 vols.; New York: The Macmillan Co., 1926–27.

CLEAVES, FREEMAN. *Meade of Gettysburg*. Norman: University of Oklahoma Press, 1960.

COLLINS, LEWIS, and COLLINS, RICHARD H. *History of Kentucky*. . . . 2 vols.; Covington, Ky.: Collins & Co., 1882.

COULTER, E. MERTON. *The Civil War and Readjustment in Kentucky*. Chapel Hill: University of North Carolina Press, 1926.

COX, LA WANDA, and COX, JOHN. *Politics, Principle, and Prejudice, 1865–66*. New York: Free Press of Glencoe, 1963.

CURRENT, RICHARD N. *The Lincoln Nobody Knows*. New York: Hill & Wang, 1958.

DODD, WILLIAM E. *Jefferson Davis*. Philadelphia: G. W. Jacobs & Co., 1907.

DONALD, DAVID. *Lincoln Reconsidered*. New York: Alfred A. Knopf, Inc., 1961.

DOWDEY, CLIFFORD. *Death of a Nation*. New York: Alfred A. Knopf, Inc., 1958.

DUBERMAN, MARTIN B. *Charles Francis Adams, 1807–1886*. Boston: Houghton Mifflin Co., 1961.

ECKENRODE, H. J., and CONRAD, BRYAN. *George B. McClellan: The Man Who Saved the Union*. Chapel Hill: University of North Carolina Press, 1941.

ELLIOTT, CHARLES W. *Winfield Scott, The Soldier and the Man.* New York: The Macmillan Company, 1937.

FISH, CARL R. "The Decision of the Ohio Valley," *Annual Report of the American Historical Association for 1910.* Washington: The Smithsonian Institution, 1912, pp. 153–164.

FRANKLIN, JOHN HOPE. *The Emancipation Proclamation.* New York: Random House–Alfred A. Knopf, 1963.

FREEMAN, DOUGLAS S. *R. E. Lee.* 4 vols.; New York: Charles Scribner's Sons, 1940.

GRAEBNER, NORMAN A. (ed.). *The Enduring Lincoln.* Urbana: University of Illinois Press, 1959.

GRAY, WOOD. *The Hidden Civil War.* New York: Viking Press, 1964.

HANDLIN, OSCAR. *Chance or Destiny; Turning Points in American History.* Boston: Little, Brown & Co., 1955.

HARRIS, THOMAS L. *The Trent Affair, including a review of English and American relations at the beginning of the Civil War.* Indianapolis and Kansas City: Bowen-Merrill Co., 1896.

HASSLER, WARREN W. *General George B. McClellan, Shield of the Union.* Baton Rouge: Louisiana State University Press, 1957.

HENDERSON, G. F. R. *Stonewall Jackson and the American Civil War.* 2 vols. in one; New York: Longmans, Green & Co., 1961.

HESSELTINE, WILLIAM B. *Lincoln and the War Governors.* New York: Alfred A. Knopf, Inc., 1948.

HOSMER, JAMES K. *The Appeal to Arms.* New York: Harper & Brothers, 1907.

JONES, W. D. *The Confederate Rams at Birkenhead.* Tuscaloosa, Ala.: Confederate Publishing Company, 1961.

JOHNSON, ALLEN, and MALONE, DUMAS. *Dictionary of American Biography.* 22 vols. and supplements. New York: Charles Scribner's Sons, 1928–36.

JOHNSTON, R. M. *Bull Run: Its Strategy and Tactics.* Boston and New York: Houghton Mifflin Co., 1913.

KIRKLAND, E. C. *The Peacemakers of 1864.* New York: The Macmillan Co., 1927.

KIRWAN, ALBERT D. *John J. Crittenden, The Struggle for the Union.* Lexington: University of Kentucky Press, 1962.

KLEMENT, FRANK. *The Copperheads in the Middle West.* Chicago: University of Chicago Press, 1960.

LEWIS, LLOYD. *Sherman, Fighting Prophet.* New York: Harcourt, Brace & Co., 1932.

LILLIBRIDGE, G. D. *Beacon of Freedom.* Philadelphia: University of Pennsylvania Press, 1955.

LIVERMORE, THOMAS L. *Numbers and Losses in the Civil War in America, 1861–1865.* 2d ed.; Boston and New York: Houghton Mifflin Co., 1901.

MCELROY, ROBERT M. *Kentucky in the Nation's History.* New York: Moffat, Yard & Co., 1909.

MCPHERSON, EDWARD. *Political History of the United States during the Rebellion.* Washington: Philip & Solomons, 1865.

MCPHERSON, EDWARD. *Handbook of Politics for 1868*. Washington: Philip & Solomons, 1868.

MARTIN, THEODORE. *The Life of His Royal Highness, the Prince Consort*. 5 vols.; London: Smith, Elder & Co., 1875–80.

MICHIE, PETER S. *General McClellan*. New York: D. Appleton & Co., 1901.

MIERS, EARL SCHENCK. *The Web of Victory: Grant at Vicksburg*. New York: Alfred A. Knopf, Inc., 1955.

MONAGHAN, JAY. *Diplomat in Carpet Slippers*. Indianapolis: Bobbs-Merrill, 1945.

MOORE, JOHN BASSETT. *The Principles of American Diplomacy*. New York and London: Harper & Brothers, 1918.

MORISON, S. E., and COMMAGER, H. S. *The Growth of the American Republic*. 2 vols.; New York: Oxford University Press, 1960.

MORLEY, JOHN. *The Life of Richard Cobden*. Boston: Roberts Brothers, 1881.
———. *The Life of William Ewart Gladstone*. New York: The Macmillan Co., 1903.

MYERS, WILLIAM STARR. *A Study in Personality, General George Brinton McClellan*. New York: D. Appleton–Century, 1934.

NEVINS, ALLAN. *The War for the Union*. 2 vols.; New York: Charles Scribner's Sons, 1959–60.

NEWTON, T. W. L. *Lord Lyons*. 2 vols.; London: Longmans, Green & Co., 1913.

NICOLAY, JOHN G., and HAY, JOHN. *Abraham Lincoln, A History*. 10 vols.; New York: The Century Co., 1909.

PALFREY, FRANCIS WINTHROP. *The Antietam and Fredericksburg*. New York: Charles Scribner's Sons, 1882.

PARRISH, WILLIAM E. *Turbulent Partnership: Missouri and the Union 1861–1865*. Columbia: University of Missouri Press, 1963.

PEMBERTON, JOHN C. *Pemberton: Defender of Vicksburg*. Chapel Hill: University of North Carolina Press, 1942.

PENNYPACKER, ISAAC R. *General Meade*. New York: D. Appleton & Co., 1901.

PERKINS, DEXTER. *A History of the Monroe Doctrine*. Boston: Little, Brown & Co., 1963.

PHISTERER, FREDERICK. *Statistical Record of the Armies of the United States*. New York: Charles Scribner's Sons, 1883.

PIERCE, EDWARD LILLIE. *Memoirs and Letters of Charles Sumner*. 4 vols.; Boston: Roberts Brothers, 1877–93.

POLLARD, E. A. *The Lost Cause*. New York: E. B. Treat & Co., 1866.

RANDALL, J. G. *Constitutional Problems under Lincoln*. New York: D. Appleton & Co., 1926.
——— and DONALD, DAVID. *The Civil War and Reconstruction*, 2d ed.; Boston: D. C. Heath & Co., 1961.

RAWLEY, JAMES A. *Edwin D. Morgan, 1811–1883*. New York: Columbia University Press, 1955.

RHODES, JAMES F. *History of the United States from the Compromise of 1850 to 1877*. 7 vols.; New York: The Macmillan Co., 1893–1900.

RHODES, JAMES F. *History of the Civil War, 1861–1865*. New York: The Macmillan Co., 1917.

SHALER, N. S. *Kentucky: A Pioneer Commonwealth*. 4th ed.; Boston: Houghton Mifflin Co., 1888.

SHANNON, FRED ALBERT. *The Organization and Administration of the Union Army, 1861–1865*. 2 vols.; Cleveland, A. H. Clark Co., 1928.

SHERMAN, W. T. *Memoirs of Gen. W. T. Sherman*. 2 vols. in one, 4th ed.; New York: Charles L. Webster & Co., 1891.

SIMKINS, F. B., and PATTON, J. W. *The Women of the Confederacy*. Richmond: Garret & Massie, Inc., 1936.

SMITH, EDWARD C. *The Borderland in the Civil War*. New York: The Macmillan Co., 1927.

SPEED, THOMAS. *The Union Cause in Kentucky, 1860–1865*. New York: G. P. Putnam's Sons, 1907.

STEVENSON, BURTON. *Poems of American History*. Boston: Houghton Mifflin Co., 1908.

STICKLES, ARNDT M. *Simon Bolivar Buckner, Borderland Knight*. Chapel Hill: University of North Carolina Press, 1940.

STILLWELL, LUCILE. *John C. Breckinridge*. Caldwell, Ida.: Caxton Press, 1936.

STRODE, HUDSON. *Jefferson Davis, American Patriot*. New York: Harcourt, Brace & Co., 1955.

SUMMERS, FESTUS P. *The Baltimore and Ohio in the Civil War*. New York: G. P. Putnam's Sons, 1939.

THOMAS, BENJAMIN. *Abraham Lincoln*. New York: Alfred A. Knopf, Inc., 1952.

TILBY, A. WYATT. *Lord John Russell, A Study in Civil and Religious Liberty*. London: Cassell & Co., 1930.

TUCKER, GLENN. *High Tide at Gettysburg*. Indianapolis: Bobbs-Merrill, 1958.

UPTON, EMORY. *The Military Policy of the United States*. Washington: Government Printing Office, 1917.

WALPOLE, SPENCER. *The Life of Lord John Russell*. 2 vols.; London: Longmans, Green & Co., 1889.

WEED, THURLOW. *Life of Thurlow Weed*. 2 vols.; Boston: Houghton Mifflin Co., 1884.

WHITE, HORACE. *The Life of Lyman Trumbull*. Boston: Houghton Mifflin Co., 1913.

WILEY, BELL. *The Life of Billy Yank*. Indianapolis: Bobbs-Merrill, 1951.

WILLIAMS, KENNETH P. *Lincoln Finds a General: A Military Study of the Civil War*. 5 vols.; New York: The Macmillan Co., 1949–59.

WILLIAMS, T. HARRY. *Lincoln and His Generals*. New York: Alfred A. Knopf, Inc., 1952.

——. *Americans at War*. New York: Collier Books, 1962.

——. *Lincoln and the Radicals*. Madison: University of Wisconsin Press, 1960.

——. *P. G. T. Beauregard: Napoleon in Gray*. Baton Rouge: Louisiana State University Press, 1955.

WILSON, HENRY. *History of the Antislavery Measures of the Thirty-seventh and Thirty-eighth United States Congresses, 1861–65.* Boston: Walker, Fuller & Co., 1865.

WOLSELEY, GARNET. *The American Civil War: An English View.* James A. Rawley (ed.). Charlottesville: University Press of Virginia, 1964.

WOOD, WILLIAM W. *Captains of the Civil War.* New Haven: Yale University Press, 1921.

YEARNS, W. B. *The Confederate Congress.* Athens: University of Georgia Press, 1960.

ZORNOW, WILLIAM F. *Lincoln and the Party Divided.* Norman: University of Oklahoma Press, 1954.

PERIODICALS

ADAMS, CHARLES FRANCIS. "The 'Trent' Affair," *American Historical Review*, XVII (April, 1912), 540–562.

BAILEY, T. A. "World War Analogues of the 'Trent' Affair," *American Historical Review*, XXXVIII (January, 1933), 286–290.

BAXTER, J. P., 3d. "The British Government and Neutral Rights, 1861–1865," *American Historical Review*, XXXIV (October, 1928), 9–29.

BREWER, W. M. "Lincoln and the Border States," *Journal of Negro History*, XXXIV (January, 1949), 46–72.

BRIDGES, HAL (ed.). "A Lee Letter on the 'Lost Dispatch' and the Maryland Campaign of 1862," *Virginia Magazine of History and Biography*, 66 (April, 1958), 161–166.

CATTON, BRUCE. "Sheridan at Five Forks," *Journal of Southern History*, XXI (August, 1955), 305–315.

———. "Crisis at the Antietam," *American Heritage*, IX (August, 1958), 54–57, 93–96.

COHEN, VICTOR H. "Charles Sumner and the 'Trent' Affair," *Journal of Southern History*, XXII (May, 1956), 205–219.

CURRY, RICHARD O. "A Reappraisal of Statehood Politics in West Virginia," *Journal of Southern History*, XXVIII (November, 1962), 403–421.

DUDLEY, HAROLD M. "The Election of 1864," *Mississippi Valley Historical Review*, XVIII (March, 1932), 500–518.

DUNNING, WILLIAM A. "The Second Birth of the Republican Party," *American Historical Review*, XVI (October, 1910), 56–63.

FERRIS, NORMAN B. "The Prince Consort, 'The Times,' and the 'Trent' Affair," *Civil War History*, VI (June, 1960), 152–156.

GLONEK, JAMES F. "Lincoln, Johnson, and the Baltimore Ticket," *The Abraham Lincoln Quarterly*, VI (March, 1951), 255–271.

HECK, FRANK H. "John C. Breckinridge in the Crisis of 1860–1861," *Journal of Southern History*, XXI (August, 1955), 316–346.

JOHNSON, ROSSITER. "Turning Points of the Civil War," *Annual Report of the American Historical Association for the Year 1894.* Washington: Government Printing Office, 1895.

JONES, ARCHER. "The Gettysburg Decision," *Virginia Magazine of History and Biography*, 68 (July, 1960), 331–343.

JONES, ROBERT HUHN. "Anglo-American Relations, 1861–1865, Reconsidered," *Mid-America*, 45 (January, 1963), 36–49.

———. "The American Civil War in the British Sessional Papers: Catalog and Commentary," *Proceedings of the American Philosophical Society*, 107 (October, 1963), 1–12.

JONES, WILBUR DEVEREUX. "The British Conservatives and the American Civil War," *American Historical Review*, LVIII (April, 1953), 527–543.

KAPLAN, SIDNEY. "The Miscegenation Issue in the Election of 1864," *Journal of Negro History*, XXXIV (July, 1949), 274–343.

MCWHINEY, GRADY. "Controversy in Kentucky: Braxton Bragg's Campaign of 1862," *Civil War History*, VI (March, 1960), 5–42.

MILNE, A. TAYLOR. "The Lyons-Seward Treaty of 1862," *American Historical Review*, XXXVIII (April, 1933), 511–525.

PIERSON, WILLIAM W., JR. "The Committee on the Conduct of the Civil War," *American Historical Review*, XXIII (April, 1918), 550–576.

The Quarterly Review. London, Vol. 112.

RANDALL, JAMES G. "Some Legal Aspects of the Confiscation Acts of the Civil War," *American Historical Review*, XVIII (October, 1913), 79–96.

RAWLEY, JAMES A. "The Nationalism of Abraham Lincoln," *Civil War History*, IX (September, 1963), 283–298.

ROBERTSON, JAMES R. "Sectionalism in Kentucky from 1855 to 1865," *Mississippi Valley Historical Review*, IV (June, 1917), 49–63.

SHALER, N. S. "Border State Men of the Civil War," *Atlantic Monthly*, LXIX (February, 1892), 245–257.

SHORTRIDGE, WILSON P. "Kentucky Neutrality in 1861," *Mississippi Valley Historical Review* IX (March, 1923), 283–301.

STRODE, HUDSON. "Jefferson Davis, His Ideals of Honor Were Born in Kentucky," in *The Civil War in Kentucky*. Louisville: *Courier-Journal*, November 20, 1960.

Times Literary Supplement, July 19, 1963.

TUCKER, GLENN. "Longstreet: Culprit or Scapegoat?" *Civil War Times Illustrated*, I (April, 1962), 5 ff.

WHITRIDGE, ARNOLD. "The 'Trent' Affair, 1861," *History Today*, IV (June, 1954), 394–402.

WILSON, CHARLES R. "McClellan's Changing Views on the Peace Plank of 1864," *American Historical Review*, XXXVIII (April, 1933), 498–505.

———. "New Light on the Lincoln-Blair-Fremont 'Bargain' of 1864," *American Historical Review*, XLII (October, 1936), 71–78.

Index

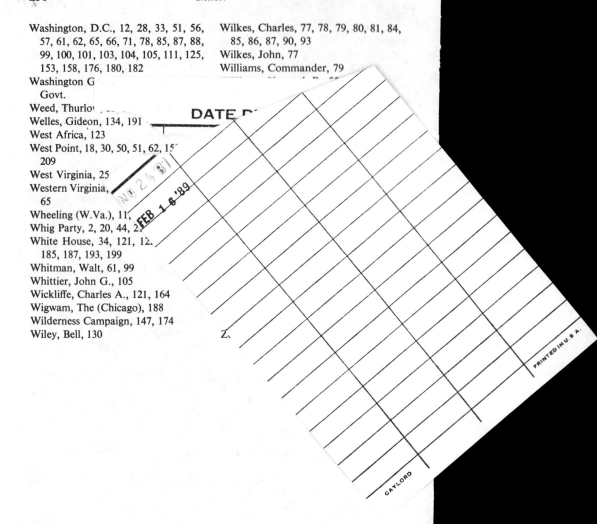

DATE D